1982

UNIVERSITY OF KANSAS PUBLICATIONS
Humanistic Studies, 53

SEMIOTIC THEMES

Edited by

Richard T. De George

Lawrence: University of Kansas Publications, 1981

PRINTED IN LAWRENCE, KANSAS, USA
BY THE UNIVERSITY OF KANSAS PRINTING SERVICE

Contents

Preface

Semiotics has a long history. But it is only in recent years that it has become an important movement. Some people see in it a threatening, imperialistic theory. They see it as an ideology, a jargon-filled fad, and as intellectual sham. Others see it as a scientific approach which might, if properly developed, serve as a unifying theory for the humanities and as a bridge between the humanities and the sciences.

Though the roots of semiotics go back to the Greeks, Charles Peirce and Ferdinand de Saussure are generally acknowledged as the modern sources from which the contemporary movement springs. The movement's development has been somewhat different in the United States and in Europe. In both places, however, it has cut across traditional disciplinary lines and has influenced linguistics, anthropology, sociology, philosophy, literary, artistic and film criticism, communication theory, and architecture, among other fields.

Semiotics has emerged on college and university campuses, sometimes as a recognized discipline, sometimes as an underground current. At the University of Kansas it became the focus of the first Faculty Development Seminar sponsored by the University's Center for Humanistic Studies and funded by a grant from the Mellon Foundation. The essays contained in this volume were initially written in conjunction with that seminar. Not all the essays from the Seminar have been included here, and most that have been included appear in revised form. They represent the range of topics covered and the diversity of views, approaches, and conclusions present in the movement as a whole.

Semiotics, despite its long history, is still a new and somewhat unproven theory and discipline. This volume is a contribution to its development.

Richard T. De George

Ferdinand de Saussure and the History of Semiotics

W. Keith Percival

The Swiss linguist Ferdinand de Saussure (1857-1913) has in many ways been the presiding genius of twentieth-century linguistics. His posthumous *Cours de linguistique générale*[1] has attained the status of a classic, and several influential theoretical schools of the past fifty years consciously formulated their ideas in relation to his. Saussure is also a remarkable figure in that his theories have attracted the attention of scholars in other fields: the anthropologist Claude Lévi-Strauss, the psychologist Jean Lacan, the philosopher Merleau-Ponty, and the literary theorists Roland Barthes and Jacques Derrida, to cite only a few examples. Indeed, it may be that his influence is now more perceptible outside linguistics than within. This is especially true in the newly established field of semiotics, where Saussure ranks along with the American Charles Sanders Peirce as one of the founders of the discipline.

The purpose of this paper is to present the fundamental features of Saussure's sign theory. Since much of what he wrote and taught on this topic was directed against traditional views, his theory will be viewed in a historical context. My aim is to put his ideas into sharper perspective and in this way to see their strengths and weaknesses more clearly.

I shall proceed by sidestepping the familiar *Cours de linguistique générale* and concentrating my attention instead on Saussure's manuscripts and on the lecture notes taken down by students of his in the three courses on general linguistics which he gave at the University of Geneva between 1907 and 1911. The *Cours,* it may be recalled, was not written by Saussure himself but compiled by his younger colleagues Charles Bally and Albert Sechehaye on the basis of students' lecture notes. In a real sense, therefore, the book is the work of Bally and Sechehaye as well as Saussure. Fortunately, it is no longer our only source of information: the extant lecture notes and Saussure's own manuscripts have been made available,[2] and a critical edition of the *Cours* has appeared in which the text is flanked sentence by sentence with the manuscript sources on which it was presumably based.[3]

In addition to examining the manuscript sources of the *Cours,* scholars

interested in Saussure have in recent years begun to look into the antecedents of his ideas. Not surprisingly, it has been discovered that many
linguists and philosophers active at the end of the nineteenth and the
beginning of the twentieth century expressed ideas similar in one way or
another to those propounded by Saussure. But the extent of his indebtedness to these forerunners is still an open question. Perhaps the most interesting hypothesis suggested so far is that he was influenced by the theories
of the French philosopher and literary critic Hippolyte Taine (1828-1893).[4]
However, I shall have little to say here about the fascinating question of
Saussure's direct antecedents.

The position of his theory in the history of semiotics is likewise a cloudy
issue. While there is no doubt that the questions posed by signs and
symbols have been an enduring preoccupation in Western philosophy from
Antiquity to the present, the development of semiotic notions has not
excited as much curiosity on the part of historians of ideas as it undoubtedly
deserves.[5] Indeed, for some periods basic research is still needed to find
and interpret the primary sources. To this extent we are still in the position
of pioneer explorers constantly tantalized by the prospect of discovering
new and uncharted lands.

We commence our exploration with Aristotle's semiotic theory;[6] specifically, with an extract from the opening chapter of the *Peri Hermēneias
(On Interpretation)*, since much subsequent discussion of semiotic questions was based on this passage. The English translation offered here is
my own.

"Spoken language symbolizes events which take place in the mind,
while writing symbolizes spoken language. Just as men do not all use the
same written symbols, so they do not all have the same language. However, the mental events which are primarily symbolized by language are
common to all mankind, as also are the things of which these mental
events are likenesses."[7]

Aristotle's position may be summarized as follows: Speech symbolizes
mental events just as writing symbolizes speech. Mental events are related
to things in the extra-mental world by being similar to them. While
mental events and things are the same for all mankind, speech is not.
Languages vary in much the same way as writing systems vary. The relation between words and mental events is, therefore, not a natural one,
and in this respect it parallels the relation between speech and writing.

Thus, the sign relation holds between words and mental events, and between speech and writing, but not between words and the things they refer to. Indeed, there is no mention of a direct relation between words and things in this passage.

Elsewhere in the Aristotelian corpus, however, the relation between words and referents is discussed. Let us consider a passage from the first chapter of the *Categories,* of which I present the following English translation:

"Things are said to be *homonymously* named if they share only the name (*onoma*) but have different definitions (*logos*) with regard to their essence (*ousia*). For example, the word *zōion*[8] may refer either to a human being or a picture, and all that a human being and a picture have in common is the name *zōion,* while they differ as regards their definition. For if somebody were to specify what constitutes being a *zōion* for a man or for a picture, he would provide a different definition in the two cases.

"Things are said to be *synonymously* named if they share the same name and also have the same definition with regard to their essence. Take, for instance, the word *zōion* in relation to a human being and an ox. Both of these have the name *zōion,* and their definitions are the same. If somebody were to specify what constitutes being a *zōion* in these two instances, he would provide the same definition in both cases."[9]

A distinction is drawn here between cases in which the same word is used to refer to things which have different essential defining attributes, like a human being and a picture, and cases in which a word is used to refer to things which share essential defining features, like a human being and an ox, which share the essential defining feature of being animals. The word used to refer to a thing is called its name (*onoma*). There is no mention here of the mental events symbolized by words, nor is the word sign (*sēmeion*) used. Thus, the theories presented in the *Peri Hermēneias* and the *Categories* differ from one another significantly.

In a third work of Aristotle's, the *Sophistic Elenchi,* yet another theory is expounded. The passage reads as follows:

"It is not possible for us to bring the actual things (*pragmata*) with us when we argue; we use names as symbols (*symbola*) instead of the things and assume, therefore, that whatever follows in the names also follows in the things, just as those who calculate do with regard to their counters."[10]

Here again words are referred to as the names of things, but the sign relation is mentioned. Hence, in this theory there is a sign relation between words and the things they refer to. However, no mention is made of the relation between words and the mental events associated with them. There is no discussion either of essential defining attributes.

We must conclude that, strictly speaking, Aristotle had three different theories of the linguistic sign. An adroit interpreter might perhaps be able to show that they are in reality different versions or facets of the same theory. Alternatively, one might concentrate on one of them and not try to reconcile it with the others. In fact, the second alternative was the more popular one, and the focus of attention was the passage from the *Peri Hermēneias*. But before considering Aristotle's commentators let us look at another major semiotic theory propounded in Antiquity, namely that of the Stoics.[11]

The passage we shall analyze is from a work by Sextus Empiricus, a Greek-speaking philosopher who lived in the early third century A.D. The Stoic school had been founded five hundred years earlier by Zeno of Citium, but since the works of Zeno and the other heads of the school have not come down to us we must rely largely on secondary sources for our knowledge of Stoic philosophy. The work from which our passage is taken is entitled *Adversus Mathematicos* (*Against the Professors*) and is devoted to a criticism of the· prevailing philosophical systems of the day. The passage reads as follows (the English translation is my own):

"The Stoics say that there are three things linked together, namely the signified, the signifier, and the referent. Of these the signifier is the sound, e.g. *Dion;* the signified is the state of affairs revealed by the signifier; and we grasp the signified as coexisting with our understanding, whereas barbarians do not understand the signified although they hear the sound. The referent is the object in the outside world, e. g. Dion himself. Two of these things are corporeal, namely the sound and the referent, and one is incorporeal, namely the state of affairs signified and expressible. This latter is either true or false."[12]

The Stoic theory clearly differs both in terminology and in content from Aristotle's. As regards the terminology, we note that two of the key terms, signifier (*sēmainon*) and signified (*sēmainomenon*), are inflected forms of the same verb *sēmainein* 'to signify' (compare Saussure's terms *signifiant* and *signifié*), while the term for referent (*tynchanon*) is unconnected with the other two.[13] As for the content of the theory, two features distinguish it from Aristotle's system. First, a distinction is drawn between meaning and referent; and second, meanings are not equated with mental events. In the Stoic view, the semantic content of a linguistic expression is its meaning; the referent, on the other hand, is whatever the speaker happens to be referring to when he uses the expression. Thus, if I say "It is night," when it is in fact day, what my statement means is at variance with the actual state of affairs, and it is this discrepancy which might lead my interlocutor to regard the statement as either factually mistaken or intentionally misleading. It is, then, the distinction between meaning and referent which enables the Stoics to account for the difference between true and false statements. All three components of Aristotle's sign situation—the sign, the mental event, and the referent—would be categorized by the Stoic as corporeal and as lying outside language; the incorporeal meaning alone resides within language.[14]

Unlike Aristotle, the Stoics also speculated about the origin of language. The earliest words, in their belief, had a natural relation to their referents, i.e., were onomatopoetic creations (like the English word *cuckoo*). This theory was, in fact, not new with the Stoics; similar ideas had already been aired in Plato's dialogue the *Cratylus*. Although the Stoics were quite aware that few words in contemporary Greek were clear cases of onomatopoeia, they believed that the whole vocabulary had been derived from an original core of imitative words. This assumption, unwarranted as it may seem to us nowadays, gave a powerful impulse to the study of etymology. But not only was the starting point—the onomatopoetic core vocabulary—a mere conjecture, no restrictions were placed on the processes of derivation. The result was unbridled speculation.[15] But to many of the Ancients the bizarre explanations arrived at in this way were accepted at their face value. The Roman antiquarians, with their strong interest in the customs of their ancestors, were especially attracted by these ingenious word-origins, and we find them faithfully reflected in the compendia and encyclopedias which late Antiquity bequeathed to the Middle Ages.

Another important development was the rise of a grammatical tradition aimed at inculcating facility in reading and writing the language of the great writers of the Periclean age. The first full-scale grammatical textbooks were written in the first century B.C., and the Romans soon followed suit. These manuals contain elaborate prescriptions covering the facts of linguistic usage, but they seldom concern themselves with semiotic notions. It was the logicians and philosophers, not the grammarians, who continued an interest in these questions. For instance, St. Augustine (354-430 A.D.) enumerates the different types of signs in his *De Doctrina Christiana,* a work which was influential in later centuries. Also of interest is the fact that St. Augustine, in the same work, depicts words as signifying concepts in the mind: "In short, among men words have achieved the pre-eminent function of signifying whatever mental concepts anybody may wish to communicate."[16]

A similar point of view is expressed by Boethius (died 524 A.D.) in his influential commentary on Aristotle's *Peri Hermēneias:* "Thus, when I say *stone,* it designates both the concept 'stone' and the stone itself, i.e., the substance itself; but it signifies the concept first, and the thing secondarily."[17] Boethius also translated several of Aristotle's works into Latin, and it was through these translations that the Latin-speaking Middle Ages first became acquainted with Aristotelian philosophy. In this way, Boethius' interpretation of Aristotle's ideas remained authoritative for many centuries. It is noteworthy, for instance, that he offered the following translation of Aristotle's definition of the noun in chapter II of the *Peri Hermēneias:* "The noun, therefore, is a sound which is meaningful by arbitrary choice (*secundum placitum*)."[18] The Greek original of this definition contains the ambiguous phrase *ḳata synthēḳēn,* meaning either 'in combination' or 'by agreement.' If J. Engels is right, Aristotle is more likely to have had the first meaning in mind here,[19] but in choosing to translate the phrase by the words *secundum placitum* 'at will, by arbitrary choice,' Boethius caused the second interpretation to become the accepted one from then on, and he thereby reinforced the impression that for Aristotle the relation between words and meanings is not a natural one.

Boethius' phrase *secundum placitum* carried another implication, which did not escape the attention of posterity, namely that an element of conscious choice was involved in the formation of words. It was by choice and general agreement that, say, the Romans called a horse *equus* while the Greeks called it *hippos.* The accepted view came to be that language was a conscious contrivance resorted to for the purpose of communicating thought. As late as the eighteenth century, language is defined in Ephraim Chambers' *Cyclopaedia* as "a set of Words which any People have agreed upon, in order to communicate their Thoughts to each other."[20]

any event, the grammatical theories of the scholastics were soon discredited, first by philosophers (notably by the followers of William of Ockham), and later by the humanist grammarians of the fifteenth century.[35] Scholastic logic itself began to lose ground and was abandoned by the end of the sixteenth century. Semiotic speculation continued in the seventeenth century in the work of Locke and Leibniz, and was maintained in the following century by such figures as Condillac. After an intermission, certain features of the Enlightenment tradition were revived by Hippolyte Taine, specifically in his *De l'intelligence,* first published in 1870. Taine's ideas created widespread enthusiasm in France in the final decades of the nineteenth century, and it was within the intellectual environment so created that much of Saussure's early linguistic theorizing took place. Hence, although he may not have been aware of this himself, Saussure stood at the end of a long tradition of semiotic inquiry.

The linguistic tradition, to which Saussure also had close ties, was an outgrowth of traditional grammar and etymology. It was born in the late eighteenth and early nineteenth centuries when scholars discovered that it was possible to make a systematic study of the way grammatical systems develop through time. By the second half of the nineteenth century linguists considered their foremost task to be that of hypothetically reconstructing the unattested proto-language of the Indo-European language family. Their interests broadened to include the more recent history of the Indo-European languages and general questions concerning the nature of language.

For most of the nineteenth century German scholars were in the forefront of the new discipline, but in the second half of the century scholars from other countries played an increasingly large role. Thus, Ferdinand de Saussure went from his native Geneva to the University of Leipzig to obtain professional training in linguistics. At the time he studied there the Leipzig linguistic fraternity was passing through a turbulent period. A group of young linguists, jocularly referred to as the *Junggrammatiker,* were propounding general theoretical views to which the older generation took violent exception. Saussure not only sided with the Young Turks, he outdid them. His *Mémoire sur le système primitif des voyelles dans les langues indo-européennes,* published in late 1878, was a brilliant piece of inferential reasoning—so brilliant, in fact, that it failed to receive the attention that it deserved.

Saussure proceeded to obtain his doctorate with a rather conventional dissertation entitled *De l'emploi du génitif absolu en sanscrit,* published in 1880, and then went in the autumn of 1881 to take up a teaching post at the Ecole pratique des Hautes Etudes in Paris, where he was entrusted with courses on Gothic and Old High German, Lithuanian, and the comparative grammar of Greek and Latin.

In 1891, he was called to the University of Geneva to occupy the newly created chair for the history of comparison of the Indo-European languages. After the retirement of his colleague Joseph Wertheimer in 1906, he gave his famous courses on general linguistics (1907, 1908-1909, and 1910-1911). In the summer of 1912 he was obliged to retire for reasons of health; he died in early 1913 at the age of fifty-five.

After the publication of his doctoral dissertation, Saussure's scholarly output was meager. It is not known for certain why this was so. As for the material he collected for his three courses on general linguistics, there is no evidence that he had any firm plans to publish it. After his death, his friends Bally and Sechehaye undertook this difficult task on the basis of notes taken down by students who attended the courses (Bally and Sechehaye had not themselves been among them). The book which resulted, appropriately entitled *Cours de linguistique générale,* appeared in early 1916.

It is strange that this modern classic on general linguistics was at first not warmly received. For example, it got two frosty reviews from Saussure's brilliant Paris student, the Indo-Europeanist Antoine Meillet. The situation did not markedly change until the 1930's, when the book became the rallying cry of the new schools of "structural" linguistics which had emerged in Denmark and Czechoslovakia. This had the bizarre result that Saussure came to be regarded *ex post facto* as the founder of structural linguistics. In Germany and in English-speaking countries his ideas were either ignored or sharply criticized. In France, the general attitude continued to be cool until after the Second World War, when something in the nature of a cult grew up around his name in intellectual circles.

Viewed as a linguistic theorist, Saussure challenged a number of notions which were widely accepted in the late nineteenth century: (1) the notion that linguistics should be primarily concerned with the study of linguistic change; (2) the notion that articulatory phonetics, the study of the physiology of the speech act, provides the foundation on which all linguistic research rests; and (3) the assumption that individual psychology is the superordinate discipline under which linguistics should be subsumed.

As for the first point, Saussure believed that language is a sign system and as such functions at a particular point in time quite regardless of its previous history. The native speakers of a language communicate perfectly well without knowing anything about its history. Linguists should, therefore, focus their attention first and foremost on linguistic systems as they function at particular periods. Hence the famous distinction between *synchrony,* the study of language states at particular chronological stages, and *diachrony,* the study of the ways in which languages change through time. In Saussure's view, synchronic linguistics should be kept insulated from diachronic considerations. Thus, the linguist describing the French spoken in the reign of Louis XIV should abstain from allowing his analysis to be influenced by his knowledge of the earlier history of the language. However, as we shall see, Saussure also insisted that one cannot comprehend the phenomenon of natural language if one fails to take into consideration the diachronic dimension *(le facteur "temps,"* as he called it).

As for phonetics, Saussure could see no utility in the minute articulatory analysis of speech sounds. In his view, the physical character of the signs in a sign system is not a primary consideration. The system functions regardless of the precise way in which the signs are distinguished physically. It follows, therefore, that phonetics is an ancillary discipline, not an integral part of linguistics.

Finally, Saussure disapproved of the excessive reliance on psychological explanation characteristic of much linguistic theorizing in the late nineteenth century. If language is a sign system, it should be studied within the context of other sign systems, in a special discipline created for that purpose. Saussure seems to have been unaware that such a discipline had already been proposed by others (notably by C. S. Peirce), and suggested that it should be called *sémiologie.*

This science of sign systems would study the situations which result whenever human beings signify their thoughts by means of a necessary convention. Saussure envisaged that it would embrace not only linguistics, but also the study of writing systems, visual signals (sign language, military and maritime signals), Braille, all marks of courtesy, rites, and ceremonies. It would, in short, investigate all systems of arbitrarily fixable values.

Saussure laid special emphasis on the social character of sign systems, including language. It is in this context that his famous dichotomy between *langue* and *parole* may be placed. *Langue* is the social product of the semiological behavior of a speech community, while *parole* is the individual facet of the phenomenon, i.e., any of the concrete acts of speech performed by members of such a community. Saussure insisted on the centrality of *langue,* the pre-eminence of the social over the individual. Indeed, he not only advocated separating the linguistics of *parole* from the linguistics of *langue,* he even denied that purely individual factors are of any importance in language. Just as ships are made to sail on the sea, languages exist for the social group and therefore need only be studied as something collective.

After this brief introduction to Saussure's ideas, we are now ready to examine some of the primary sources. The first extract we shall consider is from a set of notes for a projected book on general linguistics. Here as elsewhere, the translation is my own:

"Three things are invariably missing from what philosophers believe to be true of language (*langage*). First, there is a fact which we scarcely need to emphasize, namely that language (*langage*) is not fundamentally made up of names (*noms*). It is an accident when a linguistic sign happens to correspond to an object perceptible to the senses, like a horse, fire, or the sun, instead of an idea like [Greek] *ethēka* 'he placed.' No matter how important these cases are, there is no obvious reason why they should be considered typical of language (*langage*). In fact, the opposite is true. In a sense, this is, of course, no more than a poor choice of examples on the part of those who look at the situation in this way. But, implicitly, there is an unmistakable tendency here, one which we cannot let pass, to take a stand on what language (*langage*) is, namely to regard it as a set of names for objects (*une nomenclature d'objets*); objects given first (*d'abord donnés*).

"[In this conception] there is first the object, and then the sign. We are, therefore, given an external basis for the sign, a notion we shall always reject, and language (*langage*) is represented as involving the following relation:

$$\text{objects} \left\{ \begin{array}{l} * \rule{4cm}{0.4pt}\ \text{a} \\ * \rule{4cm}{0.4pt}\ \text{b} \\ * \rule{4cm}{0.4pt}\ \text{c} \end{array} \right\} \text{names (\textit{noms})}$$

In reality the correct way to portray the matter is this: a — b — c, with no mention of a relation of the kind * —— a, centered on an object.

"If it were possible for an object, wherever it might be, to be the factor (*terme*) on which the sign is based (*fixé*), linguistics would immediately cease being what it is, from top to bottom, and likewise the human spirit, as is clear from this discussion. But, as we have just said, this is merely an incidental reproach that might be leveled at the traditional way of approaching language philosophically. It is certainly unfortunate that people start out by making the objects referred to the main element (*élément primordial*), when in reality they are nothing of the kind. But that is merely a result of choosing bad examples, and if one replaces *hēlios, ignis,* or *Pferd* by something such as [. . .], one no longer is tempted to reduce language (*langue*) to something external.

"The second mistake generally made by philosophers is much more serious, and that is to imagine that once an object has been designated by a name (*nom*), that combination will be transmitted in toto, and that no other phenomena need be taken into consideration. If some change should occur, it will be the name itself that is more likely to be affected, as when [Latin] *fraxinus* ['ash tree'] is assumed to have turned into [French] *frêne.* But the idea is also subject to change. . . . Here we already have something which causes us to question the association between an idea (*idée*) and a name (*nom*), the minute that this unexpected factor completely ignored in the philosophical system (*la combinaison philosophique*) enters the picture, namely TIME. But we should still have nothing really striking, nothing characteristic, nothing uniquely peculiar to language, if all we had were these two types of change and the first kind of dissociation by which the idea parts company with the sign, spontaneously, whether the latter changes or not. So far these two things are still separate entities, at least for a [*lacuna*].

"What is characteristic are the innumerable instances in which the change of a sign causes a change in the idea itself and in which one immediately realizes that at any given moment there was never any difference between the set of ideas being distinguished and the set of distinctive signs.

"As a result of phonetic change two signs become confused with each other, and the ideas will become confused to a certain extent; how much they will be confused will depend on all the other elements in the system (*l'ensemble des autres éléments*).

"When a sign becomes two different signs, by the same blind process a meaning will inevitably be attached to the difference which has just arisen.

"Here are some examples, but let me immediately emphasize the futility of the approach which starts out from the relation between an idea and a sign with no regard to time or the process of transmission, for it is the factor of transmission that experimentally teaches us what the value of a sign is (*ce que vaut le signe*)."[36]

Let us first examine Saussure's complaints against the philosophers. His main charge is that they regard language as a set of names for perceptible objects and believe that the objects referred to by words exist prior to the words themselves. Second, he accuses them of ignoring the factor of linguistic change, which constantly alters the relation between words and meanings, at times creating new meanings and effacing old ones.

To what extent are these strictures justified? As regards the first point, we have seen that the predominant tradition in Western philosophy has regarded words as primarily signifying mental concepts. No semiotic theory we have considered asserts that meanings are referents *and nothing but referents*. Even John Stuart Mill confines himself to the statement that he will always refer to words as the names of things, "*not merely* of our ideas of things," which clearly indicates that he did not deny the existence of ideas. Finally, the question of whether things existed before words was never raised.

Moreover, one can reasonably ask whether Saussure's arguments are cogent. His main contention in the first paragraph is that reference to perceptible objects like horses and fire is not typical of language. He contrasts such cases of simple reference with what he calls "ideas," which he exemplifies with a Greek verb form. But it is not clear whether he is insisting that language consists of *two* types of words: names and ideas, or whether he thinks that the meaning of a word such as *horse* is the idea or concept of a horse (not a real horse), in which case all words would express ideas no matter whether they referred to perceptible objects or not. The choice of Greek *ethēka* 'he placed' is also puzzling in that what one places is often a perceptible object, and in such a situation the action of placing is no less perceptible than the object being placed. In general, both subjects and predicates may refer to something perceptible (like horses or roundness) or to something difficult or impossible to perceive (like absence or meaningfulness).

When we move on to the second part of the extract, we may note first that Saussure is probably correct in asserting that philosophers have not paid attention to the factor of linguistic change. But does this factor need to be considered if one is interested in the way propositions are expressed in words, which is the main concern of logicians? Let us examine one of Saussure's strongest arguments in this regard, namely the contention that linguistic change often creates new semantic distinctions. What he has in mind here are cases like the French words *chaise* and *chaire,* both of which go back to Old French *chaiere.* The existence of two variant pronunciations of what was earlier a single word, has, according to Saussure, resulted in their acquiring different meanings, *chaise* being used in the concrete sense 'seat, chair' and *chaire* in the more abstract meaning 'seat of authority, professorship.' This example illustrates, in Saussure's view, that the momentum of linguistic change in certain circumstances ineluctably creates semantic distinctions which did not exist before. In Old French there was one word and hence one idea, whereas in modern French there are two words and two ideas.

But the only way one can be sure that no more than one idea was expressed by Old French *chaiere* is by invoking the general principle that the sum of ideas distinguished is always equal to the sum of distinctive signs. One suspects, in other words, that even if it could be shown that Old French *chaiere* (like modern English *chair*) was used in both concrete and abstract senses, Saussure would insist that it expressed a single idea. But although we may grant him his principle for the sake of argument, he is still not out of the wood, since examples of this kind involve a diachronic dimension. Why does the semantic analyst dealing with modern French *chaise* and *chaire* need to know that they were derived from the same word in Old French? The problem of how signs function in society can be studied perfectly well without introducing historical considerations. Hence, Saussure's argument that the philosophers have erred in ignoring the factor of transmission is valid only if one violates his injunction against mixing synchronic and diachronic analysis.

The positive side of Saussure's argument in our first extract is the notion that words have important relations to one another which are worthy of scrutiny. This is certainly a fruitful idea, perhaps one of the most fruitful ones suggested by Saussure. But it is perhaps strange that he seems to regard the previous neglect of these interrelations as a by-product of the referential theory of the linguistic sign. Whether this was really so is an interesting historical question which has not so far been looked into, but it seems clear that there is no necessary connection between adopting a referential view of meaning and neglecting the interrelations of words. After all, things have relations to one another no less than words: animals fall into species and genera, human beings into age groups, occupations, races, and nations, and so forth. A dedicated referentialist could logically derive many of the interrelations of words from such factual relations, if he so wished.

Let us now examine the way Saussure presented his views of the linguistic sign to his students, specifically in his lecture of November 16, 1908. The immediately preceding lecture had been concerned with the place of language among sign systems and the place of linguistics among the sciences, and Saussure had introduced the notion of semiology, the science devoted to sign systems in general. On November 16 he went on to ask why semiology had not yet gained the recognition it deserved. In answering this question he impressed on his auditors the idea that language had not hitherto been studied from the point of view of its true nature (*sous son aspect essentiel*). One of the manifestations of this failure, in Saussure's judgment, is the fact that language has been envisaged as a system of names. At this point, let us look at the notes taken down by François Bouchardy:

"Psychologists and philosophers regard language as a nomenclature, at least when you look at the examples [they cite]. In this way, a crucial matter (*une chose capitale*) is left out of consideration, namely the way in which the values in language determine one another by their coexistence. Thus, the word *judgment* can only be defined by means of the terms which are close to it. This phenomenon is noticeable in translation: [French] *craindre* ['to fear'] and *redouter* ['to dread'] have no precise meanings other than in relation to each other. If one of them did not exist, the other one would have the meaning of the first in addition to its own. If one loses sight of the fact that all there is to study is a *system* of signs one runs the risk of not treating semiology in the correct way."[37]

Here again we encounter Saussure's attack against the referential theory, this time aimed at the psychologists as well as the philosophers. He states once more that there is a connection between regarding language as a nomenclature and neglecting the relations words have to one another.

This leads him to emphasize that a word cannot be defined in isolation, but only in terms of its near synonyms ("the terms which are close to it"). The reciprocally determined meanings of related terms he calls "values." Thus, not only are the interrelations between words more important than their relations to the extra-mental world, they are the only ones capable of definition. To take an example cited by Saussure himself, words like "dog" and "wolf" cannot be regarded as isolated signs. Another student, Léopold Gautier, writes in his notes:

"Let us go even further: if the word *wolf* ceased to exist, *dog* would immediately denote the wolf. The word depends, therefore, on the system; there are no isolated signs."[38]

Clearly, the view being advanced here has much to recommend it. One recalls, for instance, that the term "buffalo" was extended to refer to the North American bison in spite of the fact that the latter belongs to a different genus from the old-world buffalo. Similarly, according to one account,[39] when the Romans first encountered the elephant they called the unfamiliar animal *Luca bos,* i.e., a type of bovine.

But is it not the physical appearance of the animals in question that legitimizes such extensions of meaning? For when the speakers of a language come upon an unfamiliar animal which bears no resemblance to any creature known to them, they will often borrow a designation for it from a language whose speakers are familiar with it. Thus, the word *giraffe* was borrowed into European languages from Arabic, *kangaroo* from a native Australian language, *cockatoo* from Malay, and so forth. Alternatively, new descriptive terms are created from the resources of the language itself, as in the case of *rhinoceros,* a name coined by the Greeks.[40] It would seem, therefore, that semantic extensions and intra-linguistic creations are influenced to a great extent by the observable characteristics of the animal to be named.

Another valuable notion is the idea that the meanings of near synonyms tend to define themselves in relation to each other. One thinks of the recent neologism *chairperson,* which is being increasingly used in the sense of a "non-chairman," i.e. a female chairman. But Saussure surely goes too far when he suggests that the semantic relations between related terms would suffice to characterize their meanings exhaustively. For instance, to inform somebody unfamiliar with the word *buffalo* that it is closely related to the word *ox* and that whatever is referred to as an ox is not referred to as a buffalo and vice versa, would clearly be an inadequate explanation. Without a knowledge of *how* oxen and buffaloes differ nobody would feel satisfied that he understood what *buffalo* meant. It is surely no accident that dictionaries often contain pictures of many of the objects referred to in their pages. If the interrelations between words really sufficed to define them this procedure would be unnecessary.

A more detailed discussion of the notion that the value of a word depends on the value of other related words occurs in the last lecture of the third course, given on July 14, 1911:

"To capture the idea of value we have chosen to start out from the system of words, not the isolated word. We could have started out somewhere else. Psychologically, what are our ideas considered apart from language (*langue*)? They probably do not exist, or they exist only in an amorphous state. Philosophers and linguists have always believed that we would have no means of distinguishing two ideas from each other were it not for the help of language (internal language, of course). Hence, the purely conceptual mass of our thoughts, when considered in isolation and separate from language, represents a sort of amorphous cloud (*nébuleuse informe*) in which nothing could be picked out in the beginning. Analogously, in language the various ideas do not constitute anything preexistent; there are no ideas completely established and completely distinct from one another, and there are no signs for such ideas. There is nothing distinct at all in thought prior to the linguistic sign. This is the crucial point.

"Moreover, a question worth raising is whether this domain of completely nebulous ideas is matched by a domain of sound, considered in isolation from ideas, which does have distinct units. But as a matter of fact, sound has no determined units circumscribed in advance either. It is precisely between these two that the linguistic 'fact' mediates:

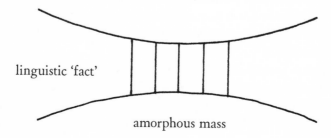

This linguistic 'fact' gives rise to values which are for the first time determined but which for all that remain values, in the usual sense of the term.

"There is something which needed to be added to the bare fact: I return to this topic now. Not only are these two domains between which a linguistic fact mediates vague and amorphous, but the act which assigns a given acoustic stretch to a given idea, the choice of a link between them, this marriage which creates value, is completely arbitrary. If that were not the case, this idea of value would have to be restricted: an absolute element would enter the picture. But since this contract is completely arbitrary, values are relative.

"Let us now return to the diagram representing the relation between the signified (*signifié*) and the signifier (*signifiant*):

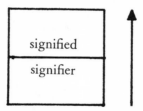

Clearly, this diagram has its raison d'être, but it is merely a by-product of value. The signified does not exist on its own—it is lost in the amorphous mass. The same thing is true of the signifier. But the signifier and the signified contract a bond by virtue of the precise values which arise from the combination of all the acoustic signs with all the countless segmentations (*découpures*) that can be made in the conceptual mass (*la masse de la pensée*).

"What would be necessary for the relation between the signifier and the signified to be given per se (*donné en soi*)? Above all, the signified, the idea, would have to be a thing determined beforehand (*d'avance*), which it is not. Therefore, this relation is merely another manifestation of the values viewed globally (*dans leur ensemble*), of the way they contrast with one another (*leur opposition*). This is true of linguistic facts of all types.

"A few examples:

1) If ideas were predetermined in the human mind prior to being values in language (*langue*), terms in different languages would correspond exactly. Where French has *cher* ['dear'], German has *lieb* and *teuer* (also in the ethical sense). There is no exact correspondence. Similarly with

French *juger* and *estimer* as compared with German *urteilen, erachten* ['judge']: the German verbs have a set of meanings which coincide only in part with those of French *juger, estimer*. We see that prior to languages (*langues*) there is no such thing as the notion "cher" per se. Thus while the diagram

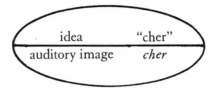

has its uses, it is only a way of expressing the fact that there exists a value "cher," circumscribed in the French system vis-à-vis other terms. It is a combination of a certain quantity of concepts and a certain quantity of sounds:

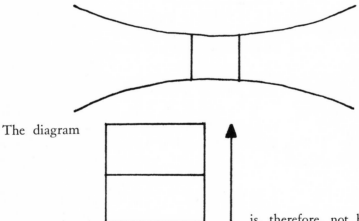

The diagram is, therefore, not basic in language (*langue*). The contours of the idea are what give us the distribution of ideas among the words of a language. Once we have these contours the diagram can be used (*entrer en jeu*).

"This example is from vocabulary, but the same is true of values of whatever kind.

2) Take, for example, the idea of different tenses, which is foreign to some languages. In the Semitic languages—in Hebrew, for instance—there are no distinctions of this kind, not even a difference between present,

past, and future. That means that these tense ideas are not predetermined but exist solely as values in particular languages. Early Germanic had no special future form; it expressed the future by means of the present. But this is only a manner of speaking. In fact, the value "present" in early Germanic was not the same as it is in French. "Present" is, therefore, a value, not a predetermined idea.

3) Likewise, in the Slavic languages, we find a pervasive distinction between the perfective aspect of the verb (action viewed apart from the notion of duration) and the imperfective action (action in the process of completion). This distinction makes these languages difficult for us to learn because we do not understand the aspectual categories. They are, therefore, not predetermined ideas, but values resulting from the opposition of terms in language (*langue*). . . .

"In a later chapter we may, if time permits, express in a different way the ideas we have included in the term *value,* by laying down the following principle: in language (*langue*), in a language state (*état de langue*) nothing exists but differences. A difference evokes in the mind the idea of the positive terms between which it holds. In language (*langue*) there are differences, nothing but differences, but without positive terms. This is a paradoxical fact. At any rate there are differences only so long as one has either the signifieds or the signifiers in mind. When one gets to the terms themselves which result from the relations between signified and signifier, one can then talk of oppositions. . . .

"This finally brings one back to the fundamental principle of the arbitrariness of the sign. If the sign were not arbitrary, one would not be able to say that in language (*langue*) there are only differences. But the fact is that it is because of the differences between signs that they can be given a function, a value."[41]

This extract is of great interest in that it contains an attempt to justify the belief that there is a one-to-one relation between distinguishable ideas and distinctive signs. This takes the form of an ingenious *Gedankenexperiment.* Imagine yourself trying to think of an idea but having no words to express it. Obviously, says Saussure, you would be at a loss. Until an idea is clothed in language it has no clear outlines. Therefore, there are no concepts prior to language. Q.E.D.

How convincing is this argument? There is at any rate this much that can be said in its favor. Language is an inestimable help in conceptualization. Even to be told, for instance, what an unfamiliar flower is called gives us a feeling of satisfaction. But the question of what our ideas would be like if language did not exist is as unrealistic as the question of whether things existed prior to the words we use to refer to them. A number such as thirty-five owes its manner of expression to the decimal system of numbering which we have used for millennia, but the number itself exists independently of that system—it could equally well be expressed in some other number system. The speakers of languages which have no tenses do not in fact lack the concepts of time and temporal succession. In general, a concept can be referred to even if there is no single unanalyzable word appropriate to it, and whenever a special term is needed for such a concept one will be created.

This is not to deny, of course, that the clarity with which we distinguish ideas is often influenced by the character of the terms we use to refer to them. But if the stranglehold of language were too tight we should have no means to overcome its restrictions. That we are aware of the power of language is surely a significant fact. Whether we are misled by language in ways which are in principle beyond our control is perhaps not an answerable question. We may concede that Aristotle was more confident of the universality of concepts than is warranted, but the opposite position—that concepts are a direct function of language—is equally unacceptable.

Another facet of Saussure's theory which needs to be carefully scrutinized is the heavy emphasis placed on the notion of arbitrariness. When the philosophers said that the linguistic sign is arbitrary, they usually meant two things: first, that there is no natural relation between words and their referents; and second, that the particular set of sounds composing a word was chosen at will. While the first of these notions is valid (except, of course, for the few imitative words which all languages contain), the second is unacceptable to us nowadays. Speakers are not free to dispose of their language as they wish. The social character of language imposes a powerful constraint on the members of a linguistic community. The idea that the speakers of each language once established a contract regulating the sounds and meanings of every word is difficult to conceive. It would seem reasonable, therefore, to restrict the term *arbitrary* to the notion "non-natural."

This Saussure does, of course, but since he has ruled out any mention of referents and regards concepts as a function of language, he arrives at a more radical kind of arbitrariness than his predecessors. The big difficulty he encounters is, in a sense, of his own making: he cannot refer to that all-important relation between sound (signifier) and meaning (signified), since he has concluded that they have no independent reality. Strictly speaking, then, he could discuss the sign relation only by stepping outside his own system and viewing the two *relata* (the signifier and the signified) in positive terms. That is to say, he needed a pre-theoretical terminology to talk about the sign relation, but was averse to creating one for fear he would seem to contradict his own theory.

Arrived at this point we are now in a position to examine the way in which Saussure set forth the basic properties of the linguistic sign in a lecture specially devoted to that topic given on May 2, 1911. This discussion is of special interest to us in that he begins by referring again to the traditional position of which he disapproved.

"People have often made the mistake of imagining that all there is in language is a nomenclature (*tree, fire, horse, snake*). This is a childish procedure (*une méthode enfantine*). If we adopt it for a minute, we shall have no difficulty in seeing what the linguistic sign does and does not consist in. One imagines oneself confronted with a series of objects and a series of names. [Drawing of a tree with the word *arbos* to the right of it, and beneath it a drawing of a horse with the word *equus* to its right.] There is an object outside the speaker (*sujet*) and the name, the other term, either vocal or mental, it is not clear which. (The word *tree* can be understood either way.) The connection (*lien*) between the two is unclear.

"Now let us adopt a different conception, the rational one. We again have two terms, but now they are inside the speaker, they are both psychological (*psychiques*), concentrated in the same place by association.

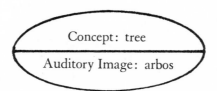

Arbos is the more material term, and *tree* the more psychological. Any attempt to link the terms differently from this we reject as a false trail in our search for the two terms which comprise the sign.

"A very simple way to realize the psychological character of our auditory images is to observe our internal speech. Without moving our lips or tongue we can, for instance, give a speech or recite a piece of poetry we have learned by heart, and we hear it internally. This is how we conceive of the linguistic sign; it is inside the speaker in the form of an auditory image. This is the material part of the sign.

"We can talk legitimately of the *sound* of the syllables, but only as syllables, i.e., as the sound of the internal auditory image. It is advisable that we should avoid certain terms; for example, *phoneme,* since this term implies the notion of vocal action, of speech (*parole*). Vocal image is another term which must be used with extreme caution.

"A general question which we admit we are unable to settle is whether to use the term *sign* to refer to the totality, i.e., the combination of concept and image, or only to the auditory image, the more material portion. In any event, if we call *arbos* a sign, we shall do so only to the extent that it conveys a concept. This is an unresolved terminological question. We really need two different words. We shall try to avoid misunderstandings, which could be serious.

"First principle or primary truth: *The linguistic sign is arbitrary.* The bond which links a given auditory image to a certain concept (*un concept déterminé*) and bestows on it the value of a sign is a radically arbitrary bond (*un lien radicalement arbitraire*).

"Nobody denies this truth, and it is not a difficult one to understand. However, it is important to enunciate it (*constater*) and place it in its proper position in the hierarchy of truths. This particular truth, which seems perfectly self-evident, is at the very top of the hierarchy. We cannot at first see all the hidden consequences that follow from this axiom. It will take us a great while to track them all down to the last detail.

"The sign is arbitrary, that is to say that the concept 'sister' [*soeur*], for example, is not connected by means of any internal relation to the sequence of sounds s + ö + r which constitute the corresponding auditory image. This concept could equally well be represented by any other sequence of sounds whatever. All one needs to do is to recall different languages. If one goes from one language to another, one sees that the concept *ox* is also represented by the sequence of sounds *bos* [in Latin].

"Written signs have the same arbitrary character. Obviously, no pre-existent connection forces us to choose the series of strokes which make up *P* to designate the sound *p* in preference to ⊓ or ⊙ . When semiology has been organized, it will have to decide whether it will concern itself with arbitrary signs only, or also with other kinds. In any event, it will deal typically with arbitrary systems, of which language is the prime example.

"One should have serious misgivings about using the term *linguistic symbol*. A symbol is never completely arbitrary or empty. There is the merest suspicion there of a connection between the idea and what serves as a sign for it. For example, the symbol of justice is a pair of scales, but it could not be replaced by a carriage without doing violence to it.

"From the same point of view, one might perhaps object to the term *auditory image,* for an image always has some connection with what it represents. It must be understood that we conceive of *image* in the more general sense of a *figure* capable of evoking something. Later we shall observe this image becoming more precisely evocative, and it is by virtue of this fact, which is not primary, that we shall retain this expression.

"Let us return to the word *arbitrary*. The sign is not arbitrary in the sense of depending on the free choice of the individual. It is arbitrary in relation to the concept inasmuch as it contains nothing which links it specially to that concept. A whole society could not change a sign once it had been established since the heritage of the past exerts a force upon it by virtue of the facts of [linguistic] development (*évolution*).

"But now, is there really no objection to this principle [of arbitrariness]? There is the vague issue of onomatopoetic words, i.e., words which are capable by their sounds of evoking (*rappeler*) the very concepts which they are supposed to represent. One might say that here there is indeed an inherent connection and that the choice is not arbitrary.

"But, first of all, people in general greatly exaggerate the number of onomatopoetic words. It is sometimes said, for example, that Latin *pluit* ['it is raining'] represents the sound of rain, but if one goes back in time a little (earlier forms are *plovit* or *plevit*), one sees that this is not the case.

"But it is nonetheless clear that we have indeed some onomatopoetic words: *tick-tock, glug-glug*. But they are so completely lost in the mass that they are treated just like ordinary words. This is shown by the fact that we often take a word to be onomatopoetic which in reality is no such thing.

"The extent of that part of the vocabulary is very limited. The same is true of exclamations. One might be tempted to claim that there is something there which is dictated by nature, and that in those words there is a connection between the sound and the concept. But in the case of most exclamations this can be shown not to be the case. Thus, to compare one language with another, [French] *aïe* [an exclamation of acute pain] does not exist in German and English. Some exclamations have developed from oaths which we know to have had quite precise meanings originally. We shall, therefore, put onomatopoetic words and exclamations aside since they are of secondary importance and their status is questionable."[42]

Here Saussure first draws a terminological distinction between "symbols" and other kinds of signs. In his system, a symbol is a non-arbitrary sign, i.e., a sign for which some connection exists between the idea conveyed and what serves as a vehicle for the idea. (Needless to say, this is not the way in which the word symbol is normally used.) Thus, for Saussure the balance is a suitable symbol of justice because it opposes equal weights, the task of the judge being to bring opposing interests into equilibrium. "True" signs, on the other hand, are arbitrary, i.e., there is no connection between the idea and what serves as a vehicle for it. The letters comprising any alphabetic writing system are signs in this sense, since there is no inherent connection between their shapes and the sounds which they designate. According to Saussure, linguistic signs also fall into this category because they are arbitrary. But whether the future science of semiology, when constituted, will deal with both arbitrary and non-arbitrary types, both symbols and "true" signs, Saussure is not sure.

Approaching the linguistic sign, he attributes two facets to it: a concept and an auditory image. He regards both facets as psychological in nature and excludes from consideration the referent, the articulatory movements responsible for producing the sound, and the sound itself qua sound. It is strange, however, that although he emphasizes that the concept and the auditory image are both psychological phenomena, he nevertheless refers to the auditory image as the more *material* part of the sign. We also see him in a terminological quandary with regard to the combination of concept and auditory image. It is clear that he would prefer to call that total combination a sign, but he is aware that in ordinary parlance the word "sign" refers to the physical aspect only. Ideally, he says, two different terms should be created.

He also feels uncomfortable with the word arbitrary, in that it connotes an element of conscious choice. But it is clearly not within the power of speakers to change their language at will. Arbitrariness must, therefore, be understood to mean no more than that there is no necessary link between the concept and the auditory image. The only restriction Saussure will concede to the principle of arbitrariness is minor, namely the existence of a small number of onomatopoetic words and exclamations in all languages. But even in these marginal cases, the link between concept and auditory image is often not very close, and the status of many supposedly onomatopoetic words is open to question, according to Saussure.

Comparing Saussure's system with the theories we examined earlier, we are struck by the following peculiarities. First and foremost, Saussure is alone in excluding all consideration of reference from the sign situation. The Stoics, we recall, banished reference from the domain of language proper, but they did not deny its ultimate relevance: without the concept of *tynchanon,* they would have been unable to explain why sentences may be either true or false. Saussure might argue, of course, that as a linguist he is not interested in the truth conditions of sentences and therefore does not need to account for them; but the role of reference is, after all, pervasive. For instance, all languages include a set of conventions to enable speakers to specify unambiguously the referents of the nominal expressions they use. If I utter the sentence *The cat has not been fed yet,* my use of the article *the* indicates that a definite cat is being referred to, and also that my interlocutor knows what cat I am referring to. Thus, reference is built into the basic grammatical texture of language.

Saussure's censorious attitude to the philosophers on this issue seems also inappropriate, for the notion that meaning is conceptual in nature puts his theory in the semiotic mainstream deriving ultimately from the key passage in Aristotle's *Peri Hermēneias* which we examined at the beginning of this paper. In this regard, therefore, Saussure can hardly be categorized as an innovator. Here, too, as elsewhere, he stated a position but failed to discuss carefully the arguments pro and contra. In general, he was ill-informed of the history of the questions he discussed: even in his manuscript notes, he theorized in a historical vacuum, often attacking positions which had never in fact been seriously maintained.

Finally, one must conclude that the theory itself is not only deficient in according no place to important elements of the sign situation, but it also contains notions which are difficult if not impossible to conceptualize. Consider the way in which Saussure attempts to combine the notions of contrast and arbitrariness. We begin with the unarguable notion that the relation between signifier and signified is arbitrary, i.e., non-natural. We are then told that the signifier and signified are in turn arbitrary in that the signifier is carved out of the raw material of perceptible sound in an arbitrary fashion and the signified is an arbitrary segment of conceptual material. Not content with that, Saussure will impute no positive features to either signifier or signified. Their mode of existence is purely negative— all that one can say about them is that they contrast with other signifiers and signifieds. But, as a former student of Saussure's trenchantly put it, "contrast pure and simple necessarily leads to chaos and cannot serve as the foundation of a *system*."[43] One might also add that chaos is impossible for human beings to conceive.

Hence, while parts of Saussure's theory contain insights into the nature of language, the theory as a whole must be rejected. Semiotics will need to be based on firmer and broader foundations. Above all, nothing but good will accrue from a closer acquaintance with the rich semiotic tradition of the past two and a half millennia. This is an area in which the history of ideas may be in a position to perform especially valuable services. In that case, Saussure will have taught us a salutary lesson: that it may sometimes pay to be familiar with one's intellectual predecessors.

Notes

1. Ferdinand de Saussure, *Cours de linguistique générale,* publié par Charles Bally et Albert Sechehaye avec la collaboration de Albert Riedlinger (Paris & Lausanne: Payot, 1916). Later editions were published in Paris in 1922, 1931, 1949, 1955, 1960, and 1968. An English translation exists: *Course in General Linguistics,* translated with an introduction and notes by Wade Baskin (New York: Philosophical Library, 1959).

2. See Robert Godel, *Les sources manuscrites du Cours de linguistique générale de F. de Saussure* (Geneva: S. Droz, 1957).

3. Ferdinand de Saussure, *Cours de linguistique générale,* édition critique par Rudolf Engler (Wiesbaden: O. Harrassowitz, 1967-74).

4. See Hans Aarsleff, "Taine and Saussure," *Yale Review,* 68 (1978-79), 71-81.

5. But see I. M. Bocheński, *A History of Formal Logic,* translated and edited by Ivo Thomas, 2nd ed. (New York: Chelsea Publishing Co., 1970); Ernst Cassirer, *Philosophie der symbolischen Formen,* Teil I: *Die Sprache,* 2nd ed. (Darmstadt: Wissenschaftliche Buchgesellschaft, 1964); Roman Jakobson, *Coup d'oeil sur le développement de la sémiotique,* Indiana University Publications, Studies in Semiotics, Vol. 3 (Bloomington: Indiana University Publications, 1975).

6. For a guide to the secondary literature on Aristotle's semantic theory, see Jan Pinborg, "Greek Antiquity," *Current Trends in Linguistics,* Vol. XIII: *Historiography of Linguistics* (The Hague: Mouton, 1975), pp. 69-126, esp. pp. 72-77.

7. Aristotle, *Peri Hermēneias* I (16a4-8).

8. The word *zōion* means either 'animal' or 'figure, image (in painting and sculpture).'

9. Aristotle, *Categoriae* II.

10. Aristotle, *Sophistic Elenchi* I (165a5-9), pp. 77-103.

11. On the Stoic approach to language, see the article by Jan Pinborg cited in footnote 6.

I am especially indebted to Hans-Erich Müller, *Die Prinzipien der stoischen Grammatik* Rostock, unpublished doctoral dissertation. The standard edition of the extant fragments of the original writings of the Stoics is Joh. von Arnim, *Stoicorum Veterum Fragmenta,* 4 vols. (Leipzig: Teubner, 1905-1924). Further textual material relating to language may be found in Rudolf Schmidt, *Stoicorum Grammatica* (Halle: E. Anton, 1839).

12. Sextus Empiricus, *Adversus Mathematicos* VIII.11. See Bocheński, p. 110; A. A. Long, *Problems in Stoicism* (London: Athlone Press, 1971), pp. 76-77; William & Martha Kneale, *The Development of Logic* (Oxford: Clarendon Press, 1962), p. 140; Benson Mates, *Stoic Logic,* University of California Publications in Philosophy, Vol. XXVI (Berkeley: University of California Press, 1953), pp. 21-23.

13. Müller, p. 17, interprets *tynchanon* as "der wirkliche Sachverhalt," as against *sēmainomenon* "der Bedeutungsinhalt eines Satzes."

14. Müller, pp. 17-20.

15. On Stoic etymological theory, see Schmidt, pp. 23-27.

16. "Verba enim prorsus inter homines obtinuerunt principatum significandi quaecumque animo concipiuntur, si ea quisque prodere velit." St. Augustine, *Corpus Christianorum, Series Latina,* Vol. XXXII, ed. Joseph Martin (Turnholti: Typographi Brepols, 1962), p. 34.

17. "Ut cum dico *lapis,* et intellectum lapidis et ipsum lapidem, id est ipsam substantiam, designat; sed prius intellectum, secundo vero loco significat rem." Boethius, *Commentaries. In librum Aristotelis Peri Hermēneias,* ed. C. Meiser (Leipzig: Teubner, 1880), Vol. I, p. 40.

18. "Nomen ergo est vox significativa secundum placitum." Aristoteles, *Categoriae et Liber de Interpretatione,* ed. L. Minio-Paluello (Oxford: Clarendon, 1966), p. 49.

19. See J. Engels, "Origine, sens et survie du terme boécien *secundum placitum,"* *Vivarium,* I (1963), pp. 87-114.

20. Ephraim Chambers, *Cyclopaedia* (London, 1728), Vol. XI, p. 428.

21. ". . . ergo illarum non sunt voces notae, sed rerum." Duns Scotus, *In universam Aristotelis logicam exactissimae questiones,* ed. C. Sarnano (Venice, 1583), f. 134ʳ.

22. See Philotheus Boehner, O.F.M., *Collected Articles on Ockham* (St. Bonaventure, N.Y.: Franciscan Institute, 1958), pp. 201-32.

23. "Signum est duplex: manifestativum et suppositivum. Manifestativum est illud quod solum indicat rem, sed pro re nihil accipitur. Sic fumus indicat ignem, hedera appensa vinum vendibile, et omnis effectus indicat suam causam. Suppositivum vero est illud quod ita significat rem ut pro re accipiatur. Sic calculi in supputatione ita significant rem quae supputatur ut pro re accipiantur. Voces igitur significant res tamquam signa suppositiva, quia pro rebus accipiuntur. Cum enim res in disputationem adducere non possimus, pro rebus verbis utimur. Sunt enim voces nomina rerum. Conceptus autem significant tamquam signa manifestativa; sunt enim voces effectus quidam conceptuum et procedunt a conceptibus sicut effectus a causa. Quare non accipiuntur voces pro conceptibus, neque sunt nomina conceptuum, sed solum indicant conceptus eo modo quo effectus indicat causam." Marcin Smiglecki, *Logica Martini Smiglecii* (Oxford: H. Crypps, 1634), p. 437.

24. "Sentio . . . tam conceptus quam voces et scripturas esse equipollentia signa res ipsas immediate significantia." Juan Caramuel Lobkowitz, *Rationalis et Realis Philosophia* (Louvain: E. de Witte, 1642), p. 9.

25. Thomas Hobbes, *Selections,* ed. Frederick J. E. Woodbridge (New York: Scribner, 1958), pp. 12-15. See also Hobbes' *Leviathan,* Part I, chap. IV, pp. 164-67 in Woodbridge's edition.

26. John Horne Tooke, *The Diversions of Purley,* 2nd ed. (London: J. Johnson's, 1798), Part 1, p. 18.

27. Tooke, p. 23.

28. Julius Caesar Scaliger, *De Causis Linguae Latinae* (Lyons: S. Gryphius, 1540), p. 2.

29. John Stuart Mill, *A System of Logic,* 3rd ed. (London: J. W. Parker, 1851), p. 24.

30. Bocheński, p. 328.

31. The terms *connotation* and *denotation* were so defined by John Stuart Mill. In non-technical parlance, on the other hand, connotations are implications in addition to the primary meaning of a word; these two uses should not be confused.

32. Mill, pp. 19-20.

33. On the history of linguistics, see R. H. Robins, *A Short History of Linguistics* (Bloomington: Indiana University Press, 1967); Hans Arens, *Sprachwissenschaft: der Gang iher Entwicklung von der Antike bis zur Gegenwart,* 2nd ed. (Freiburg & Munich: Alber, 1969); Dell Hymes, ed., *Studies in the History of Linguistics: Traditions and Paradigms* (Bloomington: Indiana University Press, 1974); Thomas A. Sebeok, ed., *Current Trends in*

Linguistics, Vol. XIII: *Historiography of Linguistics* (The Hague: Mouton, 1975). The literature on Saussure's linguistic theory is vast. A useful starting point is the excellent Italian translation of the *Cours* by Tullio De Mauro, which contains copious notes and comments: *Corso di linguistica generale* (Bari: Laterza, 1967). Valuable introductions to Saussure's ideas may be found in Robert Godel, "F. de Saussure's Theory of Language," *Current Trends in Linguistics,* Vol. III (The Hague: Mouton, 1966), pp. 479-93, and Rudolph Engler, "European Structuralism: Saussure," *Current Trends in Linguistics,* Vol. XIII (1975), pp. 829-86. The following may also be used with profit: René Amacker, *Linguistique saussurienne* (Geneva: Droz, 1975), and especially Rudolf Engler, *Lexique de la terminologie saussurienne* (Utrecht-Anvers: Het Spectrum, 1968).

34. On medieval speculative grammar, see Jan Pinborg, *Die Entwicklung der Sprachtheorie im Mittelalter* (Münster: Aschendorff in Verbindung mit dem Verlag Arne Frost-Hansen, Kopenhagen, 1967), and the same author's *Logik und Semantik im Mittelalter* (Stuttgart-Bad Cannstatt: Frommann-Holzboog, 1972).

35. On linguistic studies during the Renaissance, see my articles: "The Grammatical Tradition and the Rise of the Vernaculars," *Current Trends in Linguistics,* vol. XIII (1975), pp. 231-75; and "Changes in the Approach to Language," to appear in *The Cambridge History of Later Medieval Philosophy* (Cambridge: Cambridge University Press, 1980).

36. Saussure, *Cours de linguistique générale,* édition critique, p. 148.

37. Saussure, *Cours de linguistique générale,* édition critique, p. 50.

38. Saussure, *Cours de linguistique, générale,* édition critique, p. 50.

39. Varro, *De Lingua Latina* VII.39.

40. It meant literally 'nose-horned.'

41. Robert Godel, *A Geneva School Reader in Linguistics* (Bloomington: Indiana University Press, 1969), pp. 47-52.

42. *Cours de linguistique générale,* édition critique, pp. 147-57.

43. Sergei Karcevski, *Système du verbe russe* (Prague: "Plamja," 1927), p. 13.

Peirce and Semiotics:
An Introduction to Peirce's Theory of Signs

Arthur Skidmore

Semiotics may be characterized as the systematic study of signs or signification in general. I shall argue below that there probably cannot be a successful study, not to say a systematic science, of this kind. Yet there is a widespread supposition that a science of signs exists. And there is a great deal of writing which is based upon this supposition, as many papers in this volume testify.

Two names are most frequently mentioned in discussions of the modern foundations of semiotics: Ferdinand de Saussure and Charles Peirce. I shall say nothing further about Saussure, but I shall attempt in this paper to give an account of some of Peirce's most characteristic doctrines concerning signs and also to show in what respects Peirce's theory of signs is most obviously inadequate. I shall in passing take note of certain of Peirce's views which may shed some light on the feasibility of the semiotic enterprise.

There is today within Western philosophy, those systematic investigations begun in ancient Greece of the most general questions concerning the world and human consciousness, a split so profound that typical members of the opposing standpoints find each other's work to be literally unintelligible. One side consists in the others' eyes of obscurantists wallowing in a fantastic pseudo-scientific jargon (of which 'hermeneutic' is perhaps the best single example), while the others appear as strangely misguided mathematicians who are satisfied with playing a symbolic logic game instead of engaging in the pursuit of vital questions.

Both broad movements have roughly the same heritage, from the Presocratics up to about the beginning of the nineteenth century. By about the beginning of the twentieth century the divergent lines of inquiry have become rather clear. One path, through the great triad Hegel-Nietzsche-Husserl, what I shall call the *continental* movement, culminates in the work of contemporary phenomenologists and existentialists, typically writing in German or French, and of whom Heidegger is the most prominent example. The other movement, which I shall call the *analytic* movement, virtually rejects the nineteenth century (except possibly for John Stuart Mill) and bases itself on the great empiricist tradition of British eighteenth century philosophy and on the revolutionary developments in logic at the end of the nineteenth century beginning with the publication of Frege's *Begriffsschrift* in 1879. (This grand simplification omits Marxism altogether or construes it as a wing of continental philosophy.)

It may be said that philosophy has often wavered between being allied with *art* (especially literature and poetry) on the one hand and with *science* (especially mathematics and natural science) on the other. If this dichotomy has ever made sense, it would seem to apply with unparalleled force today. Nothing more dramatically expresses the tone or leading ideas of analytic philosophy than its close affinity for science, including the modern science of linguistics. And it appears that leading continental philosophers have a deep and significant regard for poetry and imaginative literature.

The practitioners of analytic philosophy have for the most part achieved anonymity outside their field of research scientists. Can anyone besides a student of academic philosophy name or even recognize the names of as many as six important analytic philosophers? Quine, Dummett, Kripke, Putnam, Goodman, and Davidson are not exactly names to conjure with, even among the highly literate, and yet their bearers are six of the most renowned and distinguished philosophers in the analytic tradition. Their writings resemble scientific papers much more than they do literature, and it is hopeless to try to understand any of these thinkers without first developing a solid background in mathematical logic.

Analytic philosophy seems, however, to share with the continental movement an enormous preoccupation with language. It is hardly an exaggeration to specify the question of *meaning,* understood as the question of the meaning of natural language, as *the* central question of analytic philosophy. There is accordingly a tantalizing possibility that the movements might converge around a genuine breakthrough in a general theory of signs. It is quite absurd to suppose that analytic philosophers would not be interested in a science of semiotics. The failure of analytic philosophers to embrace the work of the semioticians is based upon something far deeper than a mere lack of interest.

Charles Sanders Peirce (1839-1914) was fundamentally oriented toward science. His only graduate degree was in chemistry. He was for a time a professional astronomer who made original contributions on the subject of photometry. He worked as a physicist for the U.S. Coast and Geodetic Survey for many years. His father, Benjamin Peirce, was one of the leading American mathematicians of his time, and Charles Peirce was himself a gifted mathematician.

Peirce had the intellectual credentials to have become the leading figure of the analytic movement in philosophy. He independently arrived at the fundamental mathematical basis of modern logic, modern quantification theory, in about 1883. The co-discoverer of quantification theory, Gottlob Frege, achieved his basic result in 1879, as noted above.

Peirce is probably best known for his theory of meaning which came to be known as *pragmatism*. William James, Peirce's best and at times practically his only friend, is closely associated with something called pragmatism for which he courteously indicated his indebtedness to Peirce. Peirce rather insultingly (but apparently quite characteristically) renamed his own doctrine *pragmaticism* so that it might not be confused with what he (rightly) thought to be a trivialization of his own ideas.

It is very hard to avoid trivializing or at least simplifying Peirce's ideas. Very roughly, what Peirce meant by pragmatism is the view that the meaning, or *cognitive significance,* of a proposition consists in a subjunctive conditional of the form "If A were to be done, then B would be experienced." That is to say, even more roughly, that the meaning of a proposition consists in its *testable consequences*. An immediate consequence of this principle is that if a proposition has no testable consequences then it has no cognitive significance.

This idea is profoundly important, and it is quite characteristic of that branch of the analytic movement known as logical positivism. As is well known, the positivists asserted that entire domains of inquiry, most notably theology, ethics, and speculative metaphysics, did not admit of any testable consequences and were accordingly devoid of cognitive significance.

There are few if any unregenerate positivists among analytic philosophers today. But the attitude toward unfounded speculation entailed by adherence to the pragmatic theory of meaning is still prevalent and deep-seated. (This may explain at least in part why so much continental theorizing is viewed with such deep suspicion in analytic circles. The classic victim of pragmatism is Freudian or depth psychology, which is still viewed by many as devoid of cognitive significance, since it appears to have no testable consequences. One can easily find similar suspicions directed toward the work and theories of the German triad Hegel-Nietzsche-Husserl and especially toward Heidegger.)

The leading American analytic philosopher, Willard Van Orman Quine of Harvard, has provided the deepest and most important criticisms of Peirce's pragmatism. Quine points out (correctly, in my opinion) that strictly speaking the principle is inapplicable to single propositions (a point of which I think Peirce was eventually aware). That is, no single proposition has testable consequences all by itself, but only in conjunction with other propositions. The upshot of this is that only sets of propositions, and sometimes even whole theories, have cognitive significance. Given this revision, the spirit of pragmatism is maintained in its applications to whole theories such as Freudian psychology, General Systems Theory, and so on.

Outside of his contributions to pragmatism, fundamentally in the form of two articles in the *Popular Science Monthly,* Peirce's work remained almost totally unknown, for reasons which are worth mentioning here. Peirce did not have a very high opinion of the leading American universities of his time. He thought of Harvard, for example, as an "eleemosynary institution" for the young and idle rich. But he was intrigued by the idea behind the founding of the Johns Hopkins University (in 1876), which he thought constituted something very much like an ideal community of inquirers, and he joined the faculty in 1879 as lecturer in philosophy. To his (and our) very great misfortune, he was dismissed from this position in 1884, and he never held another university position. The precise causes of his firing remain obscure, although they may come to light in Max Fisch's forthcoming intellectual biography of Peirce. (Peirce apparently had, intellectually and practically, an almost total disrespect for authority, and he was dealing at Hopkins with some monumental egos.)

Although at the very height of his intellectual powers (recall that he had just invented modern logic, no less), he quickly and irreversibly lost touch with the philosophical community. Peirce was at that moment perhaps the greatest philosopher in the world, but he retired into a rural obscurity. His work became progressively more speculative and progressively more obscure. And this is just what one might expect, since he had no colleagues and no students to respond to his ideas.

Peirce never published a book on philosophy. He supported himself in part by writing reviews and dictionary entries, and these are filled with wonderful ideas, but they are uncritically and unsystematically developed.

His unpublished manuscripts of this period give ample evidence of his continued titanic intellectual powers, but they are highly fragmentary and profoundly elusive. Much of his writings on signs belongs to this period.

After his death, his manuscripts became the property of the philosophy department of Harvard University. In the 1930s two young academics at Harvard, Charles Hartshorne and Paul Weiss, who have since become two of the most distinguished philosophers in America, published six volumes of these manuscripts, and it has only been since then that the astonishing breadth and profundity of Peirce's philosophical achievements became widely known. Yet it was too late for the rapidly developing analytic movement to graft itself onto Peirce's foundation, and his works remain of interest primarily to Peirce scholars. As I shall attempt to show below, this is true of his writings on signs; they have become entirely superseded by contemporary developments in mathematical linguistics.

There are periodic flurries of interest in Peirce's writings, and one appears to be going on now. But the systematic development of his ideas which he so ardently hoped for has not taken place. This is largely because those most likely to continue his work find that he failed to understand the significance of the set-theoretical paradoxes and other technical logical matters. As a result, his work cannot be built directly upon by a contemporary analytic philosopher, but it would have to be reconstructed according to the prevailing paradigm. Anyone with a mind capable of both penetrating Peirce's thought and performing the necessary reconstructions would probably serve philosophy better by striking off on his own. This is, I think, the ultimate tragedy of Peirce's fate.

Peirce himself thought that his most important contribution to philosophy was his *theory of categories.* I want now to sketch a few features of this theory which are of special relevance to his theory of signs. For I do not think that Peirce's writings on signs can be understood at all without some understanding of his theory of categories.

Peirce's categories are a system of three general concepts, which he calls *Firstness, Secondness,* and *Thirdness.* These concepts in his opinion exhaustively describe or cover any field of experience or thought whatever. Peirce thought that his system of concepts would turn out to be as important as Aristotle's well-known distinctions between *potency* and *act* and between *form* and *matter,* and indeed that it would supersede them. He thought that dichotomous distinctions were a sign of immature thinking, and that thought and reality lent themselves best to his triadic analytical knife. What is more, he thought that he could prove the validity of his categories to be both universal and necessary. His argument runs somewhat as follows.

Peirce supposed that all propositions could be fully analyzed or interpreted in such a way as to reveal an ultimate logical structure. Further, every proposition contains one or more indexical parts, roughly names and definite descriptions. A *logical predicate* may be defined as that which remains when the indexical parts are removed from a fully analyzed proposition. It might seem that fully analyzed propositions could contain any number of names and hence that there could be logical predicates containing any number of blank places. For example, suppose that the following propositions are fully analyzed:

A is red.
A is next to B.
A represents B to C.
A wants B to buy C from D.

Then the corresponding logical predicates would be:

.... is red.
.... is next to ....
.... represents .... to ....
.... wants .... to buy .... from ....

Now Peirce argues that the above sequence of logical predicates ends with the third entry. He does this by an argument wherein he purports to show that all polyadic (containing three *or more* blanks) logical predicates can be reduced to complexes of triadic ones (containing exactly three blanks), and further that triadic logical predicates cannot in this way be reduced to complexes of dyadic and monadic ones, nor dyadic logical predicates to complexes of monadic ones. There are thus exactly three irreducibly distinct classes of logical predicates.

Peirce usually states his theory of categories in terms of *relations*. A relation is simply the object of a predicate, and hence the argument carries over directly to them: there are exactly three kinds of relations—monadic, dyadic, and triadic ones. Firstness is the concept of a monadic relation in general, Secondness is the concept of a dyadic relation in general, and Thirdness is the concept of a triadic relation in general.

It is extraordinarily difficult to understand the *content* of Peirce's categories. To understand what is meant by Firstness, we would have to understand what it is that is common to all monadic predicates in general. Obviously, this cannot be anything very concrete, but something like a formal character. Peirce sometimes says that this abstract content is a *quality of feeling*. The content of Firstness is not an actual feeling, which would introduce the idea of passivity (Secondness) and consciousness (Thirdness), but a qualitative possibility of a feeling.

Similarly, the content of Secondness would have to be that which all genuinely dyadic logical predicates have in common. Peirce thought that *actual brute existence* consisted sheerly in standing in dyadic relations to other things. So the content of Secondness is something like brute factuality.

Finally, the content of Thirdness is *generality* or *universality*. Examples of irreducibly triadic predicates all seemed to him to go beyond mere qualitative possibility and actual existence and to introduce an element of the really general or universal.

This may all seem terribly obscure, but the obscurity only arises when we try to arrive at intuitive content for Peirce's categories, which is after all only of secondary importance. What *is* important is that the *concepts* of Firstness, Secondness, and Thirdness as classes of logical predicates have been defined, in as clear and coherent a way as the most fundamental notions of any philosopher.

Since all of our thought is through logical predicates, everything thinkable and everything which can become an object of our experience falls under one of the three categories. Thus, in what might be called a *metaphysical* application of the theory of categories, everything must be thought of as a Firstness, a Secondness, or a Thirdness. For in order to be even a thinkable object, the object must be thinkable by means of a logical predicate. But there are exactly three kinds of these, and so the object must be one of exactly three sorts. Using the notion of the *content* of the categories, we may informally conclude that everything thinkable must be either a qualitative possibility, an actual existent, or a real general.

This metaphysical application of the theory of categories is mind-boggling stuff. For Peirce, if he is right, has succeeded in giving a rich, insightful, and highly non-trivial answer to the fundamental question of metaphysics in a relatively rigorous fashion.

An important *epistemological* application of the theory of categories stems from focusing upon the *irreducibility* of the categories. This bears directly on the possibilities of philosophical analysis. Again supposing that Peirce is right, it will not in general be possible to understand the world using only monadic and dyadic concepts. Peirce accuses most of his predecessors of having attempted to do exactly this. The term he uses for such philosophies is *nominalism*. Peirce is adamant in his insistence upon taking the category of Thirdness, and hence real universality, as philosophically ultimate and irreducible. This is perhaps the chief novelty of Peirce's theory and the source of its continuing importance for philosophy. If Peirce is right, we are as philosophers ineluctably committed to the irreducible reality of universals.

The paradigm of a genuine triadic relation for Peirce is the *sign* relation. The sign relation could also be called the *representation* relation, since it is expressed by:

.... represents .... to ....

We shall have a great deal more to say about the sign relation before long, but I should like now to remark on what has just been called the epistemological application of Peirce's theory of categories to the sign relation. Since the sign relation is irreducibly triadic, it is thoroughly an affair of Thirdness, and no account of signs, significance, language, or meaning can possibly succeed, if Peirce is right, which does not involve the reality of universals.

Since *naming* or labeling is for Peirce a characteristically dyadic relation, language cannot be understood as a system of names. The referential or naming function of a word is but a degenerate Thirdness—it can be understood in terms of the triadic sign relation, but not vice versa.

Even more important is Peirce's implicit attack on all *ideational* theories of meaning, as I shall call them. By an ideational theory of meaning I mean any theory which would attempt to account for the meaning of a sign in terms of an image or idea or mental picture in someone's mind. Suppose we say that person A has a mental picture and expresses this idea by means of a verbal sign which in turn causes to appear a similar idea in person B. If Peirce is right, this kind of account cannot possibly suffice, since it would attempt to explain the meaning of a sign in terms of two dyadic relations, between A's idea and the sign, and between the sign and B's idea.

From a slightly different perspective, we may make the same point by introducing another characteristic idea of Peirce's, that all thought is in signs. Even if we admit the function and relevance of A's and B's ideas in the above example, these ideas are themselves signs, and their meaning or significance needs in turn to be explained by any adequate theory of signs.

It is time now to take a look at some of Peirce's concrete doctrines concerning signs. I shall begin with an examination of a frequently cited definition by Peirce of the sign relation:

> A *Sign,* or *Representamen,* is a First which stands in such a genuine triadic relation to a Second, called its *Object,* as to be capable of determining a Third, called its *Interpretant,* to assume the same triadic relation to its Object in which it stands itself to the same Object. The triadic relation is *genuine,* that is its three members are bound together by it in a way that does not consist in any complexus of dyadic relations. (*Collected Papers,* 2.274)

Most of this should, I hope, make some sense. The one terminological difficulty is that the terms 'First,' 'Second,' and 'Third' here do *not* in my opinion have anything especially to do with Firstness, Secondness, and Thirdness. The First in the sign relation is I think merely the first term. It may very well be a general or universal, as Peirce explicitly asserts, and consequently may be an example of Thirdness. This definition is well worth mulling over for a while before proceeding.

One should be impressed by the extraordinary abstractness and generality of Peirce's conception of the sign or representation relation. Peirce is almost saying that representation is any genuine triadic relation. What distinguishes the sign relation from just any triadic relation is that it is *generative,* in the sense noted. I suppose an example of a genuine triadic relation which is not generative is the *giving* relation, wherein A gives B to C. In this case, C need not in turn give the same thing to someone else C'. But in the case of the representation or sign relation, when A represents B to C, it is always also true that C represents B to C' in turn. As we see, Peirce takes this formal property of the representation relation to be the defining characteristic of signs or representation.

A *sign,* for Peirce, is almost, but not quite, whatever is the first term of an instance of the representation relation. Peirce's strict usage is to call a *representamen* that which represents something to something. A *sign,* strictly, is any representamen which represents something to a *mental* something. Consider the following instructive passage, where Peirce distinguishes signs from representamens and characterizes the representation relation according to the formal feature of the above definition:

> Possibly there may be Representamens that are not Signs. Thus, if a sunflower, in turning toward the sun, becomes by that very act fully capable, without further condition, of reproducing a sunflower which turns in precisely corresponding ways toward the sun, and of doing so with the same reproductive power, the sunflower would become a Representamen of the sun. But *thought* is the chief, if not the only, mode of representation. (*Ibid.*)

In somewhat more detail, consider any instance of the sign relation: A represents B to C. The first term, A, is called the representamen or sign, as we have seen. The second term, B, is called the *object*. And the third term, C, is called the *interpretant*. According to the definition of the sign relation, C itself becomes a sign of the same object for a new interpretant C'.

The definition does not specify anything at all concerning the *nature* of A, B, and C. However, C is typically something *mental,* and in these cases C is called by Peirce a mental interpretant.

Thus for Peirce a sign is anything which stands in such a relation to its object that it is capable of determining a mental sign to stand for the same object in the same way. Accordingly, this mental sign is in turn capable of determining another sign, perhaps another mental sign in the same mind, perhaps an auditory verbal sign, perhaps a written sentence, perhaps a more elaborate sign. And any of these signs must in turn be capable of determining further interpretants.

We may feel frustrated here not to find any essential reference being made to human purposes and intentions. All the virtue, so to speak, seems to be on the side of the sign and not on the side of the human sign interpreter or sign user. It is *most* characteristic of Peirce not to make reference to human purpose when talking of signs. He seems at times to hold almost mystical doctrines to the effect that when we think we become an instance of the sign thought, that the signs in which we think have more reality than we do, and that the essence of man is literally to be a sign.

Yet one might fairly point out that it may well be precisely a matter of intention which makes a triadic relation *genuine*. For consider the case of the *giving* relation, A gives B to C. Peirce takes pains to point out that this relation does not consist merely in the transference of B from A to C. What it involves in addition is a community and a set of conventions. Similarly, human speech is not just an affair of uttering noises, but in addition there are intentions that the noises shall be interpreted in certain conventional ways.

What are we to make of Peirce's definition of the sign relation? Peirce evidently does not think that his definition is obvious, but that we may become aware of its truth when we draw inferences from his fundamental conception. It does not seem possible to find counterexamples to his definition of the sign relation simply by finding examples of signs which do not satisfy Peirce's definition.

The chief difficulty in following, much less evaluating, what Peirce has to say about signs stems from the obscurity of the term *interpretant*. To the best of my knowledge, the most coherent passage in which Peirce uses the term 'interpretant' is the following:

> A sign, or *representamen*, is something which stands to somebody for something in some respect or capacity. It addresses somebody, that is, creates in the mind of that person an equivalent sign, or perhaps a more developed sign. The sign which it creates I call the *interpretant* of the first sign. (2.228)

I gather that we may infer from this that the typical linguistic sign, say a sentence printed in a book, has the capacity to generate an equivalent sign in the mind of a reader of the book. This mental sign now has the capacity to be spoken aloud by the reader, and this sign in turn can generate a sequence of interpretant signs in the hearers, etc.

The real difficulty at this stage seems to be that of imagining what it would be like for something *not* to be a sign. What is there in the world that cannot or does not stand in the representation relation? We might suppose that something which is not interpreted as a sign is not a sign. But this pretty clearly won't do. A sentence in a book which is never read is still obviously a sign, no doubt because it is *capable* of being interpreted as a sign. But if we allow a sign to have a merely possible interpretant, then what is there in the world which is incapable of being interpreted as a sign?

When we consider Peirce's concept of *iconic* signs below, we shall discover that anything can be an iconic sign of anything it *resembles*. But then anything which is not absolutely *sui generis* can serve as an iconic sign.

Peirce is nevertheless prepared to accept this consequence of his definition: anything can be a sign. So our search for counterexamples cannot be expected to succeed.

Peirce's theory of signs proceeds by drawing a number of *trichotomies* which divide signs into classes. These trichotomies are more or less direct applications of Peirce's theory of categories discussed above. In the most common or basic formulation of his theory of signs, Peirce draws three such trichotomies:

> Signs are divisible by three trichotomies; first, according as the sign in itself is a mere quality, is an actual existent, or is a general law; secondly, according as the relation of the sign to its object consists in the sign's having some character in itself, or in some existential relation to that object, or in its relation to an interpretant; thirdly, according as its Interpretant represents it as a sign of possibility or as a sign of fact or a sign of reason. (2.243)
>
> According to the first division, a Sign may be termed a *Qualisign,* a *Sinsign,* or a *Legisign.* (2.244)
>
> According to the second trichotomy, a Sign may be termed an *Icon,* an *Index,* or a *Symbol.* (2.247)
>
> According to the third trichotomy, a Sign may be termed a *Rheme,* a *Dicisign* or *Dicent Sign* (that is, a proposition or quasi-proposition), or an *Argument.* (2.250)

The first trichotomy of signs is drawn according to the nature of the sign. This is clearly just the metaphysical application of the theory of categories applied to the first term in a representation relation. That is, everything that is is either a qualitative possibility, an actual existent, or a general or universal. Accordingly, every sign is either a *qualisign* (a qualitative possibility which is a sign), a *sinsign* (an actual existent which is a sign), or a *legisign* (a general which is a sign). It is worth pointing out that all *linguistic* signs fall into the third category. That is, words and sentences are construed by Peirce to be real generals. In this, Peirce is pretty clearly correct, and it is important to note this feature of linguistic signs. A test for something's being a general is whether it is *repeatable* as opposed to being a unique individual. It is fairly obvious that words of a human language are repeatable, that the very same word can be spoken or written many times.

The second trichotomy of signs is drawn according to the nature of the relation between the sign and its object. This trichotomy is probably the most widely discussed and referred to portion of Peirce's writings on signs. Again applying Peirce's theory of categories, we have found that there are just three possible sorts of relations. A sign may be related to its object, Peirce says, merely in a degenerate sense in which it *resembles* its object. Thus a diagram can represent something merely by virtue of its having certain properties which its object also has. Similarly, a sample represents the other things which resemble it. A sign which thus merely resembles its object is called an *icon*.

Secondly, a sign may stand in a real physical relation to its object. Signs which are connected thus to their objects are called *indices* by Peirce. Examples of indices are such things as weathervanes, shouts, and pointing fingers.

Finally, the relation between a sign and its object may be a *conventional* one. That is, a sign may represent something just because there is a convention that it do so. Such signs are called *symbols*. Linguistic signs are all symbols, since they represent their objects through linguistic conventions.

I shall make only a few remarks concerning the third of Peirce's trichotomies before returning to the second, since this trichotomy is drawn according to the nature of the interpretant, which makes it terribly difficult to understand. Further, it has not been nearly as influential as the first two trichotomies.

The third trichotomy, of *rheme, dicisign* (proposition), and *argument,* is of utmost interest for a logician, since it deals with precisely the sorts of signs with which the logician is most concerned. This should come as no surprise, since Peirce is in the end uninterested in signs which have nothing to do with human cognition. To be sure, he intends his theory of signs to be completely universal and to apply anywhere where we might find significance or representation of any kind. But he is fundamentally most interested in propositions and arguments.

What is most intriguing about the third trichotomy is that it purports to *deduce* the existence of rhemes, propositions, and arguments directly from an application of his theory of categories to his definition of the sign relation. This is indeed something rather haunting and extraordinary.

It is fairly clear that Peirce's theory of signs has begun to go haywire even at the level of the first and second trichotomies. Notice, for example, that the second trichotomy does not operate separately within each of the three classes produced by the first trichotomy. Specifically, as we have seen, linguistic signs are all conventional, and consequently they are all *symbols*. No linguistic sign can be an icon or an index, strictly speaking. Yet Peirce definitely wants this second trichotomy to apply to linguistic signs, and he frequently employs the expressions 'iconic' and 'indexical' to refer to various sorts of linguistic signs.

Peirce is himself aware of this difficulty, and when he is being especially careful he will speak of 'hypoicons' and 'subindices.'

> A possibility alone is an Icon purely by virtue of its quality; and its object can only be a Firstness. But a sign may be *iconic,* that is, may represent its object mainly by its similarity, no matter what its mode of being. If a substantive be wanted, an iconic representamen may be termed a *hypoicon.* Any material image, as a painting, is largely conventional in its mode of representation; but in itself, without legend or label it may be called a *hypoicon.* (2.276)
>
> *Subindices* or *Hyposemes* are signs which are rendered such principally by an actual connection with their objects. Thus a proper name, personal demonstrative, or relative pronoun of the letter attached to a diagram, denoted what it does owing to a real connection with its object, but none of these is an Index, since it is not an individual. (2.284)

Most of the time, however, Peirce is not careful about this matter and speaks freely of linguistic signs as icons or indices, which is strictly speaking a contradiction in terms. The ambiguity concealed in the terms 'iconic' and 'indexical' has bedeviled both Peirce and his many commentators.

Peirce would have liked to have proved that every proposition must have an indexical part, that is, a part which is an index. But a proposition is a conventional sign, thoroughly of the nature of Thirdness. All of its *parts* are also Thirdnesses. So a proposition cannot contain a part which is an index. But how then can we guarantee that propositions link up with the world?

It would be so neat, logically speaking, if only Peirce could prove that propositions referred by necessity to an object (a Secondness) in the actual world of existent objects. But he quite simply cannot prove this.

I certainly do not want to leave the impression that I think Peirce made silly mistakes or obvious blunders. I do think that once having so decisively arrived at his conception of Thirdness, it has so to speak taken hold of his thought or perhaps, to speak with my own metaphor, it has imprisoned him within a semiotic idealism from which there is no escape. Thought becomes irreducibly a matter of Thirdness alone, and the factually existent or sheerly possible become at best degenerate Thirdness.

Peirce tries to reinstitute the contingently factual or brute existent and the qualitatively possible into his universe of real generals. But there isn't really any way I can see of doing this. That symbols can refer to things which are not also symbols remains something fundamentally unintelligible. If Thirdness really is irreducible to Secondness, and symbols and thought are essentially matters of Thirdness, then we cannot in fact rationally break out of the circle of language.

Consider Peirce's dilemma in the following:

> Words alone cannot do this [provide one with an index—A.S.]. The demonstrative pronouns, "this" and "that," are indices. (2.287)

Here Peirce almost desperately tries to find a way of breaking out of the circle of Thirdness by virtually contradicting himself in two successive sentences. Words alone cannot provide one with an index, and yet we are told that the word 'this' is an index. (He does not actually contradict himself, since he is thinking of a physical connection between 'this' and its object brought about in the context of utterance.)

Peirce's very definition of the sign relation may I think be seen to apply, properly speaking, only to conventional signs or symbols. This stems from Peirce's requirement that the sign relation be a *genuine* triadic relation. A Firstness or a Secondness cannot really stand in a genuine triadic relation and consequently cannot really be a sign. Thus there aren't really any qualisigns or sinsigns, and thus the first trichotomy completely collapses: only legisigns are signs at all.

For similar reasons, there are no icons or indices either. That is, suppose that A represents B to C, and suppose further that the relation between A and B is merely one of *similarity*. Well if A is similar to B, then A is similar to B *regardless* of whether A is interpreted as standing for B. If the relation were genuine, this could not be so. In a precisely similar way, if A is causally connected to B, then the relation between A and B is what it is regardless of whether A is interpreted as representing B. Hence in both cases the relation between A, B, and C is not a genuine or irreducibly triadic relation. The relation is genuine only when A is a sign of B only because of its relation to C.

The objection I am here raising to Peirce's theory of signs is somewhat formal in nature. That is, it deals with some highly abstract definitions. Peirce's theory of signs can be criticized from an even more abstract level by criticizing his theory of categories, but I shall not pursue this topic here.

The formal nature of the criticisms I have leveled against Peirce leaves open at least one avenue of response. Peirce may *agree* that Firstnesses and Secondnesses cannot strictly speaking be signs, but at the same time respond to my criticism by pointing out that we cannot even be conscious of something which is a pure or absolute Firstness or Secondness. If we restrict ourselves to the field of consciousness, we find that everything there is a matter of Thirdness. For example, a *diagram* may be a conventional sign, and hence a Thirdness, but its mode of signification takes advantage of its qualitative features. Similarly, a demonstrative pronoun is a symbol which enables us to understand its object through a dyadic relation to what is referred to.

Although Peirce's theory can be 'saved' through considerations such as the above, the cost is very high. For if we turn Peirce's theory into an empirical, observational theory, we lose its quasi-necessary character. Remember that the startling value of Peirce's approach was that it enabled us to *deduce* the existence of the various classes of signs. From our revised standpoint it becomes a competitor to linguistic theory. There is nothing to recommend Peirce's speculative empirical theory over the work of contemporary mathematical linguists, who have found in the concept of *phrase structure* a far more useful tool than Peirce's trichotomies. Nor do I think that Peirce would hesitate a moment to adopt the methods of contemporary linguistics in preference to his own.

Peirce's theory of signs fails. I would like now to speculate a bit on the reasons for Peirce's failure. I think that the real explanation of Peirce's dilemma is the problem faced by anyone who might attempt to devise a general theory of signs. If the concept of the sign relation is to be rich and complex enough to cover human language, it is going to leave out, or be inapplicable to, non-linguistic signs such as bee dances or wax impressions. On the other hand, if one's concept of sign is to be broad enough to extend to anything that might be called significant or a sign, it will lack the subtlety and complexity required to explain anything about human language.

This fundamental dilemma is I think amply borne out by the failure of semioticians to provide us with a general account of signs which has any plausibility at all when applied to human language. One enduring value of reflecting on Peirce's writings, especially his writings on signs, is that it may help us to understand why this is so. The semiotician who theorizes from animal communication or simple dyadic models will not provide us with a theory of language. And the linguist will find his work on language not to apply to animal communication.

Peirce's theory of signs may be of value in casting serious doubt upon the feasibility of the semiotic enterprise, at least in the present state of knowledge. But the moral should not be to give up inquiry into language and into non-linguistic signification, but to pursue these perhaps essentially different inquiries *independently,* without requiring that either be shackled within the confines of a non-existent *general* theory of signs. This is to say that the linguist need not be particularly concerned with the findings of the communication theorist or the semiotician. His aim ought to be to discover the nature of human language and to follow this inquiry wherever it may lead using whatever resources are necessary. Similarly, the student of literature need not concern himself with communication theory and semiotics, but rather with scientific linguistics.

Suggestions for Further Reading

All references to Peirce are to the standard edition of Peirce's philosophical works, *Collected Papers of Charles Sanders Peirce* (Cambridge, Mass.: Harvard University Press, 8 v., 1931-35, 1958). The editors have in my opinion done an outstanding job of selecting Peirce's manuscripts, many previously unpublished, and arranging them according to subject matter, for which they have received a great deal of undeserved criticism. Peirce's reflections on signs are scattered throughout every volume, but are especially concentrated in the second volume. References to Peirce are made according to volume and numbered paragraph.

Justus Buchler's edition of selected essays by Peirce, *Philosophical Writings of Peirce* (New York: Dover, 1955), is a very handy source which covers the full range of Peirce's ideas. It probably contains all of Peirce's thought with which any student of philosophy should be familiar.

The best single comprehensive study of Peirce's philosophical development is Murray Murphey's *Development of Peirce's Philosophy* (Cambridge, Mass.: Harvard University Press, 1961). Murphey's treatment of Peirce can be criticized in detail, but Murphey thoroughly understands the main lines of Peirce's thought, and Murphey's central thesis, that many of Peirce's views changed throughout his career though his terminology might remain the same, is correct and important. Murphey does not try to simplify things, and his book is at times very heavy going.

A very useful summary of Murphey's book is his entry in Paul Edwards' *Encyclopedia of Philosophy* under the heading Peirce.

Recently two editions of Peirce manuscripts not contained in the *Collected Papers* have appeared, one an edition of Peirce's mathematical papers by Carolyn Eisele, and the other Charles Hardwick's edition of the correspondence between Peirce and Lady Victoria Welby, *Semiotic and Significs* (Bloomington: Indiana University Press, 1977). The latter contains a highly elaborate and late version of Peirce's reflections on signs.

An interesting and influential work of Peirce scholarship on his theory of signs is Douglas Greenlee's *Peirce's Concept of Sign* (The Hague: Mouton, 1973).

Charles S. Peirce and the Semiotics of Literature

John K. Sheriff

Ferdinand de Saussure, who provided the terms and concepts that have been most useful in "structuralist" linguistics, anthropology, and poetics, said that language is a system of signs, the most important among many such systems, and predicted that a science of signs (Semiology) would emerge which "would show what constitutes signs, what laws govern them."[1] Among Saussure's followers the analysis of sign systems has flourished but the definition of "what constitutes signs" has not gotten significantly beyond that provided by Saussure. The use of Saussure's basic concepts of *langue* and *parole,* of relations and oppositions, of signifier and signified for studying networks of sign relations in literature has become a major influence shaping literary theory and criticism. But as Jonathan Culler says in the preface to his *Structuralist Poetics,* "The type of literary study which structuralism helps one to envisage would not be primarily interpretive . . . . Rather than a criticism which discovers or assigns meanings, it would be a poetics which strives to define the conditions of meaning."[2] The semiotics of literature, then, tries "to analyze the system of conventions which enable literary works to have the meanings they do for members of a given culture. It asks what are the conventions that enable works to have meaning for readers."[3] If, as Culler says, "the semiotician is one who, by profession, scrutinizes meanings already known to members of his culture in the hopes of discovering the conventions which they have mastered and have no need to know,"[4] it is appropriate to ask why semiotics of literature is thus limited. The answer, it seems to me, lies with the linguistic model, particularly the inadequate definition of a sign.

This essay is an attempt to show that the theory of signs developed by Saussure's American contemporary Charles Sanders Peirce provides a frame of reference which will allow semioticians to see beyond the limitations of Saussure's analysis of the sign and will clarify many of the issues that have been problematic in the semiotics of literature. Most publications in semiotics contain an obligatory paragraph on Peirce, but few or none seriously consider the implications of his theory of signs for the semiotics of literature.

Peirce, near the end of his life, wrote in a letter to Lady Welby: "Now a definition does not reveal the Object of a Sign, its Denotation, but only analyzes its Signification, and *that* is a question not of the sign's relation to its Object but of its relation to its Interpretant."[5] If Peirce had tried to put his finger on the weakness of Saussure's definition of a sign he could not have done it better than with this statement. In light of Saussure's refusal to treat signs-in-the-mind it is understandable that structuralists have been unable to generate and evaluate interpretations of texts. No wonder their criticism reads as though the conventional sign systems are the main actors and the characters are merely nexuses of intersecting sign systems. Moreover, the mindset that divides the sign into arbitrary signifiers and signifieds leads to a misunderstanding of Wittgenstein's linguistic turn, a concept that has numerous implications for semiotics of literature, particularly in relation to reader response theory.

In order to pursue these issues, it is first necessary to provide a review of Peirce's theory of signs. In doing so, I have emphasized the aspects of Peirce's theory that remained fundamentally unchanged during his lifetime and are most important to the present discussion, that is, his definition of a sign in relation to his categories. Peirce defines a sign as follows:

> A sign, or *representamen,* is something which stands to somebody for something in some respect or capacity. It addresses somebody, that is, creates in the mind of that person an equivalent sign, or perhaps a more developed sign. That sign which it creates I call the *interpretant* of the first sign. The sign stands for something, its *object.* It stands for that object, not in all respects, but in reference to a sort of idea, which I have sometimes called the *ground* of the representamen. (2.228)[6]

An understanding of the italicized terms is essential. Probably the most ambiguous term is "ground." Peirce says that "every representamen" is "connected with three things, the ground, the object, and the interpretant" (2.229). Moreover, he says that the branch of semiotics dealing with "ground" is *"pure grammar,"* which has the task "to ascertain what must be true of the representamen used by every scientific intelligence in order that they may embody any *meaning*" (2.229).

Peirce's immediate concern in the context in which we find the above definition is to inquire into the character of signs themselves. But in a later essay entitled "Meaning" (1910) Peirce enlarges upon the idea of "ground." He says, "If a Sign is other than its Object, there must exist, either in thought or in expression, some explanation or argument or other context, showing how—upon what system or for what reason the Sign represents the Object or set of Objects that it does" (2.230). The "ground" it turns out is nothing more nor less than the context or language-game within which the sign relates to its interpretant. "The peculiarity of it [a sign], therefore, lies in its mode of meaning; and to say this is to say that its peculiarity lies in its relation to its interpretant" (2.252).

Other of Peirce's definitions of a sign describe not only the triadic relation within which a sign must be embodied in order to signify but also the generation of signs and the modes of being signs represent. In Baldwin's *Dictionary of Philosophy and Psychology* (1902) Peirce defined a sign as "Anything which determines something else (its *interpretant*) to refer to an object to which itself refers (its *object*) in the same way, the interpretant becoming in turn a sign, and so on *ad infinitum*" (2.303). And in his unpublished "Syllabus," written about the same time as the above, Peirce states:

> A *Sign*, or *Representamen*, is a First which stands in such a genuine triadic relation to a Second, called its *Object*, as to be capable of determining a Third, called its *Interpretant*, to assume the same triadic relation to its Object in which it stands itself to the same Object. The triadic relation is *genuine*, that is its three members are bound together by it in a way that does not consist in any complexus of dyadic relations .... The Third ... must have a second triadic relation in which the Rerepresentamen, or rather the relation thereof to its Object, shall be its own (the Third's) Object, and must be capable of determining a Third to this relation. All this must equally be true of the Third's Third and so on endlessly" (2.274).

The triadic relation described in the first definition of a sign quoted above may be visualized thus:

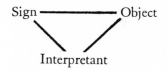

In the last statement quoted above, Peirce inserts First, Second, and Third (which he undoubtedly meant to refer to his categories of Firstness, Secondness, and Thirdness, which I will define later) in a way that may be visualized thus:

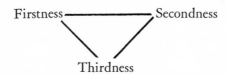

Peirce does not mean that Firstness is synonymous with sign and Secondness is synonymous with object. It is easy to become confused at this point because interpretants are, in fact, always Thirdness. But Peirce is defining here the simplest possible sign (which we learn later is a Qualisign). Peirce goes on to say in the last two definitions quoted above that the interpretant must be able to cause a second triadic connection in which the relation-of-the-sign-to-its-object in the first triad becomes the object of the interpretant (which assumes the position of a sign in the new triad). Again it may be helpful to visualize the process. I will abbreviate Firstness (F), Secondness (S), and Thirdness (T).

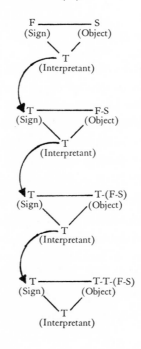

The relation-of-the-sign-to-its-object in the first triad becomes the object of the interpretant, which assumes the position of a sign in a new triad. "And so on endlessly."

"[A]nd this, and more, is involved in the familiar idea of a Sign; and as the term Representamen is here used, nothing more is implied" (2.274).

When we picture this generative nature of signs, we see the increasing complexity of the Object: "A sign may have more than one Object. Thus, the sentence 'Cain killed Abel,' which is a Sign, refers at least as much to Abel as to Cain, even if it be not regarded as it should, as having 'a killing' as a third Object. But the set of Objects may be regarded as making up one complex Object" (2.230). Furthermore, we can understand why Peirce's definition of object is so encompassing:

> The Objects—for a Sign may have any number of them—may each be a single known existing thing or thing believed formerly to have existed or expected to exist, or a collection of such things, or a known quality or relation or fact, which single Object may be a collection, or whole of parts, or it may have some other mode of being, such as some act permitted whose being does not prevent its negation from being equally permitted, or something of a general nature desired, required, or invariably found under certain general circumstances" (2.232).

Peirce's theory of signs is merely an elaboration of his definition of a sign, and his trichotomies and classes of signs make no sense and have no validity unless viewed in the light of this definition of a sign. Peirce's method is to reason "from the definition of a Sign what sort of thing *ought* to be noticeable and *then* searching for its appearance."[7]

Firstness, Secondness, and Thirdness, as the above discussion of signs implies, are central to Peirce's classification of signs. In fact, the three categories are the basis on which Peirce attempts "to outline a theory so comprehensive that, for a long time to come, the entire work of human reason, in philosophy of every school and kind, in mathematics, in psychology, in physical science, in history, in sociology, and in whatever other department there may be, shall appear as the filling up of its details" (1.1). Hence definitions and examples of these three categories abound in Peirce's papers, in at least as many different contexts as there are disciplines in the above quotation. For example, when Peirce is writing a refutation of nominalism he states: "My view is that there are three modes of being. I hold that we can directly observe them in elements of whatever is at any time before the mind in any way. They are the being of positive qualitative possibility [Firstness], the being of actual fact [Secondness], and the being of law that will govern facts in the future" [Thirdness] (1.23).

Firstness is the mode of being which consists in something being what it is without reference to anything else, the thing in itself without relation to others. The qualities of phenomena have such being. "The mode of being a *redness,* before anything in the universe was yet red, was nevertheless a positive qualitative possibility. And redness in itself, even if it be embodied, is something positive and *sui generis.* That I call Firstness" (1.25). Firstness is very difficult to talk about, "is so tender that you cannot touch it without spoiling it" (1.358), because when we talk about Firstness we turn a sign into an interpretant and thereby lose what we are seeking to grasp. The Qualisign, we shall see, is nothing but Firstness.

Secondness is the being of actual fact. "The actuality of the event seems to lie in its relations to the universe of existents . . . . Actuality is something brute. There is no reason in it. I instance putting your shoulder against a door and trying to force it open against an unseen, silent and unknown resistance. We have a two-sided consciousness of effort and resistance, which seems to me to come tolerably near to a pure sense of actuality . . . . I call that Secondness" (1.24).

Thirdness, as a category of being, consists in that tendency of things to come together in such a way as to be predictable, "to conform to a general rule" (1.26).

Perhaps the most helpful treatment of the categories for a study of signs is Peirce's treatment of these categories in consciousness: "It seems, then, that the true categories of consciousness are: first, feeling, the consciousness which can be included with an instant of time, passive consciousness of quality, without recognition or analysis; second, consciousness of an interruption into the field of consciousness, sense of resistance, of an external fact, or another something; third, synthetic consciousness, binding time together, sense of learning, thought" (1.377).

Feelings, then, comprise immediate consciousness. Immediate feelings can only be contemplated in memory which "is an articulated complex and worked-over product which differs infinitely and immeasurably from feeling" (1.379). The experience of Firstness is "an instance of that kind of consciousness which involves no analysis, comparison or any other process whatsoever, nor consists in whole or in part of any act by which one stretch of consciousness is distinguished from another, which has its own positive quality which consists in nothing else, and which is of itself all that it is, however it may have been brought about" (1.306).

Just as immediate feeling is the consciousness of Firstness, a sense of polarity or reaction is the consciousness of Secondness. Again, Peirce's examples clarify his general, often vague, statements:

> Besides Feelings, we have Sensations of reaction; as when a person blindfold suddenly runs against a post, when we make a muscular effort, or when any feeling gives way to a new feeling . . . . Wherever we have two feelings and pay attention to a relation between them of whatever kind, there is the sensation of which I am speaking (6.19).

> While I am seated calmly in the dark, the lights are suddenly turned on, and at that instant I am conscious, not of a process of change, but yet of something more than can be contained in an instant. I have a sense . . . of there being two sides to that instant. A consciousness of polarity would be a tolerably good phrase to describe what occurs (1.380).

The consciousness of a process of change negated in the above quotation is the consciousness of Thirdness:

> This is a kind of consciousness which cannot be immediate, because it covers a time, and that not merely because it continues through every instant of that time, but because it cannot be contracted into an instant. It differs from immediate consciousness, as a melody does from one prolonged note. Neither can the consciousness of the two sides of an instant, of a sudden occurrence, in its individual reality, possibly embrace the consciousness of a process. This is the

consciousness that binds life together. It is the consciousness of synthesis (1.381).

In consciousness, feelings are Firstness; reaction-sensations or disturbances of feelings are Secondness, and general conceptions are Thirdness.

Having briefly defined Firstness, Secondness, and Thirdness, we are ready to ask how these categories relate to Peirce's three trichotomies. Are these categories ontological or phenomenological? First let's review the three trichotomies.

According to Peirce's analysis of his own definition, a sign is one of three kinds (Qualisign, Sinsign, or Legisign); it relates to its object in one of three ways (as Icon, Index, or Symbol); and it has an Interpretant that *represents* the sign as a sign of possibility, fact, or reason, i.e., as Rheme, Dicent Sign, or Argument.

The answers to the questions raised can be shown easier than explained. I present the following in full awareness of the commonly held notion that Peirce is not clear about whether his categories are ontological or phenom-

Phenomenological or formal categories		Ontological or material categories		
		Firstness	Secondness	Thirdness
Firstness	A sign is:	a "mere quality" QUALISIGN	an "actual existent" SINSIGN	a "general law" LEGISIGN
Secondness	A sign *relates* to its object in having:	"some character in itself" ICON	"some existential relation to that object" INDEX	"some relation to the interpretant" SYMBOL
Thirdness	A sign's interpretant *represents* it (sign) as a sign of:	"possibility" RHEME	"fact" DICENT SIGN	"reason" ARGUMENT

enological. I do not find Peirce to be inconsistent on this matter. He shows that signs signify because of their intrinsic qualities and their relations. The material aspects are predominant in a Qualisign; the relational or formal aspects in a Symbol or Argument. A Saussurian linguist who focuses only on linguistic signs obviously sees only the relational-differential character of the sign.

Peirce holds that the material aspects of Firstness, Secondness, and Thirdness are empirically observable. The material aspect of Firstness, as we have mentioned already, Peirce calls quality, the immediate nonconceptual given of sense experience. The material aspect of Secondness Peirce calls "Thisness," the immediate, nonconceptual experience of the dynamic interaction of two things. Depending on one's definition of ontological, the concept of a material aspect of ontological Thirdness may cause some confusion. What Peirce has in mind is the experience of thought or rationality. Ontological Thirdness has much less the character of the immediate given than have the other two categories, but the material aspect of Thirdness is analogous to that of *langue* as described by Saussure.

Formally, or phenomenologically, Peirce holds that "signs may be divided as to their own material nature, as to their relation to their objects, and as to their relations to their interpretants."[8] Peirce holds that all thought is reducible to some combination of these three and that this triadic relation is irreducible. He was later to increase the number of formal categories, but never revised the concept of a triadic relation of sign-object-interpretant.

"A *Qualisign*," according to Peirce, "is a quality which is a sign. It cannot actually act as a sign (be represented) until it is embodied (in a triad of sign-object-interpretant); but the embodiment has nothing to do with its character as a sign" (2.244, the parenthetical material is mine). In the beginning was a sign, and that sign was with a quality, and that sign was a quality. All signification came into being through it and without it was no sign made that was made. The only way a Qualisign can be represented is thus:

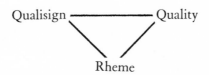

Otherwise, the Qualisign becomes part of the object of another triadic relation, such as:

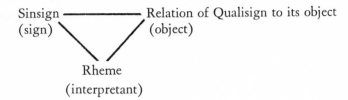

Sinsign ———————— Relation of Qualisign to its object
(sign)   (object)

Rheme
(interpretant)

Now it should be clear why pure Firstness and Secondness, Qualisigns and Sinsigns respectively, are difficult to talk about. They cannot be linguistic signs. No sign can be a word (written or spoken) until it has become a triad of Thirdnesses. A Firstness must undergo three transformations or generations before it can be represented by a word. By now I think the abbreviations for sign, object, and interpretant and for Firstness, Secondness, and Thirdness will be clear.

S   "positive qualitative possibility"

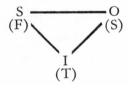

a sign in the mind (feelings) of Firstness, a Qualisign

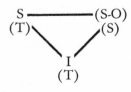

a sign in the mind of a sign in the mind, a Sinsign

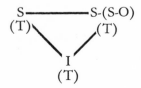

a sign or symbol (possibly a word) in the mind for a sign in the mind of a sign in the mind, a Legisign

If one understands the above he already understands Sinsigns and Legisigns. A Sinsign is a sign that is a fact. Or in Peirce's words, it "is an actual existent thing or event which is a sign" (2.245). The syllable *sin,* Peirce tells us, is taken as meaning "being only once." It can be only once in the sense that it is always and only the second transformation, that is:

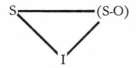

Every Legisign is a sign that represents the relation of a sign in the mind to a sign in the mind. Just as the objects of Sinsigns are embodied Qualisigns, the objects of Legisigns are embodied Sinsigns. And just as Qualisign is a sign that is a quality and Sinsign "is an actual existent thing or event which is a sign," a Legisign is "a law that is a Sign." "This law is usually established by men. Every conventional sign is a Legisign .... It is not a single object, but a general type which, it has been agreed, shall be significant" (2.246). Since it is a general law and not a quality or actual existent object, "Every legisign signifies through an instance of its application, which may be termed a *Replica* of it." "Thus the word 'the' will usually occur from fifteen to twenty-five times on a page. It is in these occurrences one and the same word, the same legisign. Each single instance of it is a Replica" (2.246). But the Replica would not be significant "if it were not for the law which renders it so" (2.246).

A quick reference to Peirce's definitions of Icon, Index, and Symbol would reveal that only a Legisign can be a symbol, i.e., "a sign which would lose the character which renders it a sign if there were no interpretant" (2.304). A Sinsign may be Index or Icon. As Index it is "a sign which would, at once, lose the character which makes it a sign if its object were removed, but would not lose that character if there were no interpretant" (2.304). As Icon it is "a sign which would possess the character which renders it significant, even though its object had no existence" (2.304). Of course a Qualisign can be only an Icon. When Peirce is describing his ten classes of signs he frequently uses the adjectival form for the signs in his second trichotomy (e.g., Iconic) because Icon, Index, and Symbol are concepts (signs) that describe the relation of a sign to its object.

Interestingly, Peirce's definition of a sign is consistent with the linguistics of Wittgenstein. In contrast, Saussure's definition of the sign as dyadic and his failure to bring the activity of mind into his treatment of signs has been an obstacle to the use of Wittgenstein's linguistic turn in literary criticism and poetics. The implication one gets from Saussure's linguistics is that language is something arbitrarily added to pre-existing objects. This concept has led frequently to a misunderstanding of the linguistic turn as merely a reversal of this process—beginning with language rather than being. It is not as though we experience language and the world as independent entities; we come to the world through language, or more precisely, through language-games—"modes of activity which involve intentional actions, in accord with rules and norms, directed toward purposeful ends."[9] This is the same argument Peirce makes for his definition of a sign as a triadic relation of sign-object-interpretant. Wittgenstein and Peirce both insist that we have no choice but to unite linguistic signs, objects, and mental activity (interpretants) in one notion and treat them as dependent rather than independent entities.

It seems to me that the linguistic turn is very much at the center of Derrida's *Of Grammatology* and that he could have communicated several of his ideas more simply using Peirce's definition of a sign. Though Derrida gives only a cursory treatment of Peirce in *Of Grammatology,* he does make a few comments that leave one wondering why he did not use Peirce more extensively. In qualifying Saussure's concept of the arbitrary nature of linguistic signs Derrida says, "In his project of semiotics Peirce seems to have been more attentive than Saussure to the irreducibility of the becoming-unmotivated" of the sign as symbol, or linguistic sign.[10] In this regard he quotes Peirce approvingly:

> Symbols grow. They come into being by development out of other signs, particularly from icons, or from mixed signs partaking of the nature of icons and symbols. We think only in signs. These mental signs are of mixed nature; the symbol parts of them are called concepts. If a man makes a new symbol, it is by thought involving concepts. So it is only out of symbols that a new symbol can grow (2.302).

He concludes that Peirce has already done much that his own work sets out to do. Derrida says of his own work, "To make enigmatic what one thinks he understands by the words 'proximity,' 'immediacy,' 'presence' . . . is my final intention in this book. This deconstruction of presence accomplishes itself through the deconstruction of consciousness and therefore through the irreducible notion of the trace (*Spur*)."[11] Therefore it is quite significant that he says "Peirce goes very far in the direction that I have called the de-construction of the transcendental signified" [i.e., presence].[12] Derrida recognizes that Peirce's definition of a sign has within it the destruction of the metaphysics of presence. Derrida's commentary on Peirce's *Principle of Phenomenology* is that it, unlike Husserl's unacceptable phenomenology, is not a theory of things but a theory of signs.

> [*M*]*anifestation* itself does not reveal a presence, it makes a sign . . . . The so-called "thing itself" is always already a *representamen* shielded from the simplicity of intuitive evidence. The *representamen* functions only by giving rise to an *interpretant* that itself becomes a sign and so on to infinity. The self-identity of the signified conceals itself unceasingly and is always on the move. The property of the *representamen* is to be itself and another, to be produced as a structure of reference, to be separated from itself . . . .
>
> From the moment that there is meaning there are nothing but signs. We *think only in signs*.[13]

It is within the context of his definition of "trace" that Derrida interjects this commentary on Peirce. The concept of the "trace" remains somewhat enigmatic in *Of Grammatology* because Derrida uses Saussure's concept of a sign to describe what he sees to be a characteristic of signs that cannot be accounted for using Saussure's definition of the sign. One wonders again why Derrida does not use Peirce's theory of signs to get beyond Saussure, particularly when he admits that in specific ways Peirce is superior. Consider, for example, some of Derrida's definitions of "trace":

> *The trace is in fact the absolute origin of sense in general. Which amounts to saying once again that there is no absolute origin of sense in general.*

> That the signified is originarily and essentially . . . trace, that it is *always already in the position of signified* is the apparently innocent proposition within which the metaphysics of the logos, of presence and consciousness, must reflect upon writing as its death and its resource.[14]

Peirce, it seems to me, makes it much clearer than Derrida in what sense all linguistic signs derive their meaning from "trace" or signs which are always already prior to consciousness. In Peircian terms, the relation of Firstness and Secondness to Thirdness (language and thought) is that they are always already a Thirdness. Moreover, a Thirdness in thought is always already another Thirdness. This is Derrida's major point. Linguistic signs are "always already in the position of the signified." Peirce would have said that signs conceal themselves in triadic relations of significance from which they cannot be separated. In that sense they are already objects as well as signs, or signifieds as well as signifiers.

I do not mean to imply that there is nothing (or that there is something), in Derrida's *Of Grammatology* that is not already implied in Peirce's theory of signs, or that Derrida's concept of "trace" is nothing more than I have mentioned herein. However, if we are going to take Derrida seriously, that is in itself good reason to take Peirce seriously. Derrida finds Saussure's definition of sign inadequate and speaks approvingly of Peirce's, though he gives no evidence of careful consideration of Peirce's complete theory of signs. Perhaps those who take it upon themselves to elucidate Derrida's work will find Peirce helpful.

What are the implications of Peirce's theory of signs for the semiotics of literature? First of all, his classification of signs shows us something

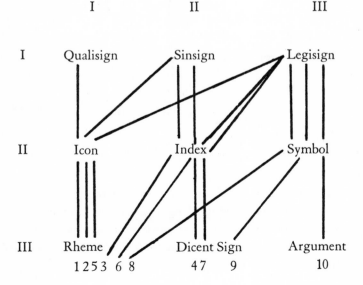

about the character of a literary text. This will become clear if we look at Peirce's ten classes of signs. The following graph is less complex than the one Peirce provides but adequate for the present purpose. Note that each line represents one of Peirce's classes of signs and the numbers indicate the order in which Peirce presents them.

Based upon the fact that Qualisigns and Sinsigns are Firstness and Secondness respectively and upon the hypothetical process of sign generation noted above, classes one through four cannot be linguistic signs, that is they cannot be words or sounds emitted from a person to signify. The interpretant of a Qualisign can be no more than a feeling. A Sinsign is already a combination of signs in that it is always an object of experience (actual existent) which points to another object of experience. Of interest here is the fact that at a more basic level of experience than the use of linguistic signs, we already have *syntax,* a combination which signifies by the nature of the relationship.

The last six classes involve Legisigns, but classes five, six, and seven, are not necessarily linguistic. ☺ I take to be an Iconic Legisign; but I cannot imagine a word that is an Iconic Legisign, except maybe one like G..d. Even when they are linguistic signs (e.g., the demonstrative pronoun "that" is a Rhematic Indexical Legisign), they are general laws, habits, conventions that as Icons and Indices picture and point, draw attention to objects other than themselves.

Classes eight, nine, and ten are all symbols; they draw attention to themselves, to their formal properties, as much as to their referential significance. In early formulations Peirce had called his interpretants Terms, Propositions, Arguments. He later changed the first two of these because at best they were only appropriate to classes eight, nine, and ten. Moreover, the class eight sign, the Rhematic Symbol can be a much more complex sign than "Term" implies, because it can embody a virtually unlimited number of objects. The difference between classes eight, nine, and ten lies principally in the different ways in which they represent their objects. "A *Rheme* is a Sign . . . of qualitative possibility, that is, is understood as representing such and such a kind of possible Object" (2.250), "a sign which is understood to represent its object in its characters merely; . . . a Dicisign is a sign which is understood to represent its object in respect to actual existence; and . . . an Argument is a Sign which is understood to represent its Object in its character as a Sign" (2.252). The peculiarity of a sign, therefore, "lies in its mode of meaning; and to say this is to say that its peculiarity lies in its relation to its interpretant. The proposition professes to be really affected by the actual existent or real law to which it refers. The argument makes the same pretension, but that is not the principal pretension of the argument. The rheme makes no such pretension" (2.252).

Generally speaking, "-logy" disciplines, such as theology, biology, anthropology, deal with arguments or theories, interpretants which are assured or verified by their "Form," their character as signs. The "-ic" disciplines, such as logic, ethics, physics, and linguistics, deal with existent relations, interpretants assured by "Experience." Saussure's conception of *Semiology* as a "science of signs" and Peirce's conception of *Semiotic* as synonymous with logic may account for the suffixes they employed. Most important to our present concern is the fact that all the arts, literary art included, are signs of qualitative possibility, interpretants assured by "Instinct" or conviction.

Peirce speaks very little about art as sign, but he makes clear in various writings that art always partakes of the mode of being of Firstness as well as Secondness or Thirdness. Literary art, being inseparable from language of course partakes of Thirdness (i.e., is a symbol), but it creates an interpretant that has the mode of being of Firstness (i.e., is a rheme). For example, Peirce says that if we allow his categories to form our conceptions of history and life, "we remark three classes of men"—men who create art, practical men who carry on the business of the world, men possessed with a passion to learn. "The first consists of those for whom the chief thing is the qualities of feelings. These men create art" (1.43). The artist is enthralled by the possible and the role of the possible. The actual interests him only to the extent that his artistic imagination can invest it with poetical possibilities. He is the archetypal intellectual who contemplates actual existence as an aesthetic spectacle, interested in it primarily as a possible instance of some universal or law. For these persons "nature is a picture" (1.43).

The second class of men "respect nothing but power, and respect power only so far as it [is] exercised" (1.43). These men seek methods to control themselves and their environments, usually in order to better fulfill their own desires.

"The third class consists of men to whom nothing seems great but reason" (1.43). Those familiar with Peirce will recognize that these are in Peirce's view the "natural scientific men" who inquire "into truth for truth's sake, without any sort of axe to grind, nor for the sake of the delight of contemplating it, but from an impulse to penetrate into the reason of things" (1.44). To the degree that the literary critic has this motivation he is in Peirce's view one of the scientists. To the degree he has an ulterior motive (to get published, promoted, etc.), he, like the chemist who studies nothing but dyestuffs because of their commercial importance, is a businessman type.

Peirce says "A Sign may *itself* have a 'possible' Mode of Being."[15] A literary work, then, is a sign of possibility experienced, according to Peirce, as rhematic symbol. Even though it may contain many propositions and arguments, as for example, a work of fiction frequently does, these must be seen in context as part of a sign of possibility. The fact that a class eight sign, a rhematic symbol, may be a word or an entire text is important to emphasize because of what that implies about the nature of literary art. Peirce's definitions of a rheme are meant to be applicable to all classes involving rhemes. Consequently he usually uses the simplest examples.

Peirce says, "A rheme is any sign that is not true nor false, like almost any single word except 'yes' and 'no,' which are peculiar to modern language." Also he says a rheme can be thought of as "simply a class-name or proper-name."[16] Wittgenstein's comments on naming seems to express the same idea. "Naming is . . . not a move in the language-game—any more than putting a piece in its place on the board is a move in chess. We may say: *nothing* has so far been done, when a thing has been named. It has not even *got* a name except in the language-game. This is what Frege meant too, when he said that a word only has meaning as part of a sentence."[17] The literary text has the same relation to ontological Secondness or Thirdness that a word has to a sentence. By itself it merely stands as a sign of possibility.

Martin Heidegger's treatment of the nature of art in *Poetry, Language, Thought* helps us to see what it means to think of art as a sign of ontological Firstness. He says, "The art work opens up in its own way the Being of beings. This opening up, i.e., this deconcealing, i.e., the truth of beings, happens in the work."[18] Heidegger has several useful analogies to explain what happens to "being" in human consciousness. For example, he says that in human cognition the world is perceived as earth and sky, divinities and mortals. The thing which is art gathers and unites the fourfold. It "stays the fourfold into a happening of the simple onehood of world."[19] This happening "cannot be explained by anything else nor can it be fathomed through anything else . . . . As soon as human cognition here calls for an explanation, it fails to transcend the world's nature, and falls short of it. The human will to explain just does not reach to the simpleness of the simple onefold of worlding. The united four are already strangled in their essential nature when we think of them only as separate realities, which are to be grounded in and explained by one another."[20] This is of course implied in Peirce's assertion that it is impossible to talk about Firstness without losing it, without relating it to Secondness and making it the object of an interpretant that is a proposition or argument.

Since a poem (any work of literature) is experienced as a rhematic symbol, it is a distortion to equate it with a proposition or argument, perhaps an enlightening distortion but a distortion nevertheless. The disdain of literary critics for moralistic and subjective interpretations of art is valid, but a little like the pot calling the kettle black. The nature of an art work as defined by Peirce's theory of signs reveals the limitations and pitfalls of the critical process. Many readers are unable to distinguish between the rhematic symbols and the arguments that are created in their minds by the reading of a text. Anytime one says anything about the rheme produced by the sign, he is unconsciously allowing the interpretant (rheme) to become a new sign (legisign) which determines a new interpretant (an argument). In other words, he turns a sign of imaginative possibility into a proposition or argument.

Strictly speaking, the critic has only a memory of experiencing a poem, and his comments are inadvertently about his memory of experiencing the poem, that is, about his memory of the poem's interpretant. The plight of the critic is that the literary work, like any other sign, conceals itself from him. It is always already something else, an interpretant, to him.

On this point, Roman Jakobson, Roland Barthes, Tzvetan Todorov, and Gérard Genette with their focus on systems and conventions, make the mistake Derrida describes in *Of Grammatology*. They seem to think that they are objectively treating the text itself when they are in fact interpreting their own interpretants with codes and language-games which are transformations of the texts. This is not to say that what these writers say about certain texts is incorrect. Peirce says that "each Sign must have its own peculiar Interpretability before it gets any Interpreter."[21] The peculiar interpretability of a literary text is responsible for the immediate interpretant (the true object of all interpretation and criticism) and is less directly but still responsible for the various interpretations or generated interpretants (each of which is different from any other).

There is no single right reading of a literary work not only because a literary work is a complex sign but also because, as is true of any sign, it is always already an interpretant that itself becomes a sign and so on to infinity. The literary text as a sign is not something fixed and permanent that will stand still to be looked at. It is always alive, unceasingly generating interpretants, always concealing itself in triadic relations of significance from which it cannot be flushed.

In the foregoing discussion we have considered a text as *a* sign in order to clarify the mode of being of a literary work and the mode of being of a discussion of that work. But we also need to come to terms with the fact that a poem or novel is not experienced as one sign. Although we attribute to it the character of being a sign of possibility, we are confronted with hundreds or thousands of signs of every linguistic type. Peirce gives an example which illustrates how many sign relations are involved in a very simple sentence.

[T]he statement, "Cain killed Abel" cannot be fully understood by a person who has no further acquaintance with Cain and Abel than that which the proposition itself gives . . . . But further, the statement cannot be understood by a person who has no collateral acquaintance with killing . . . . Of course, an Icon would be necessary to explain what was the relation of Cain to Abel, in so far as this relation was *imaginable* or imageable. To give the necessary acquaintance with any single thing as Index would be required. To convey the idea of causing death in general, according to the operation of a general law, a general sign would be requisite; that is a *Symbol*. For symbols are founded either upon habits, which are, of course general, or upon conventions of agreement, which are equally general.[22]

Peirce, it should be noted, does not deal explicitly with the question of how a literary text determines an interpretant, but his concept of the "ground" of a sign and Wittgenstein's concept of "language-game" are helpful here.

Peirce's "ground" (defined earlier) and Wittgenstein's "language-games" are similar if not exactly the same. Language-games as rule-governed activities provide the frame of reference for all use of linguistic signs. "When language-games change, then there is a change in concepts, and with the concepts the meaning of works change."[23] The truthfulness or accurateness of a statement about a poem or anything else is determined by our frame of reference or language-game. What a reader brings to a text are language-games, and most criticism is description of language-games. Northrop Frye's theory of modes, Wayne Booth's rhetoric of fiction, Roland Barthes' codes, Tzvetan Todorov's grammar of narrative come immediately to mind in this respect. Though many language-games have been identified and described, most have been learned practically and without any explicit rules.

Susanne Langer says that we have a constant need to transform all our experience into symbolic expression. "What he (man) cannot express, he cannot conceive; what he cannot conceive is chaos, and fills him with terror."[24] Apparently we will say something about the interpretant of the text we have experienced. Some ground or language-game will determine our ideas of order about the work. The French structuralists are having a heyday discovering the rules of many of these games. But to try to find the rules that control the creation of new symbols and language-games is like trying to fathom the black hole in space.

In his later years, Peirce further elaborated his theory of signs. He distinguished two objects of a sign each of which had ontological Firstness, Secondness, and Thirdness. He postulated that each interpretant could be one of three kinds and that each of these three kinds could be any of the three modes of being. Thus he came up with six trichotomies and twenty-eight classes of signs. He later suspected that there were four more trichotomies and hoped he would find only sixty-six classes though as many as 59,049 were possible. His further elaborated theory of signs, had he completed it, would not have given much more specificity to his treatment of symbols.

The character of symbols is to stand in some relation to other symbols. The possibilities of such relations are limitless. Despite Peirce's penchant for classification, there is no reason to believe he would have disagreed with Wittgenstein's demonstration of the unlikelihood of ever finding a few common rules or characteristics that will be applicable to all language-games. Below is a sample of Wittgenstein's reasoning on this matter:

> Instead of producing something common to all that we call language, I am saying that these phenomena [language-games] have no one thing in common which makes us use the same word for all,—but that they are *related* to one another in many different ways. And it is because of this relationship, of these relationships, that we call them all "language." I will try to explain this.

> Consider for example the proceedings that we call "games." I mean board-games, card-games, ball-games, Olympic games, and so on. What is common to them all?—Don't say: "There *must* be something common, or they would not be called 'games'"—but *look and see* whether there is anything common to all . . . . And we can go through the many, many other groups of games in the same way; can see how similarities crop up and disappear.

> And the result of this examination is: we see a complicated network of similarities overlapping and criss-crossing: sometimes overall similarities, sometimes similarities of detail.

> I can think of no better expression to characterize these similarities than "family resemblances"; for the various resemblances between members of a family: build, features, colour of eyes, gait, temperament, etc. etc. overlap and criss-cross in the same way.[25]

Peirce's definition of sign is consistent with the concepts of language inherent in Wittgenstein's language-games or Derrida's (and Wittgenstein's)[26] de-centering of metaphysical presence. In this regard Peirce provided a context that helps clarify the assertions of many modern intellectuals, from Sigmund Freud to Peter Handke, that man is alienated from himself, an object of his own consciousness, isolated in a prison-house of language.

On the other hand, the character of the sign as defined by Peirce provides a critique of the current trend in literary semiotics toward a concentrated focus on form. Works such as Culler's *Structuralist Poetics* and Barthes' *S/Z,* for example, practically ignore the question of meaning. The Saussurian influence with its emphasis on conventional sign systems seems to me to be largely responsible for this trend.

Peirce, though no artist or art critic, saw the significance of art to be its quality of Firstness, not its conventions of Thirdness. Wittgenstein, who did have a lifelong interest in aesthetics and used parables and fables in his own writing, said that there is fundamental difference between the use of language in mythology and art and the use of language in rational, discursive thought. In the former, language is used *indirectly* to *show;* in the latter, it is used *descriptively* to *say.* The following graph may clarify the distinction:

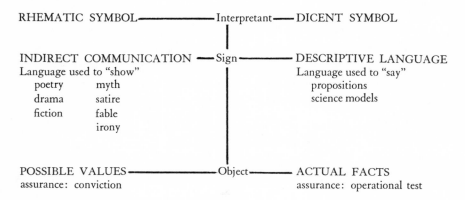

RHEMATIC SYMBOL————————Interpretant——DICENT SYMBOL

INDIRECT COMMUNICATION ——Sign———— DESCRIPTIVE LANGUAGE
Language used to "show"   Language used to "say"
   poetry   myth   propositions
   drama   satire   science models
   fiction   fable
           irony

POSSIBLE VALUES————————Object———— ACTUAL FACTS
assurance: conviction   assurance: operational test

Language (ontological Thirdness) can be used to symbolize ontological Firstness (to show) and Secondness (to say). It goes without saying that language can symbolize itself, that is, it can be a symbol that represents a symbol (i.e., argument, or Third-Thirdness) partaking of but not limited by other modes.

Allen Janik and Stephen Toulmin in *Wittgenstein's Vienna* interpret the *Tractatus* as "an expression of a certain type of language mysticism that assigns a central importance in human life to art, on the ground that art alone can express the meaning of life. Only art can express moral truth and only the artist can teach the things that matter most in life. Art is a mission. To be concerned merely with form, like the aesthetics of the 1890s, is to pervert art."[27]

And Peirce himself wrote, "So the poet in our days—and the true poet is the true prophet—personifies everything not rhetorically but in his own feelings. He tells us that he feels an affinity for nature, and loves the stone or the drop of water."[28]

Such a view of the artist and his work is rarely put forward by a structuralist. Saussure's concepts lead attention away from it. The person who comes to semiotics motivated by an interest in the meaning of human experience will find very little published to date that is relevant to his interest. But Peirce gives a theoretical basis for such an unscientific position as the following:

> All arts create symbols for a level of reality which cannot be reached in any other way. A picture and a poem reveal elements of reality which cannot be approached scientifically. In the creative work of art we encounter reality in a dimension which is closed for us without such works . . . . A great play gives us not only a new vision of the human scene, but it opens up hidden depths of our own being. Thus we are able to receive what the play reveals to us in reality. There are within us dimensions of which we cannot become aware except through symbols, as melodies and rhythms in music.[29]

There is no contradiction between this statement by Tillich and the statement that man is alienated from himself and isolated in a prison-house of language. In fact, Peirce helps us to see that the statements are complementary.

Saussure inspired his followers to meticulously survey the island of linguistic signs; Wittgenstein chose rather to survey the boundary of the ocean.[30] Peirce provides a theory of signs helpful to either endeavour. Saussurian linguists looked at literature and found structures; Wittgenstein saw in literature a manifestation of that about human experience which cannot be put into words. Peirce developed a theory of signs containing formal as well as experiential categories, and consequently is a more comprehensive model for literary analysis than the one presently in vogue that contains only formal categories.

Notes

1. Ferdinand de Saussure, *Course in General Linguistics* (New York: McGraw-Hill, 1959), p. 16.
2. Jonathan Culler, *Structuralist Poetics: Structuralism, Linguistics, and the Study of Literature* (Ithaca, N.Y.: Cornell University Press, 1975), p. viii.
3. Jonathan Culler, "The Semiotics of Poetry: Two Approaches," this volume, pp. 75-93.
4. Culler, "Semiotics of Poetry."
5. 14 March 1909, *Charles S. Peirce's Letters to Lady Welby,* ed. Irwin C. Lieb (New Haven, Ct.: Whitlocks, Inc., 1953), p. 39.
6. *The Collected Papers of Charles Sanders Peirce,* Vols. 1-6, ed. Charles Hartshorne and Paul Weiss, 1931-1935; Vols. 7-8, ed. A. W. Burks, 1958 (Cambridge, Mass.: Harvard University Press). References to *The Collected Papers* are parenthesized within the text. The

first numeral in the reference is the volume number, and the number to the right of the point is the paragraph.

7. 14 March 1909, *Letters to Lady Welby*, p. 36.

8. 12 October 1904, *Letters to Lady Welby*, p. 12.

9. Richard Fleming, review of *The Illusion of Technique* by William Barrett (New York: Doubleday, 1978), in *Auslegung: A Journal of Philosophy*, 6, No. 1 (November 1978), p. 68.

10. Jacques Derrida, *Of Grammatology*, trans. Gayatri C. Spivak (Baltimore: Johns Hopkins University Press, 1974), p. 48.

11. Derrida, p. 70.

12. Derrida, p. 49.

13. Derrida, pp. 49-50.

14. Derrida, pp. 65, 73.

15. 23 December 1980, *Letters to Lady Welby*, p. 31.

16. 12 October 1904, *Letters to Lady Welby*, p. 13.

17. Ludwig Wittgenstein, *Philosophical Investigations*, trans. G. E. M. Anscombe (New York: Macmillan, 1958), p. 24.

18. Martin Heidegger, *Poetry, Language, Thought*, trans. Albert Hofstadter (New York: Harper and Row, 1971), p. 39.

19. Heidegger, p. 181.

20. Heidegger, pp. 179-80.

21. 14 March 1909, *Letters to Lady Welby*, p. 36.

22. 14 December 1908, *Letters to Lady Welby*, p. 24.

23. Ludwig Wittgenstein, *On Certainty*, ed. G. E. M. Anscombe and G. H. von Wright, trans. Denis Paul and G. E. M. Anscombe (New York: Harper and Row, 1969), p. 10e.

24. Susanne Langer, "The Lord of Creation," *Fortune*, January 1944.

25. Wittgenstein, *Philosophical Investigations*, pp. 31-32.

26. Wittgenstein, in the *Tractatus*, trans. D. F. Pears and B. F. McGuinness (New York: The Humanities Press, 1961), p. 117, shows that "in an important sense there is no subject . . . . The subject does not belong to the world: rather, it is a limit of the world. Where *in* the world is a metaphysical subject to be found?"

27. Allen Janik and Stephen Toulmin, *Wittgenstein's Vienna* (New York: Simon and Schuster, 1973), p. 197.

28. *Charles S. Peirce: Selected Writings*, ed. Philip P. Weiner (New York: Dover Publications, 1958), p. 13.

29. Paul Tillich, *Dynamics of Faith* (New York: Harper and Brothers, 1957), pp. 42-43.

30. This image is borrowed from Paul Engelmann, *Letters from Ludwig Wittgenstein*, p. 97, quoted in *Wittgenstein's Vienna*, p. 191.

The Semiotics of Poetry: Two Approaches

Jonathan Culler

People are attracted to semiotics for a variety of reasons. For some it is a powerful technique of demystification; for others an alluring mode of mystification. To some it offers the hope of a truly rigorous methodology in the human and social sciences; to others it is attractive because they can use its vocabulary to bring together insights and observations from the most disparate disciplines. For some students of literature semiotics may seem the long-delayed response to Northrop Frye's plea for a "coherent and comprehensive theory of literature, logically and scientifically organized . . . the main principles of which are as yet unknown to us";[1] for others, who on principle consider this an *ignis fatuus,* semiotics is a new source of interpretive tools, to be exploited in *ad hoc* fashion.

Michael Riffaterre's new book, *Semiotics of Poetry,* has much to offer both of these groups. On the one hand, his theory, which he believes to be applicable to all Western literature, proposes "a coherent and relatively simple description of the structure of meaning in a poem."[2] On the other hand, in every chapter he tackles, by way of example, some of the most obscure or evasive poems of modern French literature, and he invariably produces a powerful, often startling interpretation. It is a theory which both attempts to describe how poems have meaning and seeks to produce, for every poem considered, a new and authoritative interpretation.

Of course it is not difficult in itself to devise a comprehensive theory of poetry that will generate new interpretations for every poem. Consider, for example, the theory that poems are elaborate camouflage for secret messages to the elect and that, among other things, the number of letters in a poem is a hypothesis about the number of years until the Second Coming. This general theory clearly has the power to produce for any poem an interpretation that will surprise the critic. It is also a theory that is easy to master and to apply. Riffaterre, however, is not a religious fanatic and his interpretations, surprising though they may be, are much more likely to secure the assent of the critic, even though he may despair of ever producing similar interpretations himself, for want of the immense learning and the ear for echoes which Riffaterre brings to the reading of poems.

What is the theory and how does it generate interpretations? Riffaterre begins from two well-established notions about poetry: that "poetry expresses concepts and things by indirection. To put it simply, a poem says one thing and means another" (p. 1) and that "the unit of meaning peculiar to poetry is the finite, closed entity of the text" (p. ix), which must be treated as a coherent and unified whole. These notions have played an important role in criticism, but Riffaterre takes them as rigorous and literal principles, and he combines them: the poem is an indirect and circuitous expression of something, let us call it X; and the X which it expresses is the invariant of which its elements are all variants, the invariant which, once it is discovered, makes the poem a unity. Interpreting the poem is a matter of discovering this X and showing how it determines the sentences and images of the poem.

Described in this way, Riffaterre's procedure sounds somewhat familiar, a version of the New Criticism, which also insisted on unity and which, if it avoided formulations such as "the poem says one thing and means another," nonetheless demonstrated that the poem was doing or saying something that was not immediately apparent. But the New Critics always insisted on the richness and complexity of this "total and governing attitude" which unified the poem; and though they made much of the organic nature of the poem they would have indignantly rejected the view that the poem was the exfoliation of a seed or kernel which determined its unity. For them, on the contrary, to discover the unity of a poem was not to identify the single element which generated it but to build up a sense of the complex attitude to which all of the poem's parts contribute. Unity was located not in a kernel but in an overall attitude (so complex that many pages are required to describe it). Contrast this with Riffaterre's description of the discovery of unity:

> Then suddenly the puzzle is solved, everything falls into place, indeed the whole poem ceases to be descriptive, ceases to be a sequence of mimetic signs, and becomes but a single sign, perceived from the end back to its given as a harmonious whole, wherein nothing is loose, wherein every word refers to one symbolic focus (p. 12).

There are two things to note here: first, the stress on solving the puzzle, finding the secret, discovering the element which makes everything fall into place—an emphasis which makes *Semiotics of Poetry* an unusually daring work and compels admiration while it provokes uneasiness; and secondly, the radical distinction between mimesis and another kind of meaning which Riffaterre calls "semiosis." This latter distinction is familiar, if not quite in this form. Critics are accustomed to showing that signs which claim to represent or make assertions about a state of affairs are in fact forming a different pattern, leading the reader to treat the supposed representation as a sign of another kind. Whether one sees this as a displacement of reference (for example, statements about landscape or weather usually need to be taken as an indirect way of conveying feelings, or, at another level, poetic images turn out to say something about poetry itself) or whether one stresses the formal patterns created by apparently referential signs, there is a redirection of signs. Once again, Riffaterre makes a familiar distinction more rigorous and absolute than is customary, producing a theory that takes risks.

In the initial reading of a text or "heuristic reading," one is dealing with linguistic signs—"the reader's input is his linguistic competence, which includes an assumption that language is referential—and at this stage words do seem to relate first of all to things" (p. 5). But, Riffaterre argues, the reader always encounters difficulties, or, as he calls them, "ungrammaticalities": some signs, interpreted referentially, give bizarre or contradictory results. Moreover, the results of this heuristic reading are unsatisfying for two further reasons. First, the text characteristically displays patterns (metrical, phonological, semantic) which cannot be interpreted referentially; these patterns are signs which need to be interpreted but can only be dealt with at another level. Secondly, at the mimetic level the text is a string of representations, yet the reader knows that the characteristic feature of a poem is its unity, so if he is to interpret it properly he must seek a level at which this unity can be identified—a level at which the text can become a single unit.

These difficulties give rise to a second reading—"retroactive" or "hermeneutic"—in which the obstacles that arose when one tried to read mimetically become the keys to a new reading, "the guideline to semiosis, the key to significance in the higher system" (p. 6). It is worth quoting Riffaterre's description of this process:

> The ungrammaticalities spotted at the mimetic level are eventually integrated into another system. As the reader perceives what they have in common, as he becomes aware that this common trait forms them into a paradigm, and that this paradigm alters the meaning of

the poem, the new function of the ungrammaticalities changes their nature, and now they signify as components of a different network of relationships. This transfer of a sign from one level of discourse to another, this metamorphosis of what was a signifying complex at a lower level of the text into a signifying unit, now a member of a more developed system, at a higher level of the text, this functional shift is the proper domain of semiotics. Everything related to this integration of signs from the mimesis level into the higher level of significance is a manifestation of *semiosis* (p. 4).

Riffaterre is unusually frank in his assertion that the interest of poetry lies in this overcoming of mimesis, this puzzling out of semiotic unity which, as he says, makes poetry "more of a game than anything else" (p. 14). But what is truly radical is his claim about the nature of this semiotic unity. "The poem . . . results from the transformation of a word or sentence into a text" (p. 164) and the sentences which appear to be making statements about the world must, if the poem is to be constituted as a unity, be grasped as variants of this kernel or "matrix."

> The poem results from the transformation of the *matrix,* a minimal and literal sentence, into a longer, complex, and non-literal periphrasis. The matrix is hypothetical, being only the grammatical and lexical actualization of a structure. The matrix may be epitomized in one word, in which case the word will not appear in the text. It is always actualized in successive variants; the form of these variants is governed by the first or primary actualization, the *model*. Matrix, model, and text are variants of the same structure" (p. 19).

Before we consider some examples that will illustrate this process and these concepts, it is important to emphasize that the expansion or conversion of matrix to text produces a series of signs which are apparently representational, but certain of these signs are what Riffaterre calls "poetic signs": "a word or phrase is poeticized when it refers to (and, if a phrase patterns itself upon) a pre-existent word group" (p. 23). This pre-existent word group Riffaterre calls a *hypogram;* the hypogram may be a cliché, a descriptive system, a quotation, a thematic complex. In any event, the hypogram is not located in the text but is the result of past semiotic or literary practice, and it is in perceiving a sign's reference to this pre-existing phrase or complex that the reader identifies the sign as poetic. "For the poeticity to be activated in the text," Riffaterre writes, "the sign referring to a hypogram must also be a variant of that text's matrix" (p. 23). In other words, poetic signs in a text are powerfully over-determined: they both refer to a pre-existing hypogram and are variants or transformations of a matrix.

These are strong claims. Let us look first at a relatively simple example in which Riffaterre's argument is clear and in which his revelation of the "secret" provides an interpretation which, if it lacks the richness critics are wont to seek, is nevertheless likely to be preferred to previous interpretations. The example is Rimbaud's "Fêtes de la faim":

FÊTES DE LA FAIM

Ma faim, Anne, Anne
Fuis sur ton âne.

Si j'ai du *goût,* ce n'est guères
Que pour la terre et les pierres.
Dinn! dinn! dinn! dinn! Je pais l'air,
Le roc, les Terres, le fer.

Tournez, les faims, paissez, faims,
Le pré des sons!
Puis l'aimable et vibrant venin
Des liserons;

Les cailloux qu'un pauvre brise,
Les vieilles pierres d'églises,
Les galets, fils des déluges,
Pains couchés aux vallées grises!

Mes faims, c'est les bouts d'air noir;
L'azur sonneur;
— C'est l'estomac qui me tire.
C'est le malheur.

Sur terre ont paru les feuilles!
Je vais aux chairs de fruit blettes
Au sein du sillon je cueille
La doucette et la violette.

Ma faim, Anne, Anne!
Fuis sur ton âne.[3]

Here, for convenience, is Riffaterre's translation:

> Feasts of Hunger. My hunger, Anne, Anne, run away on your
> donkey. If I have any taste, it is for hardly anything but earth's
> soil and stones. Dinn! dinn! dinn! dinn! I feed on air, rock, soil,
> iron. Turn round and round, hungers, graze the meadows of sound!
> Then the nice vibrant venom of the morning glories; the stones a
> poor man breaks, the old slabs of churches, the beach pebbles, children
> of deluge, bread loaves lying in the grey valleys! My hungers, they
> are crumbs of black air; the azure bellringer; it's my stomach that
> aches. It's unhappiness. Leaves have come out on earth! I am going
> to the flesh of overripe fruit, from the heart of the furrow I pick
> lamb's lettuce and the violet. My hunger, Anne, Anne! run away
> on your donkey.

In commenting on this poem critics have generally tried to explain individual images by supposing private associations on the part of the poet,
or else have simply given up: "Rimbaud lets himself go here in free childish association. The effect is fresh, innovative and naturally uneven"
(quoted p. 77). But Riffaterre argues that the poem can be comprehended
if it is seen as a series of images, each of which is a transformation of a
cliché and a variant of the matrix. As he writes:

> The mimetic deficiencies that have been piling up from the first
> stanza on have the appearance—to our hindsight—of accumulating
> metonyms of hunger. Starting with the self-mocking italics (line 3),
> "if I have a taste for anything (what a taste!), it is for earth and
> stones," the poem simply catalogs inedibles. More precisely, since the
> last stanza shifts to edibles, the entire poem is an expansion on two
> polar opposites, the narrative potentialities derivable from the sememe
> "hunger": a tale of unsatisfied hunger, and a tale of its satisfaction.
> *Avoir faim* has two lexical facets, a negative and a positive: you
> starve, or you have a good appetite. In either case the craving for
> food can be expressed in terms of eating, hence a matrix: *eating
> the inedible, eating the edible,* which covers the whole story of the
> poem's given (pp. 77-78).

At first, Riffaterre explains, "the reader does not catch on because each
disconcerting (and linguistically established) *exemplum* of the uneatable
is out of context" and because the items the poem lists at first are, pre-

cisely, inedible, so that the reader would be producing a contradiction if he brought them together under the heading of *eating*. But, Riffaterre claims, and this argument must be cited at some length since the comprehensiveness of his mode of explanation is what is in question,

> each variant of this non-food is in fact guaranteed by, and ritual-istically refers to, clichés. The air (line 5): *vivre de l'air du temps,* a proverbial phrase applied to impecunious individuals or dieting ladies. The puzzling *bouts d'air noir* uses *air* as a hyperbolic substi-tute for the famine cliché *des bouts de pain noir.* Whereas *air noir* is sheer nonsense referentially, it carries on the conversion by replac-ing stale and scanty crusts with the illusion of food, and, as a variant on the model of the stereotype, it makes sense. Again, the deadly convolvulus brings us to familiar warnings to children about poison-ous plants. And the revolving hungers refer to the revolving wooden horses of the carousel ("Tournez, tournez, bons chevaux de bois," Verlaine is writing at about the same time) by way of the collo-quial *manger avec les chevaux de bois* [eat when the wooden horses eat]—that is, starve. Hence too *paissez,* the verb for cattle or horses browsing on grass. Hence *sons,* a pun on the two meanings, "bran," horse fodder, and in the plural, "sounds." Sounds, of course, because of the bell in line 5, the refectory bell that summons to the table. We need not be wildly imaginative to find this a nice instance of tautology, since "dinn! dinn! dinn! dinn! mangeons" sounds like "dine! dine! mangeons!" (as we would say, "Dinner! Dinner! Let's eat!"). A hollow invitation, this being a mineral dinner—wherefore the bitterness concerning *l'azur sonneur,* which unites *l'air du temps* of our aforementioned proverb with the delusive call to dinner. Whence also the bitterness of the allusion to the Mallarmé intertext—the only possible explanation for this strange phrase—a poem in which the blue sky serves as image for a "sterile desert," a haunting empti-ness, where "l'Azur triomphe [. . .] qui chante dans les cloches [. . .] il se fait voix pour plus nous faire peur avec sa victoire mé-chante" [Azure triumphant sings in the bells; it turns itself into a voice the better to frighten us with its victorious wickedness] (pp. 78-79).

In sum, then, the matrix here is *hunger* (eating) and its expansion into a text employs first a negative then a positive converter, to yield a vision of eating, first, the inedible, and then, with an inversion of the key features of the inedible, the edible. Presumably, although Riffaterre does not explicitly say so, the sentence of lines 2-3, "Si j'ai du *goût,* ce n'est guères/Que pour la terre et les pierres," would be the *model,* since the subsequent images of eating are interpreted according to the formula made explicit here. Finally, though, for reasons I do not understand, Riffaterre chooses not to speak explicitly of external hypograms here, each representation of eating is determined by a cliché, quotation or a colloquial phrase to which it alludes or which it takes literally.

Riffaterre sums up his demonstration as follows:

> Thus, while every single representation in the poem is well-nigh incomprehensible to start with, it becomes capable of metaphorization or symbolization as soon as it is perceived as functionally identical with the others, as soon as we perceive the sequence that develops one word of the title, or rather one seme of that word, into a text. And once again, maximal catachresis at the lexematic level of individual words or phrases coincides with significance at the textual level (p. 80).

At a mimetic level the poem makes no sense, but once one shifts to the level of semiosis the poem becomes coherent: the poem is not an account of acts of eating or failure to eat but is rather organized around those possibilities and impossibilities of eating which are enshrined in discourse.

The obvious objection at this point is that "Fêtes de la faim" is a very special case—made for such a theory. Unlike most poems, it seems to be nonsense from the start and requires a key or revelation of a secret if any sense is to be made of it at all. Most poems, however, make much more sense at a mimetic level, do appear to be making statements about states of affairs, and critics can usually interpret them as coherent works of art without having recourse to a repertoire of clichés and commonplaces. Indeed, the objection might run, whereas the Rimbaud poem does seem to be enriched and made more suggestive and powerful by this kind of reading, most poems would be radically impoverished by an interpretation which treated them as the expansion, through clichés, of a kernel or matrix. It is therefore worth considering what Riffaterre does with a poem that critics have had less trouble interpreting and which is usually taken as a powerful statement of despair rather than a puzzle to be solved. Baude-laire's first "Spleen" poem from *Les Fleurs du Mal* is a good test case.

> Pluviôse, irrité contre la ville entière,
> De son urne à grands flots verse un froid ténébreux
> Aux pâles habitants du voisin cimetière
> Et la mortalité sur les faubourgs brumeux.
>
> Mon chat sur le carreau cherchant une litière
> Agite sans repos son corps maigre et galeux;
> L'âme d'un vieux poète erre dans la gouttière
> Avec la triste voix d'un fantôme frileux.
>
> Le bourdon se lamente, et la bûche enfumée
> Accompagne en fausset la pendule enrhumée,
> Cependant qu'en un jeu plein de sales parfums,
>
> Héritage fatal d'une vieille hydropique,
> Le beau valet de cœur et la dame de pique
> Causent sinistrement de leurs amours défunts.

Pluvius, annoyed at the whole city, pours torrents of dark cold out of his urn down onto the pale tenants of the cemetery next door, torrents of mortality over the foggy suburbs. On the tiling, my cat is looking for a litter to bed down on; he shifts his thin mangy body about restlessly. The soul of an old poet wanders through the rain-spout with the sad voice of a chilly ghost. The great bell is lament-ing, and the smoke-blackened log, in falsetto, accompanies the wheezy clock, the while, in a deck of cards filled with foul perfumes—fatal bequest of a dropsical old hag—the handsome knave of hearts and the queen of spades talk of their dead loves sinisterly.

Readers will doubtless agree that what unifies this poem is a feeling of dismal disagreeableness expressed or implied in various ways in the different stanzas. If there is any constant which the poem expands or of which the stanzas are variants it must be something of this kind. "The matrix I hypothesize," writes Riffaterre, "would be something like *no refuge from misery,* but the cliché *all-pervading gloom* would do as well" (p. 68). The fact that he can offer a choice of formulations suggests that what is crucial is the basic theme which both express. Elsewhere, as in the Rimbaud poem, he makes a strong claim in treating the text as derived from a matrix sentence, but here he seems to be doing no more than correctly recognizing a basic theme. In fact, the claim that he makes in his discussion of the poem is that the expansion of the matrix *all-pervading gloom* into a text is mediated by the descriptive system associated with *maison*. A descriptive system is a system of associated commonplaces, "a network of words associated with one another around a kernel word" (p. 39). The descriptive system of "home sweet home" in English involves, for example, the fireside, a peaceful pet, security, intimacy, perhaps a sunny green lawn, etc. Riffaterre's claim is that in this poem expansion of the gloomy matrix involves conversion of the various elements of the equivalent French descriptive system into negative images. The system has by convention a positive orientation. "Baudelaire's first 'Spleen' demonstrates how the inversion of that orientation turns the *maison* system into a code of the moral and physical discomfort a home is supposed to protect us against" (p. 67).

Earlier in his discussion he describes more generally what is involved in this conversion, as he calls it, of the hypogram:

> If he is to perceive the converted verbal sequence [i.e., perceive it as indirection and hence as poetic], the reader must make a mental comparison between the sequence and a hypogram that is the text imagined by him in a pretransformation state. This hypogram (a single sentence or a string of sentences) may be made out of clichés, or it may be a quotation from another text, or a descriptive system. Since the hypogram always has a positive or negative "orientation" (the cliché is meliorative or pejorative, the quotation has its position on an ethical and/or esthetic scale, the descriptive system reflects the connotations of its kernel word), the constituents of the conversion always transmute the hypogram's markers—in some cases the conversion consists of nothing more than such a permutation of the markers (pp. 63-64).

Ordinarily the *maison* system opposes a warm, protective inside to a hostile outside, but here, Riffaterre argues, "the conversion dictated by *pervasive gloom* transforms this opposition *inside* vs *outside* into an equivalence." The disagreeable discomfort that reigns outside is also to be found inside, as becomes obvious in the second stanza, where the description of the cat inverts all the features the descriptive system would lead us to expect of a sleek, contented, fireside cat: "the markers' permutation derives *maigre,* "skinny," from the ideal cat body, *galeux,* "mangy," from the ideal coat. The soft rug becomes *carreau,* and *carreau* never generates any adjective but *dur* or *froid,* which negate cosiness" (p. 69), and so on. Similarly, in the first tercet familiar sounds become harsh or dissonant, but most interesting is the transformation that takes place in the puzzling final stanza. Riffaterre argues that knicknacks, packs of cards, etc., are part of the system of *maison,* in which they are "common motifs in scenes of intimacy" and, when no one is about, "symbolize the essential continuity of living." A familiar hyperbolic variant of this motif gives these things a secret life: at night they come alive. The animation of inanimate household objects is an ever-present possibility in the case of playing cards, and love among kings, queens, and knaves is "a logical result." Riffaterre concludes:

> The whole motif, a complicated story, is verily a subsystem of the *maison* system. It has now been integrated into the overall conversion of "Spleen" and functions as a word—no matter how broad all its connotations—would function, as one constituent in a sentence, on a par with the other words. The conversion within the subsystem (adjectives and adverbs: *sales parfums, héritage fatal, causent sinistrement, amours défunts*) has no independent meaning; no symbolism of their own attaches to the details of this parenthetic story. Their complex negativizations are just a marker like the others, an embedding within the syntagmatic continuum of the sonnet's conversion. The realistic mimesis of the whole tercet has been semioticized into being one word of *maison*'s transformation into *non-maison,* that is of the transformation of *maison*'s systematic significance into a code of that significance's contrary (p. 70).

What is remarkable here, in its deviation from the conventions of ordinary critical writing, is Riffaterre's insistence on the absence of extra meaning, on the fact that this rich and mysterious little story has no other significance than its contribution to the negation of *maison.* Indeed, most readers are likely to find this confident and extreme reductionism somewhat objectionable; but in fact, it is possible to argue that Riffaterre is once again stating in a provocative way a position which critics generally slide into surreptitiously. The final tercet *is* difficult and puzzling: readers are likely to be fascinated precisely because the scene seems gratuitous, and sinister in its very gratuitousness; and though they would never say that the details are unimportant (since one of our conventions is that no detail in a good poem can be unimportant), what they respond to and what they succeed in integrating into an interpretation of the sonnet is nothing other than this general sense of the sinister and disagreeable.

A more pertinent objection to Riffaterre's reading might be that even when it does not misrepresent the way in which readers succeed in achieving unity, the method involves a predilection for the impoverishment of the text: it would prefer to see the strange opening stanza of this poem as "the conventional language of traditional allegory" (p. 67) asserting "Nature's hostility to man" rather than explore for as long as possible the strange features of this account which disrupt ordinary allegorical relationships. The emblematic figure, after all, pours cold on the inhabitants of the cemetery and mortality on the suburbs, in a zeugma whose symmetry is disrupted by the substitution of suburbs for mortals—a substitution which gives each thing poured a highly problematical relationship to the recipient. Now it may well be that readers will be unable to do anything with these oddities and will conclude, either explicitly in defeat or implicitly by passing on to the next stanza, that there is an allegory here which expresses Nature's hostility to man, but theories other than Riffaterre's would enjoin readers to dwell on these odd details and to accept this solution only *faute de mieux,* whereas Riffaterre's theory explicitly welcomes and encourages this reduction to a single thematic element or to a cliché.

The charge of reductionism will be frequently levelled at *Semiotics of Poetry,* but in fact it is a criticism that is only appropriate on the assumption that Riffaterre is offering a method for interpreting poems. When his theory is viewed in this light, then one may with some justification complain that it encourages readers to opt for simple solutions and to see images and even whole stanzas as simply traditional formulations. But if one takes Riffaterre's theory as an account of conventions of reading and interpretation—as a description of how readers can succeed in producing unity when they tackle a poem—then one can reply to any charge of reductionism that his formulations are not a summing up or even a summary of the poem. They do not purport to deliver the poem but rather to reveal a structure which enables the reader to perceive the poem as unified. The matrix and hypograms cannot be equated with the poem, much less with the experience of the poem.

Indeed, those who are worried about reductionism might wish explicitly to locate the poem's value in the experience of reading, in the process of weighing and transforming the various elements one encounters. The reader, as Riffaterre describes him, is continually being confronted with possibilities of mimetic interpretation, and reading is not so much progress towards kernels of revealed significance as

> a seesaw scanning of the text, compelled by the very duality of the signs—ungrammatical as mimesis, grammatical within the significance network. . . . In the reader's mind it means a continual recommencing, an indecisiveness resolved one moment and lost the next with each reliving of revealed significance, and this it is that makes the poem endlessly rereadable and fascinating (p. 166).

This sudden invocation of endless fascination and rereading is, one must confess, the flourish with which the book closes and must be interpreted with that in mind, but nevertheless, this sort of emphasis on the reading experience is a clear option for those who fear that Riffaterre's semiotics devalues poems by reducing them to formulae. Once separated in this way from questions of value, Riffaterre's reductionism can be seen as a provocative virtue, part of that drive towards explicitness which ought to be one of the virtues of semiotics.

From the perspective of semiotics, however, there is one feature of Riffaterre's work which is extremely puzzling, and that is the relationship between Riffaterre's theory and the interpretive activity of other readers. Semiotics generally claims that meaning is the result of the systems of conventions that make up a culture and that have been assimilated by the members of that culture who are concerned with the activity in question. The semiotic study of food, for example, would be an attempt to describe the conventions which, within a particular culture, distinguish the edible from the inedible, govern the order in which dishes are eaten, determine the compatibility or incompatibility of various dishes. It would describe the meaning various foodstuffs have within that culture. In short, it would attempt to make explicit all the implicit knowledge which members of that culture apply in their dealings with food. Similarly, the semiotics of literature would be an attempt to analyse the system of conventions that enable literary works to have the meanings they do for members of a given culture. It asks what are the conventions that enable readers to interpret works as they do.

At moments Riffaterre claims that this is his program, that his theory describes how readers produce or discover meaning. Yet much of the energy and excitement of Riffaterre's writing comes from the fact that he is urging us to read differently, to interpret texts in a new way. His interpretations are not offered as summaries of the common view. He takes pleasure in proposing new interpretations and discrediting those of other critics. And many readers, as I have suggested, will value his book precisely as guide to a new sort of interpretation. They may hope to learn how to produce similar readings themselves, but unless they possess his immense learning and his ear for echoes of clichés, descriptive systems, and colloquial expressions, they are unlikely to succeed.

Perhaps one ought to say, then, that Riffaterre's semiotics is not an account of current conventions and procedures of interpretation but that it is a description of the way a specialized and sophisticated group of readers deals with poems. That is to say, it is still an analysis of reading, but it focuses on one way of reading among many. This would be a plausible description of the project, did not Riffaterre explicitly rule out such a view. He denies that readers have this kind of freedom or may differ in their approach to texts. He insists that he is describing what readers must do. Reading is a tightly restricted, highly constrained activity. Poetic signs create patterns that cannot be ignored. "The reader's freedom of interpretation is further limited because of the poem's saturation by the semantic and formal features of its matrix; in other words, continuity and unity, that is, the fact that the semiotic unit is the text itself, forbid the attention to wander, deny the opportunities for hermeneutic deviance" (p. 165). And further, the reader "is therefore under strict guidance and control as he fills in the gaps and solves the puzzle" (p. 165).

A theory which insists to this extent on the control exercized by the text, on what readers are constrained to do, must be judged first of all for its accuracy in describing what readers actually do. If it does not correspond, then we can interpret it not as a description of what readers actually do, of how meaning is produced in their encounters with text, but as the recommendation of a new method of interpretation, an account of what they *ought* to do.

There seems, then, to be an important distinction between two approaches to the semiotics of literature. The first takes linguistics as its model: just as the task of linguistics is not to propose new meanings for the sentences of English but to describe the system of rules which enables sentences to have the form and meanings they do, so the semiotics of poetry attempts to describe the system of conventions which enable poems to have the meaning (the range of meanings) they do. Its object, as Roland Barthes once wrote, is not the texts themselves but their intelligibility: texts as sign sequences.[4] The second approach posits that there are some principles according to which poetic texts are constructed which, if we knew them, would enable us to determine the true meaning of poems. A theory of this kind, however frequently it may refer to the constitutive activity of the reader, is not a description of the interpretive process but a prescription. Indeed, a theory of this sort is almost invariably a genetic theory in that it bases its method of interpretation on claims about how the text was constructed. It is because a poem comes into being as the expansion of a matrix through hypograms that readers must read it, if they are to read properly, in a quest for the unifying matrix.

Indeed, Riffaterre's theory ought to be compared not with a descriptive semiotics or poetics which attempts to make explicit the conventions of meaning but rather with competing genetic theories such as that of Harold Bloom. Like Riffaterre, Bloom offers new and often powerful interpretations, and he grounds those interpretations on claims about how poems come into being. Both claim to reveal the secret of the text and do so by positing an act of origination (a troping on or misreading of a great predecessor in the case of Bloom, a troping on hypograms or clichés in the case of Riffaterre). Both offer, that is to say, a theory about the nature of poems (grounded on an account of how poems are produced) and both recommend that we interpret poems in accordance with this new account of their nature, arguing that this is how they ought to be read, though people have not realized this in the past.

A descriptive semiotics, on the other hand, is interested not in offering a method of interpretation or in providing new and surprising readings of literary works but rather in analysing the conventions of reading and interpretation that seem to be current within a culture, the conventions that are constitutive of the institution of literature. A brief example will illustrate both the differences between this kind of semiotics and Riffaterre's approach and the ways in which Riffaterre's accounts of the reading process might enrich a descriptive semiotics. Since Riffaterre's theory is so much concerned with unity, one might consider the problem of how readers achieve unity when interpreting a brief lyric poem like Blake's "London."

> I wander thro' each charter'd street
> Near where the charter'd Thames does flow,
> And mark in every face I meet
> Marks of weakness, marks of woe.
>
> In every cry of every Man,
> In every Infant's cry of fear,
> In every voice, in every ban,
> The mind-forg'd manacles I hear.
>
> How the Chimney-sweeper's cry
> Every black'ning Church appalls;
> And the hapless Soldier's sigh
> Runs in blood down Palace walls.
>
> But most thro' midnight streets I hear
> How the youthful Harlot's curse
> Blasts the new-born Infant's tear
> And blights with plagues the Marriage hearse.[5]

If a returning tourist were to tell us what he had seen and heard while wandering through the streets of London, we would feel no overwhelming compulsion to transform these heterogeneous sights into a unified vision, but readers of poems do. The sights and sounds must be brought together according to one of our models of wholeness. Riffaterre's unvarying model is that of a matrix sentence of which everything is a variant. This is close to the model most frequently used in interpretations of London: the synecdochic series, where a series of particulars is taken to represent a general class of which they are all members. Here the class is named in various ways by critics: real social evils of 18th century life, woes due to artificial and repressive institutions which human reason has created, distant generalized cases of suffering.[6] Riffaterre's model, which stresses the sentence rather than the fact of class membership, would force one to claim that a particular formulation is correct, but it seems to be a fact about interpretation that critics following the same conventions can name a structure in different ways.

However, there is another model of wholeness or unity that can be used in the interpretation of this poem, a model which one might call the pattern of aletheic reversal: first a false or inadequate vision, then its true or adequate counterpart. By this model, which is frequently used in other cases, one unifies the poem by identifying a shift from one vision to another. With the third stanza we gain, one critic writes, "a release from the repetitiveness of the preceding stanzas. The abstracting sameness of 'every . . . every . . . every,' the dimly realized cries and voices, give way to specifically realized human situations."[7] This model of unity gives one a certain dramatic structure and enables one to locate the significance of the poem in the realization, which can be variously described, that one must go beyond surface marks of misery to a more comprehensive, analytical or even visionary account, which includes institutions and sees more.

Whichever model of unity is employed, and there seems no reason to argue in this case that either is inappropriate, critics perform some complex imaginative operations on various details of the poem in order to fit them into the unified structure. Some of the most interesting occur in readings of the last stanza. What Riffaterre calls a mimetic reading might tempt one to say that the narrator sees a harlot curse her child for crying and curse a wedding procession, but no critic remains content with this reading, since structural conventions require that the final stanza be an appropriate conclusion. There are numerous acceptable ways a poem can end,[8] but in a poem organized as a series of perceptions, the critic's inclination is to read the final stanza as the climax of the vision, its most intense and typical moment.

These seem to be two strategies that account for most readings. Either one emphasizes the parallelism that links chimneysweep, soldier, and harlot as victims (each of whose cry taints an institution that is in some way guilty for the victim's plight), or one disregards the surface syntactical parallelism, giving precedence to the cultural convention which prevents an infant from figuring in a poem as anything but a representation of innocence, and one makes the victim of the last stanza the infant and the newly-weds, who are also the object of the harlot's cursing and blighting. The convention of unity, that is to say, leads critics to seek in the final stanza a prolongation of the pattern of victimage that has been established earlier, and depending on which convention (syntactical parallelism or traditional symbolism) is given greater weight, one makes either the harlot or the infant and marriage itself the principal victim.

These interpretations are quite different, and each can produce a social rationalization. By one argument, it is the institution of marriage itself, more particularly arranged marriages, that breeds a market for harlots, who become victims of a system of "charters." "If there were no marriage there would be no ungratified desire and therefore no harlots. Thus it is ultimately the marriage hearse itself and not the youthful harlot which breeds the pestilence that blights the marriage hearse."[9] By the other argument the harlot is the evil rather than the victim; she "blasts the prospects of innocent children and blights the healthy possibilities of marriage," for any of a number of reasons—e.g., because her very existence "is a gross parody of sanctified mutuality in love."[10] A descriptive semiotics is not concerned with the question of which reading is "correct," though of course it is interested in what conventions are appealed to and what strategies are employed in attempts to demonstrate that a particular reading is the right one. A descriptive semiotics is concerned with the attempt to understand how it is—according to what conventions of signification, structural models, and processes of inference—that this poem can be interpreted as it is by critics; and when there is a disagreement among critics, as there usually is, the task is to explain what conventions enable those disagreements to arise. Interpretation is not a random process; if it were there would be nothing to explain, but since it is not, even the most blatantly contradictory interpretations are following a logic and relying on conventions which it ought to be possible to make explicit.

Because Riffaterre does attempt to be explicit about the conventions and interpretive strategies he is following, his book has much to contribute to an analysis of reading or descriptive semiotics (in particular, his discussion of prose poems has much to say about how readers make sense of brief, laconic texts), but essentially he is concerned with devising new interpretations, not explaining the old. His genetic approach has much to offer those readers who are convinced that the purpose of literary criticism is to produce more refined interpretations of individual works; and it also has the attraction of avoiding the banality that always threatens descriptive semiotics. The semiotician always risks banality since he is committed by profession to scrutinizing meanings already known or attested within the culture in the hopes of discovering the conventions which members of that culture have mastered. It is precisely this risk—that one's labors will, if one is fortunate, lead to an explicit account of what is already implicitly known—that explains the attraction interpretation has for semioticians. Why not offer a new reading instead of trying to explain the conditions of interpretation? Why not, after all, do both? Riffaterre's rhetoric suggests that he has indeed tried to do both, but the result is a theory that is torn between its two claims: that it describes what readers do and must do; that it offers new and compelling interpretations. To save Riffaterre's theory, to appreciate what is valuable in his book, one must distinguish the two approaches to semiotics which he attempts to conflate.

Notes

1. Northrop Frye, *Anatomy of Criticism* (Princeton: Princeton University Press, 1957), p. 11.

2. Michael Riffaterre, *Semiotics of Poetry* (Bloomington: Indiana University Press, 1978), p. 1. Further quotations from this work will be identified simply by page references in the text.

3. Arthur Rimbaud, *Oeuvres,* ed. Antoine Adam (Paris: Gallimard, 1972), pp. 83-84.

4. Roland Barthes, *Critique et vérité* (Paris: Seuil, 1966), p. 62.

5. *Complete Writings of William Blake,* ed. Geoffrey Keynes (London: Oxford University Press, 1966), p. 216.

6. For further discussion of critical responses to this poem, see Jonathan Culler, "Prolegomena to a Theory of Reading," *The Reader in the Text,* ed. S. Suleiman & I. Crosman (Princeton: Princeton University Press, 1980).

7. Heather Glen, "The Poet in Society: Blake and Wordsworth on London," *Literature and History* (May 1976), p. 10.

8. See Barbara H. Smith, *Poetic Closure* (Chicago: Chicago University Press, 1968).

9. E. D. Hirsch, *Innocence and Experience* (New Haven: Yale University Press, 1964), p. 265.

10. Thomas Edwards, *Imagination and Power* (London: Chatto & Windus, 1971), p. 121.

Literary Language and Postmodern Theories of Semiotics

Louis Oldani

"You can't make a poem with ideas," said Mallarmé to Degas, "—you make it with *words!*"[1] Carlyle noted of the literary writer: "Wonderful it is with what cutting words, now and then, he severs asunder the confusion; shears it down, were it furlongs deep, into the true center of the matter; and there not only hits the nail on the head, but with crushing force smites it home, and buries it."[2] The literary writer, fashioning, even wrestling with, his sometimes intractable building blocks, chooses and arranges words with art. For literature is, according to Tzvetan Todorov, following Valéry, and can be nothing other than an extension and application of certain properties of language.[3] That emphasis is struck in the definitions of prose and poetry whereby Coleridge claimed that "prose = words in their best order;—poetry = the *best* words in the best order."[4] Swift averred that "Proper words in proper places make the true definition of a style," partaking perhaps in the more general advice of Ecclesiasticus, "Weigh your words in a balance."[5] For the Seminar I have chosen to focus discussion on some developments in semiotic theorists' views of the language of literature. William K. Wimsatt and Cleanth Brooks indicate a rationale for such choice in the following passage.

> . . . we shall have occasion to consider the question how far a close verbal analysis of poetry may fall short of doing justice to the more massive structural features of such works as novels, epics, dramas. Literary criticism of the mid-20th century in America has been raising that question with an insistence which might even be taken . . . as a discouragement of our dignifying the episode of 18th-century "poetic diction" and the Wordsworthian condemnation of it with very much notice. Both "poetic diction" and the reaction against it, however, stand out conspicuously in critical history, and we choose to dwell upon them with some deliberation. The concept of "poetic diction" is . . . a handy one both for the theorist and for the literary historian. It has at least the advantage that it reduces to a nearly definable and

testable form a good many other problems of literary criticism. "Poetic
diction" is a good small-scale model of the larger problems.[6]

Language, the medium of literature, is a shared system of sounds and
of written or printed letters representing sounds by which meaning is conveyed among people who know the system. A word begins as a blend of
noises and tones—articulated by the throat, tongue, and lips—for which
the written letters are a notation. The conventional part of a word's meaning, its denotation, is signification as verified in common usage and as
defined in a dictionary. (Such dictionaries as the *OED* and *Webster's
Third New International* present a well-nigh exhaustive account of the
conventions of meaning that undergird the system of signs which we call
words.) A word's connotations are imaginative associations and emotional
charges that the word evokes beyond what it denotes. Whereas the person
using language to communicate only information may not be attentive to
the sounds of words and may be hampered by connotations and even
multiple denotation, the poet, the playwright, or the novelist needs a multi-
dimensional vocabulary in which to denotations he adds connotations to
enrich meaning and sounds to reinforce or echo meaning. In thus signifying multiple and maximum meaning, patterns of diction reveal the imagined
world, the images of the human person, the vision of a writer as an individual artist and as a participant in, or against, a movement or school.
Diction is the means of literature: there is no way of experiencing the work
except through the words that express it. Hence Todorov's remark that
the "very fact that the literary work is a 'verbal work of art' has for a long
time moved scholars to speak of the 'great rôle' of language in a literary
work."[7]

Literature is a specialized or heightened use of word symbols communicating in a way distinguishable from the language of science, of philosophy,
and even of most daily conversation, except when the speaker is, say,
retelling a folk story or singing a song. The concern of writers of literature
is with experience, which comes to us largely through the senses. Accordingly, although literature conveys questions, statements, explanations, and
information, its peculiar mode demands sensuous words, the representation
in language of sense impressions, not only images but figures of speech—
metaphor, for one, which Cassirer interpreted as "the intellectual link
between language and myth"; symbol, the abstract or transcendent rendered
in physical form or concrete terms; synecdoche ("Always a larger signifi-

cance," Frost explained: "A little thing touches a larger thing").[8] Observing that the nature of fiction, for example, is determined by the nature of our perceptive apparatus, Flannery O'Connor pointed out that the writer of fiction "appeals through the senses, and you cannot appeal to the senses with abstractions."[9] James Joyce maintained in *Stephen Hero* and *A Portrait of the Artist as a Young Man* that literature consists of incarnations and epiphanies.

Cognizant of the work of such scholars as Brooks and Wimsatt and such artists as Coleridge and Joyce, semioticians are scrutinizing literary language from a new coign of vantage. In contrast to the long-standing analytic approach to meaning, which has focused primarily on the referents of words—patterns of imagery, for instance, or (in Samuel Johnson's aim) "the grandeur of generality" instead of the lowness of particulars—and secondarily on source—as Wordsworth's "low and rustic" persons—and on rhythm and music,[10] semioticians' operational theories stress each word's derivation of meaning directly from the language system as a whole and indirectly from other systems linked with language. I use the term *semiotics* broadly enough to include structuralism and poststructuralist deconstruction and offer the following definition: a general theory of signs and symbols as means of communication, especially the study of rules and conventions governing the relationships among the elements of language, comprising syntactics, semantics, and pragmatics.[11] In literary criticism, C. Hugh Holman comments, semiotics examines literature "in terms of its use of language as dependent on and influenced by literary conventions and modes of discourse" and "how these conventions create meanings unique to such literary expression."[12] Diverging from theorists who assess language as a textural element of the literary work, semiotic treatment of language in literature concentrates on the system of conventions which control its meanings, use, and purposes as well as the system of generic codes which enable the reader to find order and complex significance in the integral work. The semiotician's goal can be stated in a paraphrase of one of Frost's lines: "The theorist in me cries out for ensemble, for design."[13]

Robert Scholes' semiotics of literature can serve as a bridge from traditional ways of considering literary language. Starting with the six features constituting Roman Jakobson's diagram of the act of communication, Scholes explains that "we sense literariness in an utterance when any one of the six features of communication loses its simplicity and becomes multiple or duplicitous."[14] This happens when, for instance, a hiatus appears between what the speaker of a poem says and what the author implies, as in Auden's "The Unknown Citizen." But, cautions Scholes, "literariness does not equal literature until it dominates any given utterance." The sound effects and patterns of syntax as well as the ironies, paradoxes, and other figures of speech "function not to cut the work off from the world by making it a self-contained object," but "function to create a literary tension between the utterance as communication and externally referential, on the one hand, and as incommunicative and self-referential, on the other." Thus a work of literature "tantalizes us by being a mirror and a window at the same time." Although Scholes agrees that the formulation that signs refer, not to things, but to concepts has provided a useful critique of naive realism, he breaks with the position of Ferdinand de Saussure and of Roland Barthes that between words and things, sign and referent, is an unbridgeable gap. To Scholes, language is not a closed system, but one enriched by and pointing to the phenomenal world. To him, "the codes of fiction are tied to our perceptual system as well as to our language." And fiction results from "the semiotic generation of an absent context or the distortion of a present one."

> The world created by a fiction, then, whether a story, play, or poem, is one context we perceive and half create around the message that directs our thoughts. But behind that world or around it is our own phenomenal world, in which the fictional events reverberate. What we know from experience of love and lust, charity and hate, pleasure and pain, we bring to bear upon the fictional events—inevitably, because we seek to make every text our own. And what we find in fiction leaks out to color our phenomenal world, to help us assign meaning, value, and importance to the individual events and situations of our lives.[15]

Concerned also with questions of semantics, while carrying out his own brand of Derridean deconstruction, J. Hillis Miller has claimed that "Ultimately, man finds in things nothing but what he himself has imported into them."[16] To account for what is distinctive in the signification of a sign, Jacques Derrida uses the term "trace," which indicates a "simulacrum" or semblance of foregoing meanings. The sedimentation of traces which a signifier has accumulated in the history of its use constitutes the diversity in the play of its present significations. The trace "appears/disappears" and creates the "undoing/preserving" oscillation of the sign itself. Any attempt to define or interpret the significance of a sign or complex of signs amounts, for Derrida, to nothing more than "sign-substitution"—the interpreter's putting in its place another sign or complex of signs whose self-effacing traces defer, from substitution to substitution, the fixed and present meaning that the interpreter vainly seeks. Reference is interminably postponed.[17] Miller's "innocent black marks" on the pages of a text are similarly endued with traces of meaning and multimeanings. Deconstruction he defines as "a recognition that all language, even language that seems purely referential or conceptual, is figurative language."[18] Deconstruction, he adds, "is not . . . nihilism or the denial of meaning in literary texts. It is, on the contrary, an attempt to interpret as exactly as possible the oscillations in meaning produced by the irreducibly figurative nature of language."

Yet, quoting Paul de Man, Miller argues that "'the impossibility of reading should not be taken too lightly.'"[19] He claims that a "key word," for instance, signifies any and all of the heterogeneous meanings it has conveyed in varied linguistic forms throughout its recorded history, back through its etymology. Because of this multiplicity of equally signified meanings, a key word or a passage or a text is finally "undecipherable," "unreadable": "All reading is misreading."[20] Paradoxically, "any literary text, with more or less explicitness or clarity, already reads or misreads itself."[21] The end of interpretation is, therefore, an "impasse." M. H. Abrams' summary of what Miller calls "the uncanny moment"—"the moment in which the critic, thinking to deconstruct the text, finds that he has simply participated in the ceaseless play of the text as a self-deconstructing artefact"—is an accurate paraphrase of Miller's assertion: "The deconstructive critic seeks to find . . . the element in the system studied which is alogical, the thread in the text in question which will unravel it all . . . . . . Deconstruction is not a dismantling of the structure of a text but a demonstration that it has already dismantled itself."[22] Miller notes as "an essential part of the procedure" of deconstruction a "hyperbolic exuberance, the letting language go as far as it will take one."[23] For language is itself the determiner, not a "tool in man's hands, a submissive means of thinking," explains Miller. "Language rather thinks man and his 'world,' including poems, if he will allow it to do so." These few quotations from and summaries of Miller's understanding of the nature and function of language evince an outlook emphasizing a system of traces that determine meanings over which the individual user and reader each has at once little and much control: much by reason of the individual's role in initiating the deconstructive process and in finding "nothing but what he himself has imported," little by reason of the function of language itself, "not an instrument or tool in man's hands," but "rather think[ing] man and his 'world.'" Thus "Ariadne's thread makes the labyrinth, is the labyrinth. . . . [And] Criticism is the production of more thread to embroider the texture or textile already there."[24]

Some of Miller's notions were published in *Critical Inquiry's* spring 1977 exchange of views on "The Limits of Pluralism," in which questions are raised and alternatives offered by Wayne Booth and M. H. Abrams. "Nothing that anyone can say or write," Booth observes, "makes any sense unless we all believe that people can understand each other, sometimes, and that they should always try to understand."[25] Abrams objects that Miller "leaves no room for taking into account that language, unlike the physical world, is a cultural institution that developed expressly in order to mean something and to convey what is meant to members of a community who have learned how to use and interpret language."[26] Abrams argues for the existence of a "control or limitation of signification by reference to the uses of a word or phrase that are current at the time an author writes, or to an author's intention, or to the verbal or generic context in which a word occurs." I dispute the fitness of Miller's "hyperbolic exuberance." The fact that, in the most obvious sense, a text has no meaning in itself does not necessarily occasion 100% subjective readings (or "nothing" but what the reader "imports into it"). Writers can and do utter determinate signs to readers with means to determine significations, not often fully, but to a degree, as through use of the semantic system of a language to ascertain denotation and through examined ordinary living to discern connotations. Frost addressed this issue when he insisted that in composing a poem he was not writing on blotting paper on which the ink spreads out into scarcely recognizable shapes that can mean anything or nothing.[27]

For Tzvetan Todorov, the meaning of a word "is defined by the combinations in which it can accomplish its linguistic function. The meaning . . . is the entirety of its possible relationships with other words."[28] Concurring with Émile Benveniste, Todorov adds that meaning includes "the

capacity of a linguistic unit to integrate itself into a unit on a higher level."
But whereas "in speech the integration of units does not go beyond the
level of the sentence, in literature sentences are integrated again as part of
larger articulations, and the latter in their turn into units of greater dimension, and so on until we have the entire work." Words themselves,
Todorov notes, imply the absence of their referents: "Words are to things
as desire is to the desired object."[29] As he indicated in the Kansas Faculty
Semiotics Seminar, however, Todorov has sufficient confidence in the
writer's ability to produce and the reader's ability to interpret an utterance,
though it be unrepeatable, that he had developed a coherent theory of the
genre *"littérature fantastique."*

Rejecting as a means to account for meaning in literature the linguistic
model, specifically A. J. Greimas' hypothesis that minimal semantic features
combine in rule-governed ways to produce large-scale effects, Jonathan
Culler calls for "mastery of various semiotic conventions which enable
[one] to read series of sentences as poems or novels endowed with shape
and meaning."[30] In *Structuralist Poetics,* Culler focuses attention, not on the
author as source and the literary work as object, but on "two correlated
networks of convention: writing as an institution and reading as an activity."[31] From this perspective, the meaning of a sentence is "the series of
developments to which it gives rise, as determined by past and future
relations between words and the conventions of semiotic systems." To
study literary modes of writing, the reader must concentrate both on the
conventions which guide the play of differences (as understood by Derrida)
and on the conventions which guide the process of constructing meanings.
One must let the work speak to him by viewing writing itself as a "period
and generic concept." "To understand the language of a text is to recognize the world to which it refers": the historical period and its differentiae
and the literary genre plus contrasts with other genres, which includes
identifying "what features are constitutive of functional categories." Expectations connected with the conventions of genre are, Culler remarks,
"often violated. Their function, like that of all constitutive rules, is to make
meaning possible by providing terms in which to classify the things one
encounters." Thus, "to read a text as a tragedy is to give it a framework
which allows order and complexity to appear."

Using Barthes' terms "kernels" ("elements which link up with one another to form plot") and "satellites" or "catalysts" ("which are attached to kernels but do not themselves establish sequences"), Culler theorizes:

> Once we have identified the dominant structure of the *récit,* we know how to deal with whatever kernels and satellites we then postulate. . . .
>
> The goals towards which one moves in synthesizing a plot are . . . notions of thematic structures. If we say that the hierarchy of kernels is governed by the reader's desire to reach a level of organization at which the plot as a whole is grasped in a satisfying form, . . . we have at least a general principle whose effects at lower levels can be traced. The reader must organize the plot as a passage from one state to another and this passage or movement must be such that it serves as a representation of theme. The end must be made a transformation of the beginning so that meaning can be drawn from the perception of resemblance and difference. . . . One can attempt to establish a coherent causal series, in which disparate incidents are read as stages towards a goal, or a dialectical movement in which incidents are related as contraries whose opposition carries the problem that must be resolved.[32]

The crucial function of words is their role in developing the structural pattern of a work, a role that semantics cannot play.

Rhetorical figures, states Culler, are "instructions" about how to understand the text by passing from one meaning to another.[33] Figures serve as the basis of interpretation, as, for example, synecdoche "allows one to move from part to whole, from whole to part, from member to class and from class to member." Each figure must be taken in a sense different from the literal and normal meaning; each requires semantic transformation. Culler's structuralist poetics, however, is not hermeneutic: "it does not propose startling interpretations or resolve literary debates," though it offers "a theory of literature and a mode of interpretation."[34] The attempt to understand how we "make sense of a text," he adds, "leads one to think of literature not as representation or communication but as a series of forms which comply with and resist the production of meaning." Instead of a structuralist method geared for the discovery of structure in literature, Culler proposes "a kind of attention which one might call structuralist": "a desire to isolate codes, to name the various languages with and among which the text plays, to go beyond manifest content to a series of forms and then to make these forms, or oppositions or modes of signification, the burden of the text." Verbal texture is not at issue here; "language" is not to be understood as diction, but as a system making possible the production of meaning. Culler's is a view from a weather spacecraft or through an electron microscope, not a sight glimpsed by the transparent eyeball or even through colored and distorting lenses.

Maria Corti's *An Introduction to Literary Semiotics* investigates "the notion of the text as a hypersign or polysemic message."[35] She notes that T. S. Eliot anticipated current theorists in recognizing the rules of the game, or system, of literature, which "is not the sum of its texts but a kind of totality both linked and linking, and in movement."[36] Existing works of art, Eliot explained, "form an ideal order among themselves, which is modified by the introduction of the new (the really new) work of art among them." The order of works, according to Eliot, was complete before the new work arrived; but for order to persist after the introduction of novelty, "the *whole* existing order must be, if ever so slightly, altered; and so the relations, proportions, values of each work of art toward the whole are readjusted." Fundamental to the notion of a system of literature is the "fact that literature is subject to structuring on various planes and levels," some of which are implied in "the diachronic development and the synchronic articulation of a literature, resulting from the interaction of its institutional forms and genres . . . and the subtle relations that exist among literary phenomena." Levels of structuring superimposed on those just mentioned result from the relation between a writer and the whole of literature: "the individual author draws on his favorite texts . . . ; he effects connections and interrelations among these favorite texts in relation to the constitutive law of his own work" and thereby "creates the subsystem of his own sources." To show that the cause can come after the effect in this structuring, Corti quotes a paradox of Jorge Luis Borges: "The fact is that each writer creates his precursors. His work modifies our conception of the past, as it will modify the future."[37] Moreover, a semiological conception of literature apprehends a network of relations between the signs of the literary series and those of other series, such as the social models of an era or the world view.

Production of literary signs, of texts, entails the choice and use of words to span the chasm between addresser and addressee, a use motivated by the writer's personal experience and by the context. But the words are conventional symbols in a language system and cannot be arranged into art, claims Corti, "unless, as Eliot maintains, there is a critical act, 'the labour of sifting, combining, constructing, expunging, correcting, testing.'"[38] Corti views this crafting of the text as a scene in the "drama of alternatives" in which the selection of one plot carries the renunciation of alternate plots and demonstrates the writer's generative "competence" in transforming from the type the token.

The polysemic "sign-life" of the literary work Corti also examines:

Every text can support an incalculable number of decodifications or destructuralizations; in effect, every text is many texts in that the very nature of its polysemic complexity prevents identically repetitive readings even in the same cultural context. This explains why . . . in our era there has arisen the conception of readings as *variations of a basic invariant,* that is, the text.[39]

At the end of reading as characterized by Corti, the interpreter finds that the internal relationships of the text, of the words among themselves, count more than the relationships of words and things. The dynamic of reading thus corresponds to the dynamic of the text.

In Chapter III, Corti directs consideration to the following aspects of literary language and its combinatorial game of words: codes and structures which underlie the word (A.4), generative factors and extraordinary potentialities of poetic language (A.2), ungrammaticality (pages 71-73), macro- and micropolysemy (B.3), phonic-rhythmic and semantic links in the language of a poetic text (B.2), development from "pre-text"—or poetic text in progress realized through the dynamics of variants—through the several stages of execution to the closure of "the last chosen version" (B.6). Corti points out that the language of literature "actualizes the greatest number of the potentialities of language," has the status of a "supersign-function" (Umberto Eco), constitutes "a specific language-system" (Teun Van Dijk), is a form of discourse comprising lower signs of the sentence (connotations, figures, et cetera) and higher (a structure of narrative, for example, or of the poetic message) (Barthes), a priori codes (as literary genre) and a posteriori codes (produced with the message) (G. Granger), the kinds of formation and transformation proper to itself (alliteration, rhyme, specific lexicon, et cetera) (Van Dijk).[40] Literary language, Corti explains, "does not appear . . . as a codifying system but as a catalyst for the potential that resides in language itself." She regards the writer's linguistic activity as an "oscillation" between his individual idiolect and literary language, which he absorbs from living at a given time and from reading the texts of the past. In literary language the possibilities of signification and communication are realized differently than in everyday language because literary language "is a connotative system that accumulates diachronically. The word or syntagm or styleme is not only connotative in itself; it also has an extra semantic element, a surplus of significations which derives from the earlier artistic contexts in which it has occurred . . . ." Within literary language Corti distinguishes the following codes: 1) styles which belong to the various literary genres and to particular historical periods; 2) styles whose birth, growth, and death are conditioned by the dialectic of sociocultural phenomena (for instance, in some ancient literatures parataxis was a component of the plain style, whereas in the Bible it stands among the syntactic structures of a high style); 3) rhetoric, the rules and practices of which have endured through the centuries. "The ensemble of rhetorical markers as well as traditional rhetorical material and codified stylistic elements," Corti adds, "is very important for literary communication because it eases the encounter of the text and the addressee; it offers the presence of the already known alongside the newness of the message and favors communication on its first level."

Corti locates the distinctiveness of poetic language from prose language in the writer's poetic competence and creativity and in the "generative pre-text."[41] She finds in poetic language a density of signification, an "ingrained polysemy" which marks it only in the poetic context, a density connected with pre-textual processes. Inasmuch as the poet achieves a fresh vision which escapes the common "grammar" of vision, his language, too, must violate the norms of grammar of the language deriving from ordinary experience. The poet is engaged not only in ungrammaticalities, but in generative figures and the "subtle and stubborn self-imposition of a word" in the pre-text. The result is that in the finished poem "everything signifies." Moreover, the "global meaning of the text" amounts to more than the sum of partial meanings that can be isolated among the signifiers: macropolysemy, or multivalence of the text as such, exceeds the sum of micropolysemies "on the level of the single word, of the syntagm, of the styleme, which because of a particular semantic density become polyvalent." Finally,

Corti maintains, the poet's utterances in a poem are "incapable of substitution."

Thus my epitome of Corti's full-blown discussion of the language of literature, a discussion which has the merit of clarity, takes into account alternative views, is illustrated from a formidable acquaintance with world literature, and is qualified by reference to the positions of fellow semiologists and other theoreticians, some outside the semiotic circle, including a number who write literature.

CONCLUDING COMMENT. My paper synthesizes approaches to the language of literature established by semioticians, approaches which function as part of a more encompassing goal, a full accounting not only of the whole system of language as a medium of communication, but of all systems connected with language. Such a goal is not surprising in view of the guiding linguistic model, in which each language is a coherent, homogeneous entity whose codes, conventions, and structures work to make meaning possible. Like other theorists of literary language, semioticians are occupied with the multimeanings of the word and the sundry levels of textual meaning. They have contributed a further dimension, however, in the more complex explanation of the nature of allusion by the subsystem of sources or intertextuality, a concept summed up as follows by Vincent B. Leitch:

> Every text emerges out of a textual tradition. In actuality, countless sources, influences and epochs—both hidden and revealed, spoken and written—are interwoven into language itself. The very syntax and lexicon in the system of language carry the work of innumerable and often unnameable precursors. Consequently, the lineage of any text quickly approaches an impasse in the inevitable labyrinth of intertextual connections and combinations.[42]

Not only does the concept of intertextuality affix its beam on each text's genealogy, but the formulation of "pre-textual" processes illumines each text's genesis in the individual writer. Thus semioticians attend closely to genre, not as a device for classifying works of literature, but as a generative principle whereby the writer's words become a communicable message. Genre serves, then, as a correlative principle of production and therefore of interpretation. Hence Todorov's remark that "a 'Ptolemaic' discipline cannot account for a 'Galilean' genre."[43]

To semioticians the language of literature has yielded levels of relationship previously undiscovered or at least uncharted. The stress on codes, structures, and systems, on ensemble, is a constant among semiotic theories. The part is inspected as it performs in the larger configuration, without which it loses significance. In what Culler has called semiotics' "imperialism," semioticians attend to the full range of areas of study directly or indirectly linked with the signifiers and signifieds of language—including animal communication, human clothing, codes such as the Morse and braille, and chemical symbols as well as natural and written languages.[44] Granted, semioticians have treated elements not excluded from earlier approaches to the study of literature. They have nonetheless metamorphosed the study of literary language into a discipline postmodern in its partial replacement of individual creativity—"what matters most" yet "must," according to T. S. Eliot, "remain unaccountable"[45]—with enabling systems which determine individual endeavor while eluding individual control.

Notes

1. Paul Valéry, *Degas . . . Manet . . . Morisot*, trans. David Paul (New York: Pantheon Books, 1960), p. 62.
2. Quoted from X. J. Kennedy, *An Introduction to Poetry*, 4th ed. (Boston: Little, Brown, & Co., 1978), p. 32.
3. Tzvetan Todorov, "Language and Literature," in *The Structuralist Controversy: The Languages of Criticism and the Sciences of Man*, ed. Richard Macksey and Eugenio Donato (Baltimore: Johns Hopkins University Press, 1972), p. 125.
4. *Table Talk*, 12 July 1827, ed. H. N. Coleridge (1835).
5. Jonathan Swift, "Letter to a Young Clergyman," 9 January 1720, quoted from *Familiar Quotations by John Bartlett*, 14th ed. (1968), p. 389. Ecclesiasticus, XXVIII.25, paraphrased from *The Holy Bible: New American Catholic Edition* (New York, 1969), p. 684.
6. William K. Wimsatt and Cleanth Brooks, *Literary Criticism: A Short History* (New York: Knopf, 1959), p. 340.
7. Tzvetan Todorov, "Language and Literature," p. 125.
8. Ernst Cassirer, *Language and Myth*, trans. Susanne K. Langer (New York: Dover Publications, 1946), p. 84; Frost is quoted from Kennedy, p. 199.
9. Flannery O'Connor, "The Nature and Aim of Fiction," in *Mystery and Manners*, ed. Sally and Robert Fitzgerald (New York: Farrar, Straus & Giroux, 1969), p. 67.
10. Samuel Johnson, "Cowley," in *Lives of the English Poets*, ed. G. Birkbeck Hill (Oxford: Clarendon Press, 1905), I, p. 45; William Wordsworth, Preface, *Lyrical Ballads*, 2nd ed. (London: printed for T. N. Longman, 1800).
11. Derived from *Webster's New World Dictionary of the American Language*, 2nd college ed., and C. Hugh Holman, *A Handbook to Literature*, 4th ed. (Indianapolis: Odyssey Press, 1980), pp. 406-07.
12. Holman, pp. 406-407.
13. Robert Frost, "A Masque of Reason," line 261.
14. Robert Scholes, "Toward a Semiotics of Literature," *Critical Inquiry*, 4 (Autumn 1977), pp. 109-13, 116.
15. Scholes, p. 117.

16. J. Hillis Miller, "Tradition and Difference," *Diacritics,* 2 (Winter 1972), p. 12 (also p. 8).

17. For translation of Derrida's position ("La Différence," in *Marges de la philosophie* [Paris, 1972], and *La Dissémination* [Paris, 1972]), I am indebted to M. H. Abrams, "The Deconstructive Angel," *Critical Inquiry,* 3 (Spring 1977), pp. 429-32.

18. J. Hillis Miller, "The Function of Rhetorical Study at the Present Time," in *The State of the Discipline, 1970s-1980s, ADE Bulletin,* No. 62 (September-November 1979), p. 13.

19. J. Hillis Miller, "The Critic as Host," *Critical Inquiry,* 3 (Spring 1977), p. 440.

20. J. Hillis Miller: "Tradition and Difference," p. 12; "Walter Pater: A Partial Portrait," *Daedalus,* 105 (Winter 1976), p. 98; "Stevens' Rock and Criticism as Cure, II," *The Georgia Review,* 30 (Summer 1976), p. 333; "The Critic as Host," *Critical Inquiry,* 3, pp. 439-43.

21. Miller, "Walter Pater," pp. 105, 98.

22. Abrams, p. 434; Miller, "Stevens' Rock and Criticism as Cure, II," p. 341.

23. Miller, "The Critic as Host," pp. 443-44.

24. Miller, "Stevens' Rock and Criticism as Cure, II," p. 337. See also, for example, "Ariadne's Thread: Repetition and the Narrative Line," *Critical Inquiry,* 3 (Autumn 1976), pp. 57-77.

25. Wayne Booth, " 'Preserving the Exemplar' or, How Not to Dig Our Own Graves," *Critical Inquiry,* 3 (Spring, 1977), p. 422.

26. Abrams, "The Deconstructive Angel," pp. 432-33.

27. In informal discussion with faculty members, Rockhurst College, October 1959.

28. Tzvetan Todorov, "Language and Literature," pp. 129-30.

29. Tzvetan Todorov, "The Discovery of Language: *Les Liaisons dangereuses* and *Adolphe,*" *Yale French Studies,* 45 (1970), p. 116.

30. Jonathan Culler, *Structuralist Poetics: Structuralism, Linguistics and the Study of Literature* (Ithaca, N. Y.: Cornell University Press, 1975), see Chap. 4 and p. viii.

31. Culler, pp. 131-37, 148.

32. Culler, pp. 219, 221-22.

33. Culler, pp. 179-82.

34. Culler, pp. 258-59.

35. Maria Corti, *An Introduction to Literary Semiotics,* trans. Margherita Bogat and Allen Mandelbaum (Bloomington: Indiana University Press, 1978), p. x.

36. Corti, pp. 1-3, 16; T. S. Eliot, "Tradition and the Individual Talent," in *Selected Essays,* New Edition (New York: Harcourt Brace Jovanovich, Inc., 1964), p. 5.

37. Jorge Luis Borges, *Other Inquisitions* (Austin: University of Texas Press, 1964), p. 108.

38. Corti, pp. 31-33; Eliot, "The Function of Criticism," in *Selected Essays,* p. 18.

39. Corti, p. 42.

40. Corti, pp. 50-53, 58-63.

41. Corti, pp. 71-74, 79-80.

42. Vincent B. Leitch, "The Book of Deconstructive Criticism," *Studies in the Literary Imagination,* XII (Spring 1979), p. 21.

43. Tzvetan Todorov, "Bakhtin's Theory of the Utterance," this volume, pp. 165-178.

44. "Deciphering the Signs of the Times," *The Times Higher Education Supplement,* 24 September 1976, p. 15.

45. T. S. Eliot, "The Frontiers of Criticism," in *On Poetry and Poets* (New York: Farrar, Straus and Cudahy, 1957), p. 124.

A Problem of Audience: A Semiotical Approach to the Deistic Elements in *The Siege of Rhodes*

Andrew A. Tadie and James P. Mesa

Sir William Davenant's *The Siege of Rhodes* was entered in the *Stationers' Register* on August 27, 1656:

> Entred . . . under the hand of Master Thrale warden,
> a maske called *The Siege of Rhodes made a representacion by the art of prospective in scenes, and the story sung in recitative musicke* by Sr Willm
> Davenant, acted at ye back pte of Rutland House, at
> ye upper end of Aldersgatestreet.[1]

The publisher is listed as "Hen. Herringman."

The play, which was published in quarto a few days later, was not only welcomed by the English reading public who had been deprived of their plays by Parliamentary ban, but it also advertised that in a few days hence, in September of 1656, the play was to be acted. The advertisement promised the public even more than a play; it promised a spectacle of music and machinery, a spectacle with the richness of the royal masque but which now was no longer to be reserved for the court. William Davenant was able to accomplish this rather amazing feat of obtaining from the Puritan rulers permission to produce a public spectacle only because of his shrewd political and theatrical savvy.

In some respects *The Siege of Rhodes* is the most epoch-marking play in the language because no single play has had a greater number of significant innovations which were subsequently adopted by English drama: it was the first opera produced in England;[2] it used elaborate moveable scenes and employed a proscenium arch for the first time on the English public stage; it included what is generally considered the first appearance of an actress on the English public stage;[3] and it was the first libretto which derived its plot from modern history instead of from classical history or mythology.[4]

If his introduction of operatic conventions to England were the principal dramatic innovations that Davenant introduced, there were two other innovations which could not go altogether unnoticed by his 17th century audience. The first is the character of Solyman. He is emperor of the Ottoman Empire and the pagan enemy of Christendom, but in this play he is more virtuous than Alphonso, the Christian hero. The second innovation is the apparent violation of the Terentian Five-Act Structure. Not only was this the recognized dramatic structure for English drama since the 1570's, but Davenant's formulation of the Terentian Five-Act Structure in the introduction to *Gondibert* was a widely known statement regarding dramatic structure. Davenant's violation of this structure in not bringing closure to the main action, the political war, cannot have gone unnoticed. Yet to leave unresolved what had hitherto been regarded as the main action must force the reader to look elsewhere for the main action. What is thereby heightened is the relationship between the characters, especially the newly married lovers.

The question arises as to why the 17th century's leading formulator of the Terentian Five-Act Structure would construct a play which would clearly violate its presumed guiding principles. There are two possibilities that would explain this. Either Davenant lacked the imagination and talent to construct *The Siege of Rhodes* in accordance with this structure, or, which is the more reasonable explanation given Davenant's dramatic background and political activism, he was about some purpose which could not be contained by adhering to that structure.

In order to offer a plausible explanation as to why *The Siege of Rhodes* did not adhere to the Terentian scheme, our encounter with the text would have to yield some element which would have been discernible to Davenant's own audience. Now every encounter with a text, such as *The Siege of Rhodes,* is conditioned by what may be called the conceptual framework or *semiotic set* of the encountering-interpreter and the structural integrity of the encountered-text. The outcome of the encounter of the text and interpreter is the *interpretant.* The interpretants of different interpreters can be homologous only to the extent that the text is encountered with homologous semiotic sets. Communication between interpreters about a text is possible only to the extent that these "semiotic systems"[5] possess a shared semiotic set.

The problem identified in this paper involves semiotic systems encountering a text in two distinct historical eras. In an earlier work, "Sir William Davenant's *The Siege of Rhodes* and the Popularization of English Deism"[6] (portions of which are incorporated into this paper) we claimed that *The Siege of Rhodes* embodies the five basic tenets of Deism which were first set forth by Edward Lord Herbert of Cherbury. This claim is based on a critical study of the text *The Siege of Rhodes,* Herbert's *De Religione Laici,*[7] a review of texts both contemporaneous and scholarly, and a survey of historical conditions in which the two principal texts arose, which is to say that the study utilized normal biographical, historical, and critical methods in the treatment of the text.

The claim that *The Siege of Rhodes* embodies deistic tenets was then expanded to the position that the play contributed to the popularization of Deism in 17th century England. It is this judgment about *popularization* which gave rise to problems concerning semiotic process: the judgment implies that the interpretants which resulted from our encounter with the text, *The Siege of Rhodes,* are homologous to the interpretants produced by the text on 17th century English interpreters, specifically those who saw the play when it was first performed.

Every encounter with text is existential and as such is related to the interpreter's present semiotic set. However, some encounters with text can occur in what might be called a "diachronic" mode (not to be identified with Saussure's technical use of the term). The text is encountered in the present precisely for the reason of appropriating some past semiotic set. This encounter in a diachronic mode is, of course, synchronic for the interpreter himself. It becomes diachronic when he purports to possess as part of his own semiotic set a semiotic set, or at least relevant dimensions of it, which existed for some past interpreters.

Thus a claim that *The Siege of Rhodes* relates to the popularization of Deism implies that a contemporary critic has possession of the relevant elements of the semiotic set which the original audience possessed. It implies something of an identification of minds from two different historical periods. It is taken as a given that such an appropriation of past semiotic sets is realizable to some degree. Indeed, this is the same assumption that lies behind the acceptance of the reality of communication. It is also taken for granted that there is a law-like character to the semiotic process.[8] An account of how this appropriation or communication in general is possible is properly an epistemological-ontological task.

Our purpose in this paper is more modest, namely to locate within the semiotic process itself the touch-points between the interpreter encountering the text of *The Siege of Rhodes* in a diachronic mode (we as 20th century readers) and the interpreter encountering text in a "synchronic" mode (the 17th century audience). This will allow for mutual interpretants produced by a text. In order to accomplish this we require an outline of a theory of interpretants which emphasizes the dynamics of the semiotic process. Such an outline will enable us to discern parallels and differences in diachronic and synchronic encounters with a text. The model given is a Peircean one as utilized by James Collins in his *Interpreting Modern Philosophy:*[9]

I. Interpretants:

> Proper significate effects or outcome of action of sign, determining an interpreter toward objects thus signified.

II. Kinds of Interpretants:

1. *Immediate:*

> peculiar interpretability of each sign, its own possibility of specifying an interpreting process.

2. *Dynamical:*

> direct effect actually produced upon the individual interpreting mind or minds, distinctive actual uses of sign as:
> (a) *emotional:* feeling of recognition and familiarity.
> (b) *energetic:* action, especially mental effort with signs.
> (c) *logical:* development of meaning of intellectual general concepts, telically ordered toward ultimate interpretant.

3. *Final or Ultimate Logical:*

> self-analytical habit deliberately formed, that effect which a sign would produce on any mind if the sign were sufficiently considered, worked out, and brought to fully developed meaning. Teleological unity of immediate and dynamic interpretants in a continuing, unrestricted community of interpreters.

III. Semiosis:

> action of signs, their influence upon the interpreter as achieved through several kinds of interpretants.

This Peircean model will help clarify the position of the two kinds of interpreters that we are comparing. A general account of *interpretants* has already been incorporated in the previous paragraphs under the designation of the "semiotic set." The semiotic set is the total of interpretants possessed by the interpreter at any given time; it is the sum of effects of the actions of all signs that have determined the interpreter to objects signified. A semiotic set exists *prior to* the encounter with the text and so there will be significant differences in this regard between the critical scholar and Davenant's contemporaries. For example, the respective semiotic sets account for the differences in the reasons why the encountering interpreters approached *The Siege of Rhodes* precisely as a complex sign promising in meaning. The authors approached the text in an academic setting which presented the text as an object for ongoing critical and historical study. Davenant's contemporaries would have approached it for completely different reasons, some of which will be considered subsequently.

Furthermore, it must be kept in mind that *The Siege of Rhodes* is a performed presentment, and the pre-eminent synchronic interpreters are those members of Davenant's audience who came to see the play because they had read it, the play being published as an advertisement prior to the production. As a result, the interpreter of today will be a *reader* whose interpretants are much closer to the 17th century reader who did not see the play than with either the auditor who did read the play or the auditor who did not.

If we use the divisions of interpretants given in the Peircean model, we begin to get a sense of the enormity of the problems that attach to accounting for the possibility of comparing or reconstructing the interpretants of readers, auditors and reader-auditors. With respect to their respective immediate interpretants, there will be great differences among these interpreters depending on whether they encountered *The Siege of Rhodes* as a concrete definite which is a printed text or as a concrete definite which is a dramatic presentment. The immediate interpretant, as the initial and unanalyzed possibility of further interpretants, is the encounter with sign precisely as a sign pregnant with as yet undisclosed meaning. The importance of the nature of the sign as a concrete definite is clearly recognized by contemporary semioticians in their discriminations between the semiotics of gestures, cinema, music, etc.[10] These divisions have their foundations in the complex unconscious physiological-psychological processes of perception, the study of which, with great relief, we acknowledge to be the province of our colleagues in psychology.

The interpretants of the scholar and the 17th century audience, after the initial encounter with *The Siege of Rhodes,* would ultimately have to be similar in some respects in order that a claim can be made that the popularization of Deism is a function of the play. The respective interpreters would have to come to some shared non-arbitrary understandings about this play. These understandings would be the logical interpretants, one of which would have to be the proposition, "*The Siege of Rhodes* promotes Deistic tenets." (Peirce held that logical interpretants could be concepts, propositions or arguments [5.491].)

The development of logical interpretants is dependent upon factors which are readily identifiable by the scholar and which are to some extent those shared with the 17th century audience. The emotional interpretants of these disparate interpreters would be alike in significant respects; both would recognize the text as being a book containing a play written in the English language. There would be a sense of recognition, a feeling of familiarity (5.475 and 8.185). A sense of being "at home" with the text is born and is then nourished through energetic interpretants wherein the interpreter engages in activities as simple as picking up the text, leafing through the pages, reading random passages, and so on. These activities feed back on the emotional interpretants, increase the sense of recognition, and sustain the immediate interpretant. As the interpreter becomes more at home with the text and becomes increasingly aware of the interpretability of the text, the logical interpretants begin to develop.

The relationship between the energetic interpretants of the scholar and those of Davenant's audience is perhaps more distant than their emotional ones. The reason for this is that the energetic interpretants of the scholar in approaching *The Siege of Rhodes* are all almost completely self-conscious. He is not at all likely to approach *The Siege of Rhodes* with the same casualness and ease as the synchronic interpreter: trips have to be made to the library, card catalogues must be perused, histories and commentaries read, notes taken, notes compared, and so on. For Davenant's audience *The Siege of Rhodes* was a topic of unusual current interest; it was an attempt to test the limits of governmental censorship in the name of morality, much as a pornographer of today incites public interest in testing the limits of governmental censorship in the name of freedom of the press. The energetic interpretants of the reader of today are likely to be exercised for more scholarly or critical reasons, *The Siege of Rhodes* no longer being on our current best-seller lists. With respect to the logical interpretants, the scholar may well attend to this aspect more arduously and self-consciously than the synchronic reader, and certainly more than the synchronic auditor.

We are, of course, presenting in a very brief and simple fashion an account of what is in fact an incredibly rich and complex process. The dynamical interpretants are the warp and woof of a single fabric. Indeed, the interpreter engaged in the semiotic process of encounter with text is unlikely to be aware of the distinctions between the interpretants. The distinctions themselves are products of other semiotic processes which are then applied not to the encounter with text but to reflections about such encounters.

The Peircean model identifies the logical interpretant as telically ordered to the final logical interpretant. At the heart of the matter is Peirce's belief that a sign, or in this case a text as sign, could be penetrated by a community of interpreters after an indefinite amount of criticism over an indefinite amount of time. That is, that object, or objects, toward which a sign determines an interpreter can be realized. For every sign with cognitive dimensions (Peirce realized that not all signs have logical interpretants, 5.482) there are logical interpretants upon which a community of critical interpreters would be fated to agree. This is not to say that such an agreement would in fact ever occur, but it does serve to exclude the position of relativism, namely that one logical interpretant in relation to some given sign is as good as any other. The sign itself, within the context of the sign system in which it occurs, places constraints upon the conclusions of the community of interpreters; for example, it does not allow the logical interpretant that *The Siege of Rhodes* is a clarion call to capture the Kansas Turnpike.

It should be noted that Peirce's final logical interpretant is not the sum of logical interpretants but is a "habit." The verbal formulations of propositions merely express the final logical interpretant which is itself the "living definition" (5.491). Peirce has in mind something comparable to the Aristotelian virtue of science ($\epsilon\pi\iota\sigma\tau\eta\mu\eta$). Science is not a body of dead propositions collected in books which gather dust on library shelves. Science is not found in books; rather, science is the dynamic perfection of the theoretical abilities of reason. Science is an *activity* in conformity with the nature of reason. And like Aristotle, Peirce is aware that the human reason is bound to the conative dimensions of human nature and so the final logical interpretant as activity cannot be separated from the emotional and energetic interpretants (5.476-7, 5.486-7, and 5.491). Our claim about the Deistic tenets in *The Siege of Rhodes* would be an expression of that habit formed in relation to that sign.

From the point of view of the librettist, Davenant as a practical and accomplished poet must surely have realized that what he intended to be part of the meaning of his opera would not be manifested exactly. His intention would not correspond exactly to what he would write, and thus the diachronic reader can only understand the mind of the author imperfectly. Secondly, Davenant must have realized that his task at hand was more complex than just writing a poem or composing a libretto. With *The Siege of Rhodes* the text must work successfully as a libretto, that is, it must produce a good operatic performance, and it must work as a dramatic poem to those who read it. *The Siege of Rhodes* had to be constructed in order to be successful in two modes, and by contemporary accounts Davenant succeeded. Allowing for some differences in emotional and energetic interpretants then, some of the logical interpretants of Davenant, of the synchronic interpreter, and the diachronic interpreter should correspond. Their views would all finally correspond if all of them were a part of that ideal community of interpreters.

With this limited application of the Peircean account of interpretants to the historically separated interpreters of *The Siege of Rhodes* having been accomplished, we can see more clearly the ways in which the synchronic reader and auditor approached the text differently than we diachronic readers approach it. Just what specific concepts Davenant's contemporaries were able to bring to their encounter with *The Siege of Rhodes* is a matter for literary scholarship; the present state of scholarship also defines the initial limits of the diachronic reader's understanding of *The Siege of Rhodes*. What follows is in effect an unfolding of some dynamical interpretants which have resulted from the authors' encounter with a text.

Davenant's contemporary was likely to know that William Davenant was born in England some 50 years before *The Siege of Rhodes* and, as every biographer of Davenant relates, that Shakespeare was a frequent houseguest of the Davenants. Some of them were aware that William Shakespeare was not only William Davenant's legitimate godfather but perhaps his illegitimate father as well. This claim may have been initiated by

William Davenant himself, who, as Aubrey related, found his own poetic spirit more akin to Shakespeare's than to his father's:

> Sir William would sometimes, when he was pleasant
> over a glasse of wine with his most intimate friends
> . . ., say, that it seemed to him that he writt with
> the very spirit that did Shakespeare, and seemed
> contented enough to be thought his son.[11]

Davenant was known as a prominent Royalist who received his early education in Oxford. He had left Oxford to become a page first to Frances, first Duchess of Richmond, and afterwards to Sir Fulke Greville. After Greville's murder in 1628 Davenant sought the preferment of court by writing plays and poems.

Over 25 years earlier Davenant had written his first dramatic work, *The Temple of Love,* a masque which was published and produced in 1634; this was Davenant's first important work. It was important because it had been acted by the Queen and her court at Whitehall; but more significant than the cast was the instruction which Davenant received from Inigo Jones, who constructed the scenery for the play and who was, with Davenant, a co-author. Davenant produced this play under the patronage of Charles I, and he remained under royal patronage until civil insurrection curtailed royal entertainments.

Although Davenant's audience had never seen one, they knew that the masque was a favorite royal entertainment. Unlike the drama which they had seen, the masque was a drama based upon the Italian and French courtly entertainments, the *Mascherata, Trionfo, Mascarade,* and *Ballet de cour* and was more of a spectacle than their drama had been. The spoken word, the plot, and the characterization were not nearly as important as the spectacular effect of the formal processions, the music, the baroque scenes, and the stunning machinery. These entertainments were often enacted by players in elaborate costumes who represented mythical characters rather than the more realistic characters of the Jacobean stage. The masque, an elaborate compliment to nobility, was an expensive and extravagant private entertainment of and for the court.[12]

Visual and aural splendor were the special attractions of the masque, and it was these appeals that Davenant said he incorporated in *The Siege of Rhodes.* For this reason *The Siege of Rhodes* promised to be more closely related to the entertainment of Charles I's court than with the popular drama of the earlier 17th century. In the masques the virtues given the greatest emphasis are civility and gentility. The dramatic conflict was between classical or mythological characters who represented either good or evil, the good or ideal characters often representing the king or queen or other members of nobility. Thus, in addition to entertaining the members of the court, the masque also flattered them.

There was no doubt in the Puritan mind that Davenant had always been a royalist and needed to be watched. Davenant had successfully collaborated with Inigo Jones in writing several masques. The Queen herself had taken part in some of these, and she was so well pleased with Davenant that he was afterwards allowed to title himself "Her Majesty's Servant." In 1639 Davenant had set down his pen and, still in the King's service, had taken up the sword. In this and in the following year the court had to face a military insurrection which the Puritan had every reason to believe in 1656 he had won totally. Davenant was a member of the vanquished but valiant opposition.

By June of 1645 military victory had been won by Parliament's new model army. The King made one last desperate attempt to gather strength by appealing to the Scots, but it was the Scots who later turned Charles over to Parliament for execution. With the ascendancy of Charles II, the royal cause had taken a new direction. Under the able advice of Lord Clarendon, the royal cause became less military and more political. The new direction allowed for compromise with Parliament. Davenant, a poet and a soldier, had little to do with this new tact; so, late in 1646 Davenant, with the rest of the Queen's entourage, began a rather sedentary life of exile in Paris.

Probably much of what Davenant promised to present in *The Siege of Rhodes* he learned about in France. The new Italian art form, the opera, was performed there, and literary coteries were engaged in the most public of controversies. These French literary circles were reasserting the primacy of the epic as a literary form and adherence to the classical dramatic unities. This surely influenced Davenant in writing a new-style epic which would be modeled upon the Terencian five-act play. This epic poem, *Gondibert,* was well known in England. *Gondibert* had an elaborate moral purpose which Hobbes endorsed. *The Siege of Rhodes* promised to be a similar enterprise. It would have as its purpose the portrayal of a virtuous hero who would serve as a model of conduct for the audience. Stories would be devoid of both gods and figurative language, and evil would be treated as some misapplication or excess of virtue. In this way even the portrayal of evil could be a good example to the reader. This all had the appearance of staunch puritan thinking, but it could not be overlooked that Davenant had been arrested and formally charged with treason in 1650.

Davenant had soon set up household in Rutland House and devised a means to establish a legitimate drama. *The Siege of Rhodes* was the first fruit of these efforts. The published text of *The Siege of Rhodes* was an unabashed advertisement for a forthcoming performance. Davenant's first production was designed to test cautiously the way for full-fledged dramatic, or rather operatic, productions. The text promised epic-modeled entertainment: *The Siege of Rhodes, Made a Representation by the Art of Prospective in Scenes, and the Story Sung in Recitative Music.* Davenant did much to satisfy Parliament: the performers were not actors but known musicians; an orchestra would accompany the singers and chorus and would perform between the acts; the story of the drama would not be spoken but would be sung throughout in recitative, and no one had heard such a thing in England before.

The diachronic reader-scholar may with the aid of historical research discover more aspects of the details surrounding *The Siege of Rhodes* than the synchronic reader did, but almost certainly the synchronic reader was aware of additional meanings that the diachronic reader-scholar has yet to construct. He has discovered, what the original synchronic reader and auditor could never know, that *The Siege of Rhodes* would enjoy a great popularity throughout Davenant's lifetime. Davenant's work was, no doubt, popular for several reasons, and although the music has not survived, it was not the least reason for the popularity. The music of the play was popular in its own time as Samuel Pepys attests.[13]

After the September, 1656, performances *The Siege of Rhodes* enjoyed several revivals. The revivals occurred in 1659, 1661, 1663 and 1667. The first revival, in 1659, was at the Cockpit. At this time Davenant published a new edition of *The Siege of Rhodes,* an edition based on the 1656 edition. Consequently, it is likely that the players followed this version rather than the expanded version which probably had not yet been written.

In August, 1660, with the return of monarchy to England, Thomas Betterton and a small number of actors formed an acting company, and, by agreement with Davenant, they acted at Salisbury Court and at the Cockpit. This was the company for which Davenant in 1662 acquired a nearly exclusive license to act.[14] This was the Duke's Company which acted at Lincoln's Inn Fields.

The first work acted by the Duke's Company was an expanded version of *The Siege of Rhodes*. This was followed by a sequel, the second part of *The Siege of Rhodes*. Davenant's new style of theater was so popular that the term "opera" was soon applied by the public to any serious play which the Duke's Company performed. Modern English drama would have developed into a far different type of entertainment were it not for *The Siege of Rhodes* and the other similar presentments which Davenant produced during the Interregnum and well into the Restoration.

Davenant resided at the playhouse in Lincoln's Inn Fields as a successful impressario until his death on April 7, 1668. He was buried in Westminster Abbey.

The elements of spectacle in the play have received critical attention, but the theme of the play and the way it is manifested in the construction and development of the plot have been given almost no critical attention. One of these aspects which has yet to be treated critically is the influence of the Deistic tenets on Davenant when he developed the plot and theme of *The Siege of Rhodes*.

There is ample evidence for Davenant's interest in the religious and philosophical issues of his day. Davenant's epic poem, *Gondibert,* as already mentioned, was written to establish new epic conventions according to the new philosophy. The "Preface" of the poem was written by Thomas Hobbes himself who was a close friend of Davenant and who had met and was well acquainted with Lord Herbert of Cherbury, the founder of Deism, and Davenant knew Lord Herbert's brother who was the censor for public entertainments.

Although much has been said about the reason why Deism never enjoyed a vogue as a philosophical system, very little attention has been given to the influence Lord Herbert had on those who promulgated Deism and made its tenets popular, especially the poets and dramatists of the period. It is true that John Dryden, in his didactic poetic treatise, *Religio Laici,* written well over 50 years after Lord Herbert's *De Veritate,* argues against the tenets of Deism,[15] but the influence that is our concern here is not with John Dryden, the greatest English poet between Milton and

Pope, but with Sir William Davenant, mentor to Dryden and close friend to Thomas Hobbes.

By the mid-17th century there were many attempts made in England to answer the religious skepticism that had for so long pervaded English philosophical and literary thought. Richard Hooker and the established Church appealed to a moderating ecclesiastical authority; the Puritans appealed to scripture. These two appeals were long established in Christian tradition. They were certainly current a hundred years earlier at the Protestant disengagement. However, there was a third kind of answer to the skepticism of the period which was truly novel and had also a sense of that toleration which had made skepticism so persuasive. This third answer was English Deism. Its founder and original proponent was Lord Herbert of Cherbury, who early in his life formulated the tenets of a "true" basis for religious belief. Lord Herbert spent his entire life promoting these tenets and gathering disciples.

Lord Herbert, who was a minor social and political figure that served as an English ambassador to France from 1618 to 1624, is notable not for any significant technical contribution to philosophical thought, but for perhaps being the first to insist ". . . that in order to be valid, faith (and faith of course implied authority, for no individual unsanctioned faith was recognized) must be justified by completely unhampered reason."[16] Insistence for such justification is understandable given the strained intellectual and religious climate which was attributable to the revival of the classical Greek skepticism, as exemplified in the thought of Michel de Montaigne, and to the spectre of the religious revolution throughout Europe. All claims to truth in science, morality, and religion were placed in jeopardy by the skeptical onslaught.[17] Traditional ecclesiastical structures were challenged to provide credentials for their long presumed authority. Cherbury stepped into the breach with his attempt to identify basic religious truths and a proper attitude toward institutionalized religion.

Cherbury's *De Veritate* (1624) is a response to "skeptics and imbeciles" and purports to identify the kinds of truth that exist and the manner in which they can be obtained. The bulk of Cherbury's account is awkward and of little influence. What is of interest to our purpose is the class of intellectual, self-evident, and indubitable truths known as the "Common Notions." These truths are said to be in the possession of all sane and rational persons, and serve as the criteria for all other truths. Cherbury's basic test as to whether a proposition is a Common Notion is that it has the universal assent of normal persons. There are immediate and obvious difficulties which we need not develop here, but we may note in passing that Cherbury has the dubious distinction of being the only thinker explicitly named by John Locke in his attack on innate ideas.[18]

Concerning religion there are five Common Notions which Cherbury calls the Catholic Articles. These constitute the heart of Cherbury's thought, which is in fact a philosophy of religion.

> 1. That there is some supreme divinity. 2. That this divinity ought to be worshiped. 3. That virtue joined with piety is the best method of divine worship. 4. That we should return to our right selves from sins. 5. That reward or punishment is bestowed after this life is finished.[19]

> (1. *Esse aliquod Supremum Numen.* 2. *Numen illud coli debere.* 3. *Virtutem cum pietate conjunctam optimam esse rationem Cultus Divini.* 4. *Resipiscendum esse a peccatis.* 5. *Dari Praemium vel Poenam post hanc vitam transactam.*)

> For what teaching, purged of its obscurities and mysteries, does not incline that way? What mystery, indeed, has no regard to this? What finally is urged, because of God's mercy to mankind, but *love and fear of God, charity towards one's neighbor, repentance, and hope* of a better life?[20]

> (Quae enim illuc non vergit suis Ambagibus, Mysteriisque soluta Doctrina? Quodnam non huc spectat Mysterium? Quid tandem nisi *Amor, Timorque Dei, Charitas in proximum, Paenitentia, Spesque* melioris Vitae, ex Dei misericordia in humanum Genus suadetur?)

These Articles were first identified in the concluding section of the *De Veritate* and remained constant and insistent in the remainder of Cherbury's works, notably in the *De Religione Laici* (1645) and the *De Religione Gentilium* (1663).

The *De Religione Laici* is addressed to the wayfarer or layman and gives counsel on how to decide what is the best religion. It encourages a comparative study of doctrines which yields some basic propositions that are evident to the intellect as true, and about which there is general agreement. These are again the five above mentioned Common Notions or

Catholic Articles. "By these truths alone is the universe governed, and disposed to a better state; these therefore consider the catholic truths of the Church."[21] Any additional doctrines in any religion, and any matters of ritual, are only products of "priest-craft" and custom. Since additional doctrines are not known to be true by reason, and since the rituals are accidental to the five Catholic Articles, they can be supported solely by appeals to miracles and authority, and by threats of damnation.

Cherbury does not claim that religious doctrines and practices are pernicious *per se,* but only that they are not known to be true and are really not necessary. He requires that they be compatible with the Catholic Articles. Consequently, the strident claim of religions to some exclusive franchise on salvation is impossible and contrary to reason. Salvation must be universal. The honest and thoughtful wayfarer is not able to ". . . worship a divinity which has deliberately and painstakingly created and permeated souls doomed to perish."[22] The wayfarer, the layman or true searcher after truth, is different than the priest who is only a preserver of religious mores and cultural practices. The capable wayfarer does not so much examine the validity of the claims of competing religions as devote himself to acts of virtue and piety, for worship consists primarily in acts of virtue and piety, and these serve as the basis for the best part of all religions.

> It will be argued . . . that if the people are steadfast only in the catholic truths something at least will be lost to religion. Perhaps. But nothing, certainly, will be lost to a pious life or to virtue; yet by virtue is God so well worshiped that I have called that religion the best which is best squared to its rule.[23]

In his *Autobiography,* Cherbury notes that one of the reasons that he insisted on these Catholic Articles was "that I found nothing that could be added to them which could make a man Really more vertuous and good when the afforesaid five points were rightly explicated."[24] Only a religion which is in keeping with the Catholic Articles can foster virtue and piety. It should be noted that Cherbury does not refer to virtue as being a criterion for the true religion but for the best religion. Thus, since all doctrines and all forms of worship are accidental to the tenets of the Catholic Articles, doctrines and rituals are matters of indifference, except perhaps for personal, social and cultural reasons.

One last observation is in order before moving to a further consideration of Davenant. In his *Autobiography,* Cherbury makes the following observation which is reflected in *The Siege of Rhodes:*

> . . . I dare say That a vertuous man [or, in the play, a woman] may not onely goe securely through all the Religions but all the Lawes in the world and whatsoeuer obstructions he meete obtayne both an Jnward peace and outward wellcome among all with whome hee shall negotiate or Converse.[25]

Virtuous individuals, regardless of their religion, will respect one another and live in harmony with one another because their religion and conduct are grounded in the shared Catholic Articles. In *The Siege of Rhodes* Davenant fashioned his plot to promote a Deistic point of view in his audience.

The plot of *The Siege of Rhodes* is divided into two closely woven parts. The first deals with the conquering of the Christian isle of Rhodes by the Turkish conqueror, Solyman the Magnificent. This part only provides a dramatic setting for the second part because the play ends before the military conflict is resolved. The central part of the play deals with the relationship of Alphonso, the Christian hero, his wife Ianthe, and Solyman himself.

The play opens with the Grand Master of Rhodes and his Marshall debating with Alphonso, the hero. They see no reason why the newly married visitor should remain in Rhodes and fight what will be a losing battle with the Turks. In the meantime, Ianthe, Alphonso's wife and true model of virtue in the play, has sailed to Rhodes to assist her husband. However, she is captured by the Turkish fleet, the captain of which is so impressed with her virtue that he presents her to Solyman himself. Her virtue also overwhelms Solyman, who is no lusty polygamist in this play. He allows her to go to her husband and with a generosity inspired by Ianthe's virtue gives her and her new husband free passage from Rhodes back to their home.

When Ianthe joyfully greets her husband with the good news, Alphonso has doubts about her conduct with what he considers a lecherous, pagan emperor. She tries to convince Alphonso of her virtue but is unsuccessful. In this debate neither is able to convince the other; so both resolve to die at Rhodes, Alphonso because he thinks he is a cuckold and is dishonored, and Ianthe because she has lost the love of her husband.

Meanwhile, Solyman in preparing his attack on Rhodes debates with his two officers over the fate of the two lovers who have spurned his generosity, and he resolves that neither shall perish when he conquers Rhodes. The climax of the play occurs in the heat of battle. Alphonso must choose whether to save his former teacher or his wife who has been wounded in the fight. He finally decides that he has misjudged his wife's virtue, and he saves her. With the lovers reunited, the play ends even before Solyman conquers the island.

The first act is in Rhodes. The problem is that Solyman will soon come and lay siege to Rhodes. Alphonso, the hero, will stay and fight because the pagan, barbarian infidels must be stopped.

> My Sword against proud Solyman I draw,
> His cursed Prophet and his sensual Law.[26]   (I,i)

The chorus ends the scene echoing:

> Our Swords against proud Solyman we draw,
> His cursed Prophet and his sensual Law.   (I,i)

In the second act there is the same hostile note, but this time in the opposing camp. Solyman says that Christians are

> . . .° oft misled by mists of Wine,
> or blinder love the Crime of Peace.
> Bold in Adult'ries of frequent change;
> And ev'ry loud expensive Vice;
> Ebbing out wealth by ways as strange
> As it flow'd in by avarice.   (II,ii)

Immediately after these words Ianthe, the model of virtue, is brought before Solyman. He recognizes the virtue of this woman and immediately sees her virtuous love as transcending his previous understanding of Christianity. Ianthe comes before Solyman veiled, which shows her respect for Islamic customs regarding feminine modesty. Solyman responds to this gesture and to Ianthe's willingness to share her husband's fate in a way that is precisely opposed to his earlier beliefs about Christians; he responds to Ianthe's virtue in a virtuous way.

> In vertuous Love, thus to transcend thy Lord?
> Thou did'st thy utmost vertue show;

> Yet somewhat more does rest,
> Not yet by thee expressed;
> Which vertue left for me to do.
> Thou great example of a Christian Wife,
> Enjoy thy Lord and give him happy Life.
>
> .   .   .
>
> And as thy passage to him shall be free,
> So both may safe return to Cicily. (II,ii)

As we would expect, in the second act the forces of white, that is, Ianthe, appear to overcome the forces of black Solyman's regard for virtuous conduct, and her bravery overcomes the belief that a foreign religion unlike one's own is inferior. Yet while Solyman recognizes Ianthe's inspirational virtue, in the third act Alphonso believes his wife's actions are hardly virtuous at all. It appears at the end of the act that, in spite of Ianthe's virtue, all may well come to be lost because of Alphonso's jealousy. Alphonso believes that it was Ianthe's physical beauty, not her virtue, that moved Solyman.

> It could even *Solyman* himself withstand;
> To whom it did so beauteous show
> It seem'd to civilize a barb'rous Foe.
> Of this your strange escape, Ianthe say,
> Briefly the motive and the way. (III,ii)

Ianthe explains that she is free because Solyman is no barbarian at all but is as civil as the most gracious Christian king.

> All that of Turks and Tyrants I had heard,
> But that I fear'd not Death, I should have fear'd.
> I, to excuse my Voyage, urg'd my Love
> To your high worth; which did such pitty move
> That strait his usage did reclaim my fear;
> He seem'd in civil France, and Monarch there:
> For soon my person, Gallies, Fraight, were free
> By his command. (III, ii)

Alphonso's reply is filled with dramatic irony:

> This Christian Turk amazes me, my Dear! (III, ii)

Alphonso's assessment is that no enemy, no barbarian, no leader of the

Islamic religion with a carnal view of heaven could be motivated by anything but lust and power.

> And *Solyman* does think Heav'ns joys to be
> In Women not so fair as she.
> 'Tis strange! Dismisse so fair an Enemy?
> She was his own by right of War.
> We are his Dogs, and such as she, his Angels are.
> O wondrous Turkish chastity!
>
> . . .
>
> Oh *Solyman* this mistique act of thine,
> Does all my quiet undermine. (III, ii)

The climax does occur as expected in the fourth act. The jealous Alphonso orders his wife to leave him and return to Sicily while he will stay and die at Rhodes. Still not overcome by Ianthe's virtue as Solyman was earlier, he and the chorus vow to

> Drive back the Crescents, and advances the Cross,
> Or sink all humane Empires in our loss! (IV, iii)

By the fifth act the audience knows Alphonso to be wrong, that the Turks are certainly as humane as the Christians. Davenant has convinced his audience that virtue and morality transcend all particular religions. The fifth act itself is a spectacular battle scene during which Alphonso learns that his wife has stayed to defend Rhodes, and so doing has been wounded. Alphonso, realizing his wife's virtue, leaves to save her from being over-run by the Turks. He, wounded in the process, is taken to Ianthe:

> Tear up my wounds! I had a passion, course,
> And rude enough to strengthen Jealousie;
>
> . . .
>
> Who knows but I ill use may make
> Of pardons which I should not take
> For they may move me to desire to Live. (V, iii)

Ianthe recognizes that his jealousy "was but over-cautious Love," or as Davenant said in *Gondibert*, excessive virtue. Alphonso responds:

> Draw all the Curtains and then lead her in;
> Let me in darkness mourn away my sin. (V, iii)

Thus the play ends with Alphonso repentant and Ianthe reconciled to her husband.

Davenant has in this play created a plot that is unlike the conventions of earlier English Renaissance drama. Certainly virtuous heroines and jealous husbands are nothing new, but Solyman is another matter. Turks are not altogether unknown in English Renaissance drama: Atheists (i.e., irredeemable natural man), Mohammedans, and Christians engage in the most serious of military conflicts in the two parts of Marlowe's *Tamburlaine;* and the difference between Christian and Islamic religion and custom contribute to the deception and downfall of Othello.

Davenant's Solyman differs from the Turks which appear in earlier English dramas because Solyman comes to understand, as do the other major characters of the play, that the virtue and piety of a natural religion is superior to the intolerance and persecution characteristic of those religions which claim a direct and exclusive relationship with God. To develop this concept dramatically, Davenant has applied Herbert's systematic treatment of the five Common Notions which are, he says, the foundation of all natural religion.[27] It is upon these five Common Notions that Davenant constructs his plot. The five tenets, again, are *"Amor, Timorque Dei, Charitas in proximum, Paenitentia, Spesque melioris vitae. . . ."* Both the Islamic and Christian religions promote love of God (*Amor*) and a belief in duty to God (*Timor dei*), the Moslems because of Mohammed, the Christians because of Christ. In the play it is Ianthe's virtue that prompts Solyman and Alphonso to broaden their understanding of the other's religion, a broadening which causes a greater sense of toleration and understanding between the two men (*Charitas in proximum*). Alphonso, after he realizes the error of his jealousy, feels extremely guilty and penitent (*paenitentia*). The forgiving Ianthe, alone, can give him hope (*Spes*) for a better life. Her virtue and piety have transcended the limit and even false beliefs which are generated by differing cultures and differing religions. At the end Davenant's characters Ianthe, Alphonso, and Solyman realize, as perhaps some of Davenant's audience have been led to believe, that natural virtues transcend the opposing doctrines of different religions. In this way Christianity can be finally reconciled with what was once considered barbarism.

Davenant's treatment of deistic tenets in his play is not at first reading obvious, even to those synchronic readers who knew the works of Lord

Herbert. This is part of his dramatic art. Davenant could not afford to be too obvious about the matter because the Puritans were not to be offended at any cost. Secondly, Davenant prepared a libretto, not a philosophical treatise, and being an accomplished poet, he knew that he must keep his genre integral.

If his introduction of operatic conventions to England were the principal dramatic innovations that Davenant introduced, there were two other innovations which could not go altogether unnoticed. The first is the character of Solyman, who is one of the first examples of the "Good Sultan" motif. He is the pagan enemy of Christendom, but in this play he is more virtuous than Alphonso, the Christian hero. The second is the apparent violation of the Terencian Five-Act Structure. Not only was this the recognized dramatic structure for English drama since the 1570's, but Davenant's formulation of the Terencian Five-Act Structure in the introduction to *Gondibert* was one of the most widely known statements regarding dramatic structure, save Aristotle's, until the end of the 19th century. Davenant's violation of this structure in not bringing closure to the main action, the political war, cannot have gone unnoticed. Yet to leave unresolved what had hitherto been regarded as the main action must force the reader to look elsewhere for the main action. What is resolved is the relationship between the characters, especially the newly married lovers.

Davenant with this innovative dramatic gesture implies that true religious norms for virtue reside within man himself. The recognition and practice of virtue is not limited to a particular culture or religion. Instead it is natural to man, and models for true virtue can be found anywhere.

This rather lengthy discussion began with a presentation of the fundamentals upon which we make our claims about the presence of Deistic tenets in *The Siege of Rhodes* and its relation to the popularization of Deism. It was prefaced by the remarks that it was an unfolding of "Dynamic Interpretants" which resulted from the writers' encounter with text. The hub of our activity resided in the pragmatic dimensions of the "Dynamic Energetic Interpretants." These increased our sense of recognition and familiarity with the text, and led to specific "Logical Interpretants," i.e., our claims about Deism, which in turn presented signs within the text which further determined the interpreters toward objects thus signified. The domain of interpretants cannot be conceived narrowly nor statically.

In reflecting on our findings in terms of the Peircean model, the reader will no doubt be aware of the complexity of the process. The interpretants unfolded in the previous pages are presented as relative to the text *The Siege of Rhodes,* but within that process other signs, other texts were encountered to which the same Peircean model would apply. Further, the relation of *The Siege of Rhodes* as sign for the reader is a new factor in his semiotic process, as will be our discussion.

The treatment of the text, *The Siege of Rhodes,* is given order and meaning within the Peircean teleological account of interpretants: signs determine interpreters toward objects and the relation of sign and interpreter is ordered to an ultimate logical interpretant. This serves to evoke what William James has called the "strenuous mood"; it encourages the reader of historically important texts to continued efforts in interpreting text and provides meaning to the links with the efforts of other interpreters. Only with the positing of something like an ultimate logical interpretant can the interpreter hope that his efforts make genuine contributions to literary criticism.

Notes

1. *A Transcript of the Registers of the Worshipful Company of Stationers: From 1640-1708 A.D., in Three Volumes,* Vol. II—1655-1765 (New York: Peter Smith, 1950), p. 81.

2. Richard Flecknoe may have written a libretto before Davenant but it was never produced.

3. See Ann-Mari Hedbäck's edition of *The Siege of Rhodes* (Uppsala: University of Uppsala, 1973).

4. Monteverdi's *L'incoronazione di Poppea* is the only opera before Davenant's which had an historical and not a mythological plot. But Monteverdi's plot was from classical Roman not modern history.

5. See Rudolf Jander, "General Semiotics and Biosemiotics," this volume, pp. 225-250.

6. Presented at the meeting of the Rocky Mountain Medieval and Renaissance Association, 1979.

7. Lord Herbert of Cherbury, *De Religione Laici,* ed. and trans. Harold R. Hutcheson (New Haven: Yale University Press, 1944).

8. Consider the efforts of Jander in this regard, this volume, pp. 225-250.

9. This model is based on the following texts: *Collected Papers of Charles Sanders Peirce,* ed. C. Hartshorne, P. Weiss, and A. Bourke, 4.536 (from "Prolegomena for an Apology for Pragmatism"), 5.470-91 (from "A Survey of Pragmatism"), 8.184-85 (note on Lady Welby's *What Is Meaning?*), 8.343 (partial draft of letter to Lady Welby; and James Collins, *Interpreting Modern Philosophy* (New Haven: Yale University Press, 1972), p. 361.

10. Professor Sebeok sees some relationship between the semiotics of theatre and Paul Bouissac's *Circus and Culture: A Semiotic Approach* (Bloomington: Indiana University Press, 1976).

11. John Aubrey, *Aubrey's Brief Lives,* ed. Oliver Lawson Dick (London: Secker and Warburg, 1950), p. 85.

12. See Paul Reyher's *Les Masques anglais* (New York: Benjamin Blom, Inc., 1909, 1964).

13. *The Diary of Samuel Pepys,* ed. Henry Wheatley (London: G. Bell and Sons, Ltd., 1913), Vol. VI, p. 134.

14. See Leslie Hotson's *The Commonwealth and Restoration Stage* (Cambridge, Mass.: Harvard University Press, 1928), pp. 401-03. See p. 207 for Davenant's contract with those of his company.

15. Much attention has been given to Dryden's position regarding Deistic thought a generation after Davenant. See Phillip Harth's *Contexts of Dryden's Thought* (Chicago: University of Chicago Press, 1969) and G. Douglas Atkins' response, "Dryden's *Religio Laici:* A Reappraisal," *Studies in Philology*, LXXV (Summer 1978).

Davenant's achievements with the heroic style influenced subsequent heroic drama especially in handling this type of debate. He created a type of dialogue which was striking in its use of antithesis and juxtaposition of differences, contraries, or opposites. Dryden remarked that *The Siege of Rhodes* was especially effective with scenes "of Argumentation and Discourse, on the result of which the doing or not doing of some considerable actions should depend." The reason which Dryden cites for Davenant's effectiveness is "the quickness of Reparties, . . . it [heroic couplet] has so particular a Grace, and is so aptly Suited to them, that the suddain Smartness of the Answer, and the Sweetness of the Rhyme, set off the Beauty of each other." (John Dryden, *Works*, the dedication of *The Rival Ladies*, Vol. VIII [Berkeley: University of California Press, 1962], pp. 100-101).

In his essay "On Heroic Plays" John Dryden, the acknowledged master-writer of the heroic play, explained his own and the Restoration theater's indebtedness to Davenant:

> For heroic plays . . . the first light we had of them, on the English theatre, was from the late Sir William D'Avenant. It being forbidden him in the rebellious times to act tragedies and comedies, because they contained some matter of scandal to those good people, who could more easily dispossess their lawful sovereign than endure a wonton jest, he was forced to turn his thoughts another way, and to introduce the examples of moral virtue, writ in verse, and performed in recitative music. The original of this music, and the scenes which adorned his work, he had from the Italian operas; but he heightened his characters (as I may probably imagine) from the example of the . . . French poets. In this condition did this part of poetry remain at his Majesty's return; when, growing bolder, as being now owned by a public authority, he reviewed his *Siege of Rhodes,* and caused it to be acted as a just drama. But as few men have the happiness to begin and finish any new project, so neigher did he live to make his design perfect: there wanted the fulness of plot, and the variety of characters to form as it ought; and, perhaps, something might have been added to the beauty of the style. All which he would have performed with more exactness, had he pleased to have given us another work of the same nature. For myself and others, who come after him, we are bound, with all veneration to his memory, to acknowledge what advantage we received from that excellent groundwork which he laid. And, since, it is an easy thing to add to what already is invented, we ought all of us, without envy to him, or partially to ourselves, to yield him the precedence in it."

(From John Dryden, "On Heroic Plays, An Essay," *Essays of John Dryden*, Vol. I, ed. by W. P. Ker (Oxford: Clarendon Press, 1900), pp. 149-50.

16. Lord Herbert of Cherbury, *De Religione Laici*, p. 29, introductory essay by Harold R. Hutcheson.

17. See Richard H. Popkin, *The History of Scepticism from Erasmus to Descartes* (Assen: Van Gorcum, 1964), esp. chapters 1-4.

18. John Locke, *An Essay Concerning Human Understanding*, I, 3.

19. Lord Herbert of Cherbury, *De Religione Laici*, p. 129.

20. Lord Herbert of Cherbury, *De Religione Laici*, p. 101. Emphasis in English translation supplied editorially.

21. Lord Herbert of Cherbury, *De Religione Laici*, pp. 89-91.

22. Lord Herbert of Cherbury, *De Religione Laici*, p. 119.

23. Lord Herbert of Cherbury, *De Religione Laici*, p. 109.

24. Lord Herbert of Cherbury, *The Life of Edward, First Lord Herbert of Cherbury*, ed. by J. M. Shuttleworth (London: Oxford University Press, 1976), p. 30.

25. Lord Herbert of Cherbury, *The Life of Edward*, p. 24.

26. This and subsequent quotations from the play are from Ann-Mari Hedback's recent edition of *The Siege of Rhodes* (Uppsala: University of Uppsala, 1973).

27. See Harold Hutcheson's analysis of the relationship between Deism and natural religion in his edition of Herbert's *De Religione Laici*, pp. 66-69.

The Sign as a Structure of Difference: Derridean Deconstruction and Some of Its Implications

G. Douglas Atkins

A major force to be reckoned with in contemporary literary criticism is Jacques Derrida. Derrida's star has risen precipitously since his participation in 1966 in a Johns Hopkins international symposium, where he took structuralism, and particularly Lévi-Strauss, to task and inaugurated deconstructive criticism in America. The following year he published *La Voix et le phénomène: introduction au problème du signe dans la phénoménologie de Husserl, De la grammatologie,* and *L'écriture et la différence,* all of which are now available in English. In 1972 Derrida published three more books: *La dissémination, Positions,* and *Marges de la philosophie.* His monumental, and probably untranslatable, *Glas* appeared in 1974. That these books and various essays, several already available in English, are changing the face of literary criticism is apparent in several ways: Derrida and his theories have been embraced, in varying degrees, by such influential American critics and theorists as Paul de Man, Geoffrey Hartman, and J. Hillis Miller, all of Yale, where Derrida teaches each fall; numerous essays and books have begun to appear from others influenced by Derrida, including Joseph Riddel's study of William Carlos Williams, Pietro Pucci's recent book on Hesiod, Naomi Schor's study of Zola, and Howard Felperin's *Shakespearean Representation;* sessions on deconstruction have become prominent at the annual meeting of the Modern Language Association; journals devoted to deconstructive criticism, such as *Glyph,* are now published, and deconstructive criticism regularly appears in *PMLA* and *Diacritics;* and, not least important, frequent attacks on Derrideanism by traditionalist critics and scholars appear in publications ranging from *The New York Times* to *The New Republic* to *Critical Inquiry.*

Among the charges in these attacks are the claims that Derrida and his followers are needlessly obscure and that deconstructive criticism is nihilistic and deeply antithetical to the so-called humanist tradition. Many of these charges stem, in my view, from a misunderstanding of Derrida. His work is admittedly complex, his arguments often convoluted, and his style increasingly difficult. Still, I hope to shed some light on Derrideanism and to clear away some of the confusions surrounding the theory that so many regard as threatening and dangerous. Though my effort here will be limited, I hope to provide the kind of general introduction and consideration that has rarely been attempted on Derrida; most discussions in which Derrida figures prominently assume a basic knowledge of his thought or else proceed to offer an alternative without themselves evincing a grounding in that thought.

One cannot hope to understand Derrida apart from his undoing/preserving of the concept of the sign central to modern linguistics. Modern linguistics is often said to begin with Ferdinand de Saussure's *Cours de linguistique générale*. Probably Saussure's most important argument was that no intrinsic relationship obtains between the two parts of the sign, the signifier and the signified. In his own words, "The bond between the signifier and the signified is arbitrary. . . . *the linguistic sign is arbitrary*."[1] This is due to the differential character of language. Because the sign, phonic as well as graphic, is a structure of difference, signs being made possible through the *differences* between sounds, that which is signified by the signifier is never present in and of itself. Word and thing, word and thought, sign and meaning can never become one.

Derrida plays constantly with this discovery that the sign marks a place of difference. But whereas Saussure and Saussurian semiology rest with the binary opposition signifier/signified, Derrida puts such terms *sous rature,* that is, "under erasure." He writes a word, crosses it out, and prints both word and deletion, for though the word is inaccurate it is necessary and must remain legible. This idea of *sous rature* is an analogue of the undoing/preserving play that everywhere characterizes, indeed creates, Derridean thought ("Neither/nor is at once *at once* or rather *or rather*"[2]) and so distinguishes it from Saussurian.

Derrida carefully analyzes the sign and the concept of difference, noticing several things. He recognizes, first of all, that the possibility of the sign, the substitution of the sign for the thing in a system of differences, depends upon deferral, that is, putting off into the future any grasping of the "thing itself." But space as well as time bears on the concept of difference in a fundamental way. The temporal interval, the deferring into the future of any grasping of the thing, irreducibly divides all spatial presence. In other words, if perception of objects depends upon perception of their differences, each present element *must* refer to an element *other* than itself. The never-annulled difference from the completely other precisely opens the possibility of thought. As Jeffrey Mehlman has remarked, "Derrida's effort has been to show that the play of difference, which has generally been viewed as exterior to a (spatial or temporal) *present,* is, in fact, always already at work *within* that present as the condition of its possibility."[3]

Involved in the constitution of the sign, according to Derrida, is the "trace" of a past element that was never fully present. That element was never fully present because it must always already refer to something other than itself. This "trace" refers to what can never become present, for the interval separating sign from thing must always reconstitute itself. Now it would seem that Derrida has unarguably gone beyond Saussurian linguistics, for as Alan Bass has written, "Any other alternative, any attempt to save the value of full presence would lead to the postulation of a point of origin not different from itself (an in-different origin), thus destroying the essentially differential quality of language."[4] Derrida coins the word *différance* to describe the structure of the sign, which is always already marked by both deferring and differing (both senses occur, of course, in the French verb *différer*).

A few more remarks may be in order here on the important "trace," which creates the undoing/preserving that I have called fundamental to Derrida's thought. After defining "trace" as "the part played by the radically other within the structure of difference that is the sign," Gayatri Spivak proceeds to term it "the mark of the absence of a presence, an always already absent present, of the lack at the origin that is the condition of thought and experience."[5] Because the structure of the sign is determined by the "trace" or track of that other which is forever absent, the word "sign" must itself be placed "under erasure." Derrida writes, "the sign ⱪ that ill-named t̶h̶i̶n̶g̶, the only one, that escapes the instituting question of philosophy: 'what is . . . ?'"[6] The "trace" thus destroys the idea of simple presence, the desire of which, argues Derrida, characterizes Western metaphysics. The idea of origin is similarly destroyed, for origin is always other than itself, the idea of origin depending upon the production of temporal and spatial difference that must precede any origin.

Derrida would thus replace semiology with grammatology. "The sign cannot be taken as a homogeneous unit bridging an origin (referent) and an end (meaning), as 'semiology,' the study of signs, would have it.

The sign must be studied 'under erasure,' always already inhabited by the trace of another sign which never appears as such."[7] The term "grammatology" is itself expressive of Derridean strategy, for it reflects an unresolved contradiction. Whereas the "grammè" is the written mark, the sign "under erasure," "logos" is at once "law," "order," "origin," and "phonè," the voice. What the "grammè" does, as I have suggested, is precisely to deconstruct the authority of the "logos" and so of the privilege always afforded to the spoken word, itself supposedly an indication of presence. Grammatology is, then, as a term an example of *sous rature,* of the undoing yet preserving of apparent opposites. The undoing is, of course, no more necessary than the preserving, for without the latter another term would be privileged in a new hierarchy, simple opposition being maintained though reversed, and the "trace" ignored. With the "trace," however, one thing is defined not simply by its difference from another but by its difference from itself, a "trace" of the radically other always already being present. Derrida is perhaps most forceful on this point in his 1966 deconstruction of Lévi-Strauss, where he undoes yet preserves the latter's well-known binary opposition engineer/ *bricoleur:* "From the moment that we cease to believe in such an engineer . . . as soon as it is admitted that every finite discourse is bound by a certain *bricolage,* . . . the very idea of *bricolage* is menaced and the difference in which it took on its meaning decomposes."[8]

It is fair to say, with Spivak, that Derrida is thus asking us "to change certain habits of mind: . . . the origin is a trace; contradicting logic, we must learn to use and erase our language at the same time."[9] The implications of this are numerous and radical, for they reach, attack, subvert the roots of Western thought, defined by Derrida as logocentric and fundamentally desirous of presence. The desire of presence appears, in J. Hillis Miller's words, as "Time as presence, the other as presence, the presence of consciousness to itself, language as the pure reflection of the presence of consciousness, literary history as a history of consciousness, the possibility of reaching an original presence from which all the others derive."[10] Since Miller has admirably described the way in which Derrida deconstructs this fundamental desire of presence at every turn, and since it should be clear from my own account above how *differance* renders presence in these senses impossible, I shall not dwell on the point but turn instead to others not so well treated in the commentary.

We might begin with the question of truth. In brilliant analyses of

Plato,[11] Derrida associates writing, the structure of difference marked by the "trace," and so the disappearance of a present origin of presence, with the Platonic idea of *epekeina tes ousias* (the beyond of all presence). Because Plato posits that which cannot be viewed directly (i.e., the sun) as the origin of the visible, Derrida is able to demonstrate that the presence of the thing itself, the unity of referent and signified, is inseparable from the concept of grammatical difference. If the origin of the thing itself is, as Plato asserts, the invisible "beyond" of all presence, the thing itself can obviously never be present. Truth defined as absolute presence, as presence of the *eidos,* thus becomes simultaneously possible and impossible. As the "trace" requires, the thing itself is doubled, true and not-true. This duplicity, born with the "trace," is what makes truth possible, thereby destroying truth. Contradicting logic, Derrida thus undoes/preserves "truth." I might point out in passing that such alogical moments in Derrida, and they are obviously basic to his thought, render him suspect in traditionalist minds, but what is too easily neglected is the exacting and rigorous nature of these deconstructions. Nothing could be less subjective and less arbitrary.

An important immediate consequence of the never-annulled "trace," and so of truth/untruth, is the ubiquity of textuality. That "the central signified, the original or transcendental signified" is revealed to be "never absolutely present outside a system of differences . . . extends the domain and the interplay of signification *ad infinitum.*"[12] Bass is correct in stating, "Once one has determined the totality of what is as 'having been' made possible by the institution of the trace, 'textuality,' the system of traces, becomes the most global term, encompassing all that is and that which exceeds it."[13] According to Derrida, there is simply nothing outside textuality, outside ". . . the temporalization of a *lived experience* which is neither *in* the world nor in 'another world' . . . not more *in* time than *in* space, [in which] differences appear among the elements or rather produce them, make them emerge as such and constitute the *texts,* the chains, and the systems of traces."[14] Derrida proposes, in fact, a "double science," a science of textuality. Once we rethink the metaphysical concept of "reality" in "textual" terms (there are no philosophical regulations of truth, the thing itself being a sign and all "facts" being in "fact" interpretations, as Nietzsche argued), we are left with a world of texts, all of which possess a certain "fictive" or "literary" quality. In this situation of the fictionality of things, literature seems to occupy a privileged place, though now all texts, including philosophical and scientific ones, come to be understood as also fictive.

In this pervasive breakdown of the relationship to truth and reality, literary criticism is no more exempt from textuality than philosophical and scientific works. Whether or not it has traditionally done so, criticism now decides the meaning of a text. Criticism too is a desire of presence. But "meaning" as a privileged term refers to something outside textuality, outside the system of differences: "a text's meaning is the truth that is present 'behind' or 'under' its textual surface that criticism makes fully present by placing it before us."[15] The "trace," of course, makes meaning so conceived, like truth and presence, impossible. To repeat, there is no originating, privileged signified outside the system of differences and so no "meaning."

The deconstructive critic, in practice, tries to avoid the strong ultimate temptation to seek meaning. Such a temptation is inevitable, for we naturally want to resolve contradictions and to break out of the endless chains of substitutions, which "condemn" us to endless interpretation. We desire a haven outside contingency and temporality, which "meaning," "truth," and an originating signified offer. Indeed, the fact of *differance* seems responsible for this situation: it generates the desire to do the impossible, to unify, to locate a reference outside the system of differences that will bestow meaning, "making equal" as Nietzsche puts it (his term is *Gleich machen*). In any case, author and critic share the desire, and the deconstructive critic must be acutely conscious of the desire in both the authors he studies and in himself. As Spivak writes, "The desire for unity and order compels the author and the reader to balance the equation that is the text's system. The deconstructive reader exposes the grammatological structure of the text, that its 'origin' and its 'end' are given over to language in general . . . by locating the moment in the text which harbors the unbalancing of the equation, the sleight of hand at the limit of a text which cannot be dismissed simply as a contradiction."[16]

The deconstructive critic, therefore, aware of the differential quality of language and recognizing the fact of the "trace," seeks the moment in any text when its duplicity, its dialogical nature, is exposed. Here, as elsewhere, Freud anticipates deconstructive procedure. In *The Interpretation of Dreams,* for example, he suggests that the reader or interpreter should direct his gaze where the subject is *not* in control: "There is often a passage in even the most thoroughly interpreted dream which has to be left obscure. . . . At that point there is a tangle of dream-thoughts which cannot be unravelled and which moreover adds nothing to our knowledge of the content of the dream." Derrida extends this point, modifying it: it *is* the case that such a tangle adds nothing to our knowledge of the content of the dream-text in terms of what it sets up by itself. "If, however, we have nothing vested in the putative identity of the text or dream, that passage is where we can provisionally locate the text's moment of transgressing the laws it apparently sets up for itself, and thus unravel—deconstruct—the very text."[17] The deconstructive critic thus seeks the text's navel, the moment when any text will differ from itself, transgressing its own system of values, becoming undecidable in terms of its apparent system of meaning.[18] "Reading must always," says Derrida, "aim at a certain relationship, unperceived by the writer, between what he commands and what he does not command of the patterns of the language that he uses. This relationship is not a certain quantitative distribution of shadow and light, of weakness and force, but a signifying structure that critical reading should produce."[19] This undoing, made necessary by the "trace," and so by the duplicitous quality of words and texts, must not be confused with the simple locating of a moment of ambiguity or irony that is somehow incorporated into a text's system of (monological) meaning; rather, it is the moment that threatens the collapse of that entire system.

Nor is it enough simply to neutralize the binary oppositions of metaphysics. Derrida insists that there is always "a violent hierarchy. One of the two terms controls the other (axiologically, logically, etc.), holds the superior position. To deconstruct the opposition is first . . . to overthrow the hierarchy."[20] But only first, for another necessary step follows in which the reversal just effected must be displaced and the apparent winning term placed *sous rature*. To reverse the hierarchy, then, only in order to displace the reversal; to unravel in order to reconstitute what is always already inscribed. As we have seen at every point, the "trace" creates this undoing/preserving oscillation. It is an oscillation that continues endlessly, for one deconstructive act leads only to another, a deconstructive reading being subject itself to deconstruction. No text, it is clear, is ever fully deconstructing or deconstructed.

Having discussed some of the important implications of Derrideanism, I wish now to consider major charges levelled at the position. Earlier I mentioned three specific charges brought against Derrida and his followers (obscurity, nihilism, and threatened destruction of humanistic values), and to these I return.

Undeniably, Derrida's work, as well as that of his "disciples," is demanding and difficult. It is also different from the prose we in America and England are accustomed to. I submit, however, that Derrida *et al.* are not perversely obscure. Part of the problem is that Derrida draws on authors we know hardly at all, notably Nietzsche and Heidegger and, moreover, that he deals with abstract issues alien to the Anglo-American empirical tradition. Another real difficulty lies, I think, in our expectations as readers, for most of us, more influenced by British empiricism than we would care to admit, expect language, and especially literary-critical language, to be a mirror reflecting truly the nature and contents of the "object" being described. Derrida's point, as we have seen, is precisely that writing is never a simple means for the presentation of truth. What this means, in part, is that even criticism and philosophy must be read scrupulously and critically, teased for meaning; they must, in other words, be interpreted and in exactly the same way as poetry, for example. Language always carries the "trace," whether the text in question be poetic, critical, philosophical, psychological, or what have you. Language may be a medium in a ghostly sense (as Geoffrey Hartman puckishly suggests), but it cannot be a medium in the sense of a neutral container of meaning. Derrida and his followers not only advance this argument but they also frequently, increasingly, express these points in the form in which they write. In *Glas,* for example, Derrida consciously cultivates a *plural* style, à la Nietzsche, as a way of confounding apparent opposites and switching perspectives.

Sometimes linked with the charge of obscurity is the claim that Derrideanism leads to the abandonment of the usual interpretive procedures. This claim, as well as the charges of nihilism and antihumanism, is made by, among others, M. H. Abrams in a response to J. Hillis Miller's review of the former's *Natural Supernaturalism*. Abrams' essay, entitled "The Deconstructive Angel," is perhaps the most influential attack on Derrideanism to date.[21] According to Abrams, deconstructive criticism places even the most arbitrary reading on an equal footing with the most rigorous, for there appears no way of determining right from wrong readings. But Miller, for one, explicitly denies that "all readings are equally valid or of equal value. Some readings are certainly wrong. Of the valid interpretations all have limitations. To reveal one aspect of the work of an author often means ignoring or shading other aspects. Some approaches reach more deeply into the structure of the text than others."[22] In practice deconstructive criticism is certainly not arbitrary or slipshod. A look at such deconstructionists as Miller and Paul de Man will show just how rigorous and exacting such an interpretive procedure can be. The theory itself, on which this practice depends, insists, despite what Abrams says, on using customary interpretive procedures. Deconstructive criticism goes *with* traditional reading, preserving as well as undoing. According to Spivak, a deconstructive critic first deciphers a text "in the traditional way," and Derrida is even more direct on this point: "[Without] all the instruments of traditional criticism, . . . critical production would risk developing in any direction at all and authorize itself to say almost anything. But this indispensable guardrail has always only *protected,* it has never *opened,* a reading."[23] Failing to understand the "trace," Abrams, like other opponents of Derrida, focuses on the undoing side of the undoing/preserving oscillation.

Should deconstruction allow for the creation in a text of simply any meaning the reader or interpreter wished, it would, I think, deserve the epithet "nihilism." I am giving the name "nihilism" to that situation wherein the mind is regarded as the arbiter, even the creator, of all values. According to Miller, in a book written before he knew Derrida, "Nihilism is the nothingness of consciousness when consciousness becomes the foundation of everything."[24] I wish now to consider the question of nihilism in Derrida, hoping that we will emerge with a better understanding of his position. I shall focus on nihilism in the sense given above, believing that the results of such an inquiry will at least suggest the way a response would go to other aspects of nihilism.

As I remarked in passing earlier, the original and originating differentiation seems to generate the dream of primal and final unity, which is, however, always deferred, never present here and now. We can never "make equal" or get outside the generating system of differences to locate a reference that will bestow order and meaning. There is no Transcendental Signified, we might say, only incarnation. Myth, though, as Herbert N. Schneidau well argues, serves to make us think that totalization and meaningfulness are possible, comforting us with reassurances regarding a "cosmic continuum."[25] But still the gap remains, no matter how hard we try to close it. Perhaps the humanistic tradition is best described as one attempt at closure, positing a meaningful world.

For Derrida, like Nietzsche before him, this attempt reveals the force of desire and the will to power. Whether we speak of a written text or life, to have meaning reflects the will to power. Miller puts it well in his review of Abrams' *Natural Supernaturalism,* the oxymorons of which title express "the force of a desire" for unity: "The reading of a work involves an active intervention on the part of the reader. Each reader takes possession of the work for one reason or another and imposes on it a certain pattern of meaning." Miller goes on to point out that in the third book of *The Will to Power* Nietzsche relates "the existence of innumerable interpretations of a given text to the fact that reading is never the objective identifying of a sense but the importation of meaning into a text which has no meaning 'in itself'."[26] According to Nietzsche, "Our values are interpreted *into* things"; " 'Interpretation,' the introduction of meaning—not 'explanation' (in most cases a new interpretation over an old interpretation that has become incomprehensible, that is now itself only a sign)"; "Ultimately, man finds in things nothing but what he himself has imported into them"; "In fact, interpretation is itself a means of becoming master of something."[27] Man gives—creates—meaning, then, expressing a will to power as he attempts to improve upon the way things are.

For Nietzsche and Derrida the question is what to do with the recognition that meaning is a construct brought by the "subject," a fiction made by the force of our desire. Subjectivists and at least some hermeneuticists and Bultmannians seem all too ready to accept a situation which appears to privilege the autonomous consciousness, reversing previous hierarchies and installing fiction in the place of truth and reality. Taken only so far, Nietzsche himself may be viewed as agreeing with this sense of the fictionality of things whereby "believing is seeing" and interpretation is all there is. Clearly, Derrida is not nihilistic in the sense I defined above, for he insists throughout that consciousness is no origin, no foundation, there being *no* foundation. He undoes the truth/fiction, reality/consciousness polarities but not, with the advocates of the autonomous consciousness, so as to set up the second term in the place of the first. Fiction can no more exist without truth than truth without fiction; they are accomplices, the system of differences and the "trace" making truth (im)possible. By the same token, the subject "in itself," as center, origin, and goal, is no more possible than the object "in itself."

In Derrida, Miller, and others appears a radical understanding of the fictionality of things, which goes beyond nihilism and the autonomous consciousness to a recognition of the doubleness of what is, of the complicity of truth and fiction. Deconstructionists wish to avoid the interpretive mastery or closure that imports meaning *into* texts and the world. Dangers lurk, of course, including the strong possibility that "the desire of deconstruction may itself become a desire to reappropriate the text actively through mastery, to show the text what it 'does not know'." Even the deconstructive critic forgets that his own text is necessarily self-deconstructed. He assumes that he at least means what he says. Indeed, even if he declares his own vulnerability, his statement occurs in the controlling language of demonstration and reference. The situation is frustrating but humbling—and inescapable—allowing still another glimpse of the vanity of human wishes. Struggling with the desire of deconstruction, Spivak describes the situation as follows:

> a further deconstruction deconstructs deconstruction, both as the search for a foundation (the critic behaving as if she means what she says in her text), and as the pleasure of the bottomless. The tool for this, as indeed for any deconstruction, is our desire, itself a deconstructive and grammatological structure that forever differs from (we only desire what is not ourselves) and defers (desire is never fulfilled) the text of our selves. Deconstruction can therefore never be a positive science. For we are in a bind, in a 'double (read abyssal) bind,' Derrida's newest nickname for the schizophrenia of the 'sous rature.' We *must* do a thing *and* its opposite, and indeed we desire to do both, and so on indefinitely. Deconstruction is a perpetually self-deconstructing movement that is inhabited by differance. No text is ever *fully* deconstructing or deconstructed. Yet the critic provisionally musters the metaphysical resources of criticism and performs what declares itself to be *one* (unitary) act of deconstruction.[28]

Still, deconstruction may disillusion us about mastery as it demonstrates just how precarious our grasp on meaning is. We are and are not masters, therefore no masters. But we must be careful not to fall into the trap of believing in linear progress, supposedly resulting from this enlightenment and demystification. Nor should we pine with a Rousseauistic (and humanist?) nostalgia for a lost security as to meaning which we never in fact possessed. Rather than with either faith in progress or nostalgia for "lost" presence, Derrida would have us look with a "Nietzschean *affirmation*—the joyous affirmation of the freeplay of the world and without truth, without origin, offered to an active interpretation . . . . [This affirmation] plays the game without security." This "interpretation of interpretation," Derrida adds, which "affirms freeplay . . . tries to pass beyond man and humanism, the name man being the name of that being who, through the history of metaphysics or of ontotheology—in other words, through the history of all of his history—has dreamed of full presence, the reassuring foundation, the origin and the end of the game."[29]

For Derrida, as for Schneidau discussing the mythological consciousness, the humanist tradition represents mastery, totalization, closure, nostalgia for a full presence, and the desire of meaning. The charge that Derrida threatens this tradition is, obviously, valid. Yet, as we have seen, that threat is by no means either nihilistic or simply negative. For many, Derrideanism offers a way through—if not out of—what Schneidau calls "the bankruptcy of the secular-humanist tradition."[30] Indeed, in *Sacred Discontent* Schneidau links Derrida with a very different tradition, the Yahwist-prophetic, arguing that Derrida's work is consonant with the Biblical message, which always goes counter to the mythological sense of a "cosmic continuum." Derridean deconstruction, according to Schneidau, is akin to the way in which the Bible insists on the fictionality of things, alienating us from the world, which it empties of meaning, reminding us constantly of the vanity of human wishes. Yet the Bible's attitude is always ambivalent, at once criticizing and nourishing culture. Schneidau's highly suggestive, and somewhat surprising, argument is far too complex for me to summarize here. A good idea of the nature of that argument, however, may be gleaned from the end of the chapter "In Praise of Alienation," which presents *differance* as far from nihilistic and which sees Derrida as, like the Bible, a positive alternative to mythological and humanist understanding:

we are [always] open to sudden revelations of meaninglessness or arbitrariness. . . . Sooner or later we are afflicted by the feeling that nothing matters, or "makes any difference," *i.e.,* that we are unable to supply the differentiations which in primitive cultures are articulated by myth, so that our lives and purposes are reduced to entropy. We may flee to various cults, but doubt will have its turn at these. Thus latent Yahwism works within us, leavening all the lump. We are condemned to freedom, not because God is dead but because he is very much alive, as an agent of disillusionment in a basic sense. In this condition, it is not remarkable that we are nihilistic: what is remarkable is that we can become aware of it and can acknowledge intermittently the "nothingness of consciousness when consciousness becomes the foundation of everything." So with all self-deceptions: their extent is not as remarkable as our awareness of them. We have reached out for the apple of self-knowledge, and in doing so have alienated God, nature, and each other; but by pressing our self-awareness to its extreme, where we become alienated from ourselves, we find that this is not the end of the story. The Fall is only the beginning of the Bible. To be thus "decentered" (and . . . to be acutely conscious of the fictionality of things) is the precondition of insight: thus it is a *felix culpa,* good news for modern man of a somewhat unlikely kind.[31]

Whether Schneidau is right about the ultimately Biblical and Yahwist nature of Derrida's thought is a most important question but beyond the scope of this paper to determine. What we can say here is that Schneidau does not come to grips with Derrida's insistence that *differance* "is not theological, not even in the most negative order of negative theology. The latter . . . always hastens to remind us that, if we deny the predicate of existence to God, it is in order to recognize him as a superior, inconceivable, and ineffable mode of being."[32] For our limited purposes in the present essay, whether Schneidau is right or wrong about Derrideanism (despite reservations I, for one, think he is in the main correct) is less important than the possibility he suggests of Derrideanism as an attractive, and positive, alternative to nihilism, the autonomous consciousness, and "the bankruptcy of the secular-humanist tradition."

It may be, as Schneidau suggests, that Derrida offers a long-awaited alternative to certain forms of nihilism. Certainly the challenge he offers cannot be ignored. Since it is unlikely that either benign neglect or wishing will make deconstruction go away, we must come to grips with it, explore its implications, and evaluate it fairly. There are signs that just this kind of thoughtful analysis is underway in religion and theology as well as in criticism and philosophy.[33] Much remains to be done, the work will be difficult, but the prospects are exciting.[34]

Notes

1. Ferdinand de Saussure, *Course in General Linguistics,* trans. Wade Baskin (New York: McGraw-Hill, 1959), p. 67.

2. Jacques Derrida, *Positions* (Paris: Minuit, 1967). Parts of this book, the whole of which is due soon from the University of Chicago Press, have been translated in *Diacritics,* 2, No. 4 (Winter 1972), pp. 6-14, and 3, No. 1 (Spring 1973), pp. 33-46.

3. Introductory note to Derrida's "Freud and the Scene of Writing," which Jeffrey Mehlman translated for his collection, *French Freud, Yale French Studies,* 48 (1973), p. 73.

4. Alan Bass, " 'Literature'/Literature," in *Velocities of Change,* ed. Richard Macksey (Baltimore: Johns Hopkins University Press, 1974), p. 345. Bass's essay, to which I am much indebted, first appeared in *MLN* in 1972.

5. Gayatri Spivak, "Translator's Preface," in Jacques Derrida, *Of Grammatology* (Baltimore: Johns Hopkins University Press, 1976), p. xvii.

6. Derrida, *Of Grammatology,* p. 19.

7. Spivak, p. xxxix.

8. Jacques Derrida, "Structure, Sign, and Play in the Discourse of the Human Sciences," in *The Structuralist Controversy: The Languages of Criticism and the Sciences of Man,* ed. Richard Macksey and Eugenio Donato (Baltimore: Johns Hopkins University Press, 1972), p. 256.

9. Spivak, p. xviii.

10. J. Hillis Miller, "Georges Poulet's 'Criticism of Consciousness'," in *The Quest for Imagination,* ed. O. B. Hardison, Jr. (Cleveland: Case Western Reserve University Press, 1971), p. 216.

11. See esp. Jacques Derrida, *Writing and Difference,* trans. Alan Bass (Chicago: University of Chicago Press, 1978); "La pharmacie de Platon" in *La dissémination* (Paris: Seuil, 1972), pp. 69-197; and "White Mythology," trans. F. C. T. Moore, *New Literary History,* 6 (1974), pp. 1-73.

12. Derrida, "Structure, Sign, and Play," p. 249.

13. Bass, p. 349.

14. Derrida, *Of Grammatology,* p. 65.

15. Bass, p. 350.

16. Spivak, p. xlix.

17. Spivak, p. xlvi. The Freudian passage is quoted on this page.

18. That the "trace" makes texts undecidable means that they can never be saturated with meaning. At some point syntax must overflow the apparent meanings, syntax being the principle of textual arrangement, of differentiation.

19. Derrida, *Of Grammatology,* p. 158.

20. Translation as it appears in *Diacritics,* 3, No. 1 (Spring 1973), p. 36.

21. M. H. Abrams' "The Deconstructive Angel" appeared in *Critical Inquiry,* 4 (1977), pp. 425-38. J. Hillis Miller's review was "Tradition and Difference," *Diacritics,* 2, No. 4 (Winter 1972), pp. 6-13.

22. J. Hillis Miller, *Thomas Hardy: Distance and Desire* (Cambridge: Belknap Press of Harvard University Press, 1970), p. ix.

23. Spivak, p. lxxv. Derrida, *Of Grammatology,* p. 158.

24. J. Hillis Miller, *Poets of Reality: Six Twentieth-Century Writers* (1965; rpt. New York: Atheneum, 1974), p. 3.

25. Herbert N. Schneidau, *Sacred Discontent: The Bible and Western Tradition* (Baton Rouge: Louisiana State University Press, 1976).

26. Miller, "Tradition and Difference," pp. 6, 12.

27. Friedrich Nietzsche, *The Will to Power,* trans. Walter Kaufmann (New York: Vintage Books, 1968), pp. 323, 327, 342.

28. Spivak, pp. lxxvii-lxxviii.

29. Derrida, "Structure, Sign, and Play," pp. 264-65.

30. Schneidau, p. 180.

31. Schneidau, pp. 48-49.

32. Jacques Derrida, "Differance," in *Speech and Phenomena and Other Essays on Husserl's Theory of Signs,* trans. David B. Allison (Evanston: Northwestern University Press, 1973), p. 134.

33. See esp. John Dominic Crossan, *Raid on the Articulate: Comic Eschatology in Jesus and Borges* (New York: Harper & Row, 1976); Robert Detweiler, *Story, Sign, and Self: Phenomenology and Structuralism as Literary-Critical Methods* (Philadelphia: Fortress Press, and Missoula, Mont.: Scholars Press, 1978); and Andrew J. McKenna's review of Crossan's book, "Biblioclasm: Joycing Jesus and Borges," *Diacritics,* 8, No. 3 (Fall 1978), pp. 15-29.

34. I gratefully acknowledge the generous support of The School of Criticism and Theory, the University of Kansas Center for Humanistic Studies, and the University of Kansas General Research Fund.

Toward a Poetics of the Ironic Sign

Leon Satterfield

In 1924, the American poet Edwin Arlington Robinson found out the hard way about the fragility of the ironic sign: he published a sonnet, "New England," which was generally regarded in his hometown, Gardiner, Maine, as an attack on his native region. A counterattack in the form of chauvinistic versifying and angry letters came in the local weekly newspaper, and Robinson finally felt obliged to explain in a page-one letter to his townsmen that his sonnet was supposed to be ironic, an attack not on his homeland, but upon the "patronizing pagans" who are "forever throwing dead cats at New England. . . ." He concluded his detailed explication of his own sonnet with this rueful observation: "Interpretation of one's own irony is always a little distressing. . . ."[1]

Robinson's difficulty is familiar to anyone who has ever taught a literature class. Irony gives us trouble, pervading as it does our modern literature.[2] Because the ironic sign is by nature unstable, we find it confusing—when we find it at all. And because what it implies often opposes what it says explicitly, ignorance of the conventions by which it functions can be disastrous to anyone trying to make sense of a work.

What I propose here, in a tentative and partial way, is the formulation of a poetics of the ironic sign, something like what Jonathan Culler calls for when he argues that "the task of literary theory . . . is to make explicit the procedures and conventions of reading, to offer a comprehensive theory of the ways in which we go about making sense of various kinds of texts."[3]

Some have denied that you can *do* that with irony, which D. C. Muecke calls "a phenomenon so nebulous that it disappears as one approaches."[4] J. A. K. Thomson traced irony to its Greek origins, but he makes no effort to talk about it in the abstract: "There is, in fact, no such thing as Irony in the abstract . . . whatever generalizations we may permit ourselves to make can never (to be worth anything) be based on *a priori* considerations. . . ."[5] And A. E. Dyson, in his introduction to a collection of essays on irony, writes: "My main contention is that no embracing theories or criteria are possible and that the attempts to seek for them are invariably misplaced."[6]

One more misplaced attempt will probably do no permanent harm. I propose, then, to consider the following questions: What is an ironic sign? How can the reader or listener know when he's in the presence of one? How does one go about decoding the ironic sign? What are its typical forms? And finally, a qualitatively different kind of question: What is signified by the use of irony?

While the questions may not have been phrased as they are here, they have been dealt with implicitly if not explicitly by any number of critics and theorists. Two of the most important and most recent book-length treatments of the subject are Wayne Booth's *A Rhetoric of Irony* (Chicago, 1974) and Muecke's *The Compass of Irony* (London, 1969), both of which I lean heavily upon here. Booth's book in particular engages the issue in the way that Culler calls for (while also engaging it in ways beyond Culler's call); that is, it attempts "to make explicit the procedures and conventions" of irony and to explain "the ways in which we go about making sense" of it.

I do not propose to deal with all kinds of ironic signs, but rather with those which are a part of the world of discourse, the kind which always imply an ironist. To poke at the scab of a psychic wound by way of a personal example of what I'm not going to deal with: Recently I dug a grease pit in my garage (or rather I had my son dig a grease pit in my garage) in order to save on automotive expense by working on my car myself. A few months later, I accidentally drove my car into the grease pit, thereby incurring additional automotive expense to extricate it, and thereby vastly amusing my son. Clearly, there are ironic signs there, but they are in the real world, not the world of discourse.

Nor do I intend to deal with the kind of ironic sign talked about by New Critics like I. A. Richards, Cleanth Brooks, and Robert Penn Warren. That group has broadened the meaning of the term "irony" to the point that it is seen as a mark of all good literature. The term, as Richards uses it, means "bringing in of the opposite, the complementary impulses. . . ."[7] Brooks and Warren admit that they have perhaps been "guilty of wrenching the word from its usual context,"[8] and Brooks even sees irony in Wordsworth's Lucy poems.[9] That kind of ironic sign has very little to do with more traditional kinds and it will not be discussed here.

And at the risk of offending those who are quick to be offended by the intentional fallacy[10] and the affective fallacy, I will insist here upon considering both the ironist's intentions and the effect of the ironic sign on the reader who perceives it. Irony so private that nobody save the ironist sees it is none of my concern here. And without authorial intention, there *is* no irony as I am using the term. The writer who is unintentionally ironic is not ironic at all, Muecke tells us:

> a work can be ironical only by intention; being ironical means deliberately being ironical. It is only events and situations which may be unintentionally ironic (a man may say something which we see as ironic though he does not; but this is not being ironical; it is an ironic happening of which he is a victim.[11]

Irony as I am using the term here is discourse which appears to be moving in one direction while really moving in another. It is "the art of saying something without really saying it," a kind of dissembling, a "double-layered or two-storey" kind of discourse in which the surface is opposed or warped by the subsurface in such a way that some innocent is taken in.[12] It is "the sport of bringing about a conclusion by indicating its opposite."[13] It is destructive of easy meaning, no part of any effort to make things perfectly clear.

None of that, of course, means much until we emerge from clouds of abstraction to specific cases. But first, a division so obvious that it comes to mind almost immediately: the distinction between verbal or rhetorical irony and situational irony. By the first, I mean irony of manner, irony that lies in the language of the ironist; by the second, I mean irony of matter, irony that lies in the ironist's created situations and responses to situations. In the first kind, words do not mean what they appear to mean; that is, their meaning is undone by the ironic configuration of the text. In the second the language itself is non-ironic, a "straight" account of events which *are* ironic; here meaning is not subtracted from the words (as in the first variety), but is added on to the events in the sense that they are understood by the initiated as having more significance than is explicitly given them.

What the two have in common is "duality, opposition of the terms of the duality, and real or pretended 'innocence.' "[14] In verbal irony, the opposition is between what the author seems to be saying and what he really says (or intends that the reader understand). In situational irony, the opposition is between what is expected by the innocent victims (which may include the reader) and what actually occurs, the opposition thus residing in the events rather than in the language of the recounting of the events.

The Rhetorical Ironic Sign

What Roman Jakobson says of poetry, that it is "organized violence committed on ordinary speech,"[15] may also be said of the rhetorical ironic sign. Such a sign is a word or cluster of words to be taken literally by the innocent while discounted by the initiated who understand that the intended meaning is in some kind of opposition to the literal meaning. It is in that class of discourse (along with lies, errors, and hallucinations), Tzvetan Todorov tells us, "in which a discrepancy appears between reference and referent, between designatum and denotatum. . . ."[16] The ironic sign, Michael Riffaterre says, represents "but one special case of marker permutation" whereby the "set of representations represent something else than it does in common usage."[17] The ironic sign occurs "when we speak from one point of view, but make an evaluation from another point of view," in Boris Uspensky's formulation.[18]

Those statements make sense enough to a reader who has already detected a given ironic sign, but they don't help much in the detection. That job would be simpler, though the effect would be hideous, had anyone taken seriously a proposal made in 1899 by one Alcanter de Brahm that ironists let their readers know where in the text they were being ironic by making the sign explicit—that is, by inserting a punctuation mark like a question mark turned backwards (ʕ) which he called "le petit signe flagellateur."[19] Simply labeling a writer or a work as ironic does not help much, since the ironist is not *consistently* ironic. How do we separate the ironic signs within a work from the others, the straight ones? How do we recognize, in Booth's words, "an ironic invitation when we see one"?[20]

Culler tells us that "we are in a position to detect irony whenever the text appears to offer judgements with which we would not concur or whenever, with apparent disinterestedness, it does not pass judgement where we think a judgement would be appropriate."[21]

We begin to detect the ironic sign, Booth says, when we notice elements in a text which cause us to make the following inference about the author's intentions: "If the author did not intend irony, it would be odd, or outlandish, or inept, or stupid of him to do things in this way" (52-53). He gives us five categories of "clues" to the presence of the ironic sign:

1. "Straightforward warnings in the author's own voice"—through titles ("Gullible's Travels," "The Hollow Men," *The Dunciad* are examples), prefatory epigraphs, or postscripts—each such direct statement being "at best

only a hint" and not sufficient evidence in itself of the ironic sign (53-57).

2. "Known Error Proclaimed"—a betrayal by the narrative voice of ignorance or foolishness that is "simply incredible," through botched clichés ("You could a heard a bomb drop," James Thurber has his narrator say of a moment of silence in "You Could Look It Up"), misstated historical "facts," or stupid or outmoded conventional wisdom (57-61).

3. "Conflicts of Facts with the Work"—for example, Anatole France's "Les Pingouins avaient la première armée du monde. Les Marsouins aussi" ("The penguins had the most powerful army in the world. So had the porpoises" [61-67]).[22]

4. "Clashes of Style"—sudden departures from normal style, as in parody of some other writer, or Jane Austen's narrator of "The History of England" saying "It was in this reign that Joan of Arc lived and made such a *row* among the English," or Twain's description of the Greek chapel in *Innocents Abroad* as "the most roomy, the richest and the showiest chapel in the Church of the Holy Sepulchre" (67-73).

5. "Conflicts of Belief"—conflicts between beliefs the text expresses and those "we hold *and suspect the author of holding";* an example from Twain's "Baker's Bluejay Yarn": "I know that he could [talk with animals] because he told me so himself" (73-75).

Booth understands that even with such clues, detection of the ironic sign is uncertain; he would agree with Culler's statement that "irony always offers the possibility of misunderstanding . . . for a sentence to be properly ironic, it must be possible to imagine some group of readers taking it quite literally."[23] One reader's clues to the ironic may be another's clues to the sublime, especially in the following circumstance:

> Every reader will have the greatest difficulty detecting irony that mocks his own beliefs or characteristics. If an author invents a speaker whose stupidities strike me as gems of wisdom, how am I to know that he is not a prophet? If his mock style seems like good writing to me, what am I to do? And if his incongruities of fact and logic are such as I might commit, I am doomed. None of us can tell how many ironies we have missed in our lives because we share ignorance, stylistic naïveté, or outlandish beliefs with the ridiculed mask. For this reason all of the tests I have described are highly fallible. No complex piece of irony can be read merely with tests or devices or rules, and

it would be a foolish man who felt sure that he could never mistake irony for straight talk (p. 81).

Later he cautions against seeing irony where it does *not* exist, and talks about "five major kinds of crippling handicap" that get in the way of our perception of the ironic sign: "Ignorance, Inability to Pay Attention, Prejudice, Lack of Practice, and Emotional Inadequacy" (222).

But assuming that the reader and the writer are sufficiently attuned to one another's sensibilities and that the reader is sensitive enough to the clues that he detects the ironic sign, how does he proceed? How does he decode the ironic sign? What is the process necessary to its provoking in the reader's mind what was in the writer's mind? Ironology—Booth and Muecke both use the term a little self-mockingly, I think—begins where accounts of the function of non-ironic signs leave off. The latter tell us how the language-user encodes what he wants to say and how his reader or listener decodes in order to get at what was intended. With the ironic sign, another step is necessary: after decoding, the reader must re-decode. That is, he decodes the straight sign or apparent meaning of the ironist, then because he finds it unsatisfactory, sets about to get at the meaning that is under *that* meaning. Culler's account of the process:

> The perception of verbal irony depends upon a set of expectations which enable the reader to sense the incongruity of an apparent level of *vraisemblance* at which the literal meaning of a sentence could be interpreted and to construct an alternative ironic reading which accords with the *vraisemblance* which he is in the process of constructing for the text.[24]

Booth elaborates on that process and calls it "reconstruction." What is transformed, of course, is not the text, but the reader who moves from an innocent or naive understanding to a sophisticated understanding. As Booth renders the process, there are four different steps involved, and they may occur nearly simultaneously:

1. Rejection of the literal meaning, not just because the reader may disagree with it, but because "he is unable to escape recognizing either some incongruity among the words or between the words and something else he knows" (10).

2. Testing alternative interpretations or explanations: "I missed something earlier, or that word must mean something I don't know about," etc.,

accepting the alternative that the writer was simply "careless or stupid or crazy" only as a last resort in the absence of more plausible explanations (11).

3. Making a decision about the knowledge or beliefs of the author—not the flesh-and-blood author, but what Booth calls the "implied author" whose identity resides only in the work itself, "the creative person responsible for the choices that made the work" (11).

4. Choosing a new interpretation, reconstructing the meaning so it will harmonize with "the unspoken beliefs that the reader has decided to attribute" to the author, the end result being something like this: "In contrast with the statement Voltaire pretends to be making, which implies beliefs that he cannot have held, he is really saying such-and-such, which is in harmony with what I know or can infer about his beliefs and intentions" (12).

The reconstruction process has neither the laboratory's "modes of proof" nor its certainty, but Booth finds in the activity an "astonishing communal achievement" of complexity shared between reader and author: "The wonder of it is not that it should go awry as often as it does, but that it should ever succeed" (13).

I do not intend to offer an exhaustive classification of the forms in which the rhetorical ironic sign might be manifested. Muecke's *The Compass of Irony* does that in an admirably comprehensive and erudite way. Instead, I offer some typical forms of the ironic sign and its function within them.

The simplest form of the rhetorical ironic sign, that kind we most likely think of first, involves inversion ("antiphrasis" the old rhetoricians called it); the sign denotes one thing and means the opposite. Reconstruction simply consists of seeing that the literal statement is so drastically opposed to the context that its opposite is what is really meant. It usually, but not always, blames through apparent praise, and at its most heavy-handed becomes sarcasm (the 16th century term for it was the "dry-mocke").[25] Antony's repeated references to the conspirators as "all honorable men" taken in context with the rest of his funeral oration is an example. Even Antony's audience (as opposed to Shakespeare's) understands after about the third use of the term that he means the conspirators are anything but honorable.

Almost as common a form as inversion is understatement ("meiosis") in which the ironic sign expresses not the opposite of the intended meaning, but an exaggerated reduction of the intended meaning. Ezra Pound's comment that "Mutton cooked the week before last is, for the most part, unpalatable"[26] is an example, as is what David Worcester cites as Artemus Ward's "grave meditation": "The wick of an unlighted candle may safely be manipulated, but if you light the wick and thrust your hand into the blaze and keep it there half an hour a sensation of excessive and disagreeable warmth will be experienced."[27] Reconstruction begins when the reader sees that "for the most part, unpalatable" and "excessive and disagreeable warmth"—even though they are not the opposite of the intended meaning—are woefully inadequate to the context in their level of intensity.

Another kind of ironic sign results when the writer adopts a pose of someone whose skill or values or understanding differ considerably from those of the implied author. Chaucer, for example, portrays himself in *The Canterbury Tales* as a laughably inept poet whose "drasty rymyng is nat worth a toord!" in the pungent phrase of Harry Bailly. That he appears in a masterpiece of which he is himself the author makes our reconstruction easy. The method is similar to the one Socrates used—or is reported by Plato to have used—for purposes of argument. The ironic sign in the Socratic method is well known: with disarming admissions of ignorance and a great show of humility, Socrates asks his opposition a series of simple questions, the answers to which refute the opposition's contentions. The method is, as Worcester puts it, a kind of mental "jiu-jitsu" by which "the expert presses gently and the victim ties himself into knots."[28] By pretending ignorance, Socrates disguises his strength as weakness.

An increasingly popular form of the ironic sign—and one closely related to the form just discussed—occurs when the author temporarily disappears and lets his characters, who differ from the author in the same ways the voice of the author-as-poseur differs from the voice of the implied author, unwittingly reveal themselves. Muecke gives an example from Carson McCullers' *The Heart is a Lonely Hunter:* wrongdoers are being discussed and one of the characters wishes aloud that "I could round up some people and kill those men myself."

> "That ain't no Christian way to talk," Portia said. "Us can just rest back and know they going to be chopped up with pitchforks and fried everlasting by Satan."[29]

The reconstruction process is simple enough there. All the reader need assume is that the implied author cannot believe such things, that he therefore is implicitly condemning—or at least being amused by—Portia's religious hypocrisy. But reconstruction becomes more difficult when the author disappears completely and turns the telling of the story over to one of his characters. When the narrator's skill or values or understanding are not those of the author, there must be what Booth calls "a secret communion of the author and the reader behind the narrator's back."[30] When the gap between author and narrator is great, there's not much difficulty. For example, when Huck Finn, Twain's narrator, decides to go to hell rather than betray Jim, his judgement that *not* betraying a runaway slave is punishable by eternal damnation is a judgement so clearly undercut by the rest of the novel that we know the implied author does not share it. But we are less certain of the irony when Gulliver tells us in Book IV that after his return from Houyhnhnmland, the sight of his wife and children "filled me only with hatred, disgust, and contempt," and "when I began to consider that by copulating with one of the Yahoo species I had become a parent of more, it struck me with the utmost shame, confusion, and horror." Those views are not so different from those that could reasonably be imputed to the implied author throughout the rest of the book. Whether the gap between narrator and author is immense or slight, reconstruction of the ironic sign consists of the reader's rejecting the identity of the narrator's views with the author's, then plunging ahead in the four-step process to finally determine what the latter's views are.

The Situational Ironic Sign

While the rhetorical ironic sign is a word or group of words, the situational ironic sign is an event, a group of events, or a condition. Just as rhetorical ironic signs have double meanings—one for the naive and one for the sophisticated—so situational ironic signs have double meaning, although reconstruction, as Booth uses the term, is not necessary because the language describing the ironic event is non-ironic and can be taken at face value. But there is a sense in which ironic events as signs are more difficult than ironic words as signs. That's because we are used to thinking of words as signs, but we are not so accustomed to thinking of events as signs. What are they signs of? Certain events or conditions—a policeman's holding us back or motioning us on at an intersection—are clearly signs, as are columns of smoke rising in the distance. It follows that if an event can be seen as a straightforward sign, it may also function as an ironic sign. A policeman motioning us into the intersection just in time to be struck broadside by a firetruck—that could be considered an event constituting an ironic sign. The sign appears to be telling us that now is the time for safe passage through the intersection; the firetruck gives the lie to that expectation. The event *seems* to be signalling (that is, it establishes an expectation that a certain outcome, safe passage, is at hand), but the anticipated referent of the sign is replaced by one in opposition to the expectation (being struck by the firetruck, an event in opposition to safe passage). One can argue that if there is no irony without ironic intentionality, I need to show that the policeman, the originator of the ironic sign, intended that the expectations it aroused would be thwarted. I would argue, however, that if the policeman is a literary creation, that is, if he is a puppet whose strings are being pulled by the author who has created him, his intention is not vital to the irony. The author's volition will do to satisfy Muecke's need for intentionality: he sends out the ironic sign through the policeman.

The situational ironic sign then is a condition, an event, or series of events that establishes an expectation that is thwarted; one outcome is signalled, another in opposition to the expected one occurs, and victims (who may include certain readers as well as certain characters) are taken in.

For example, in Stephen Crane's "The Open Boat," four men—a correspondent, a ship's captain, the ship's cook, and an oiler who tended the ship's machinery—are drifting about in a life boat after the ship has sunk. The ironic sign is the physical condition of the men: the oiler is clearly the strongest; the captain is injured and both the correspondent and the cook are unaccustomed to hard manual labor. When the life boat is swamped a few hundred yards off shore and they must swim for their lives, the expectation is that the oiler is least likely to drown. But he is caught in the tide and is the only one who does *not* make it safely ashore; the others are washed up on the beach, as Crane shows us a nature that is arbitrary and unfeeling, caring not at all for human notions of the predictability or fitness of things.

What is called dramatic irony differs only in that the audience, because of prior knowledge, is aware of the outcome long before the victimized characters. We watch as the characters interpret an event in one way while we know that the event is leading to an opposing conclusion. Often the characters act in a way they think is leading to the conclusion *they* see in the offing, while *we* see that they are really helping to bring about a condition they do not expect. A standard example is Oedipus' vowing at the beginning of Sophocle's play to exile the murderer of Laius before he can do Oedipus harm, while we, knowing as Oedipus does not that he is talking about himself, groan in anticipation of the final scene in which the self-mutilated king leaves his kingdom to live out his life in exile. Sometimes dramatic irony involves superior knowledge that comes from what we know of history, as in Anatole France's portrait of Pontius Pilate as an old man who says "Jesus? . . . Jesus the Nazarene? I don't recall."[31]

In what is called cosmic irony, the writer posits the notion that the unexpected or inappropriate does not just happen, but that there is a Prime Mover who is having a sardonic laugh at the expectations and puny efforts of his puppets. The author of cosmic irony in effect creates an ironic creator. Hardy indulges in cosmic irony at the end of *Tess of the d'Urbervilles* when he has the President of the Immortals making "sport" of the human ruin below. Frost is implying the same kind of irony in his couplet:

> Forgive, O Lord, my little jokes on Thee
> And I'll forgive Thy great big one on me.

In romantic irony, the author deliberately destroys Coleridge's "willing suspension of disbelief" by self-mockery. The ironic sign is the verisimilitude of the narrative itself, a series of events which signal "This is reality," thus setting up the expectation that what follows will be real. But what follows clearly is a demonstration that "This is artifice." It is, A. R. Thompson tells us, "fundamentally a simple and trivial thing: the hand of the manipulator, as Tieck expressed it, thrust into the puppet stage."[32] That is, the romantic ironist "creates a serious mood and then deliberately pokes fun at himself for doing so"[33]—as Sterne does in *Tristam Shandy* when he tells us of the lamentable death of Parson Yorick, then includes as a tribute a page that is completely black, or when he leaves out a ten-page chapter because the writing in it is "so much above the style and manner of anything else . . . in this book, that it could not have remained in it, without depreciating every other scene."

Having looked at ironic signs, some typical forms and contexts, we can now examine an altogether different kind of question: What is irony itself a sign of? That is, what metaliterary sign does the ironist send out about himself? To answer that question is to answer by implication several others: What risks does the ironist run when he uses irony? What can he hope to gain by its use? What are its effects? Those are large questions; I offer only partial answers.

The sign emanating from the use of irony imitates the ironic sign itself—that is, it is two-layered and the two layers are in opposition. One such manifestation of that double sign is what the ironist seems to be saying about his degree of commitment. Another is what he seems to be saying about his relationship to the reader.

The ironist signifies himself, at least on the surface level, as cool and detached. His utterances are not those of the emotionally involved. "Hey, Hey, L.B.J./How many kids did you kill today?" is not the chant of the ironist, but the outraged invective of those caught up in apparent (but not necessarily unreal) commitment, so intense they lose all emotional distance, all dispassion, as they surrender their language wholly to direct and naked expression of their outrage. The ironist, by contrast, signifies himself as always in control of his expression, always distant in his scorn, always penurious with his emotion (hence, irony is, as someone has pointed out, an effective inoculation against sentimentality). He is unflappable, almost, one might believe, uncommitted. And he thus runs the risk of alienating his reader. He may appear a nihilist, his mood "attuned to ridicule, rejection, mockery, even despair," Dyson tells us.[34] Because of his indirection, he may seem to be using his irony as a shield, a prudent device to avoid exposing his own position to attack.[35] When the reader gets that impression, the ironist is seen as a cynic committed, William Van O'Connor writes, only "to the view (although rarely, if ever, in an absolute way) that everything is wrong, in the worst of all possible worlds."[36] Such cynicism does not wear well; as Worcester writes of this particular danger of irony, "No one grows more trying than the acquaintance whose shoulders are set in a perpetual shrug, whose superior smile flows in hateful tolerance around every idea. . . ."[37]

But of course the reader who picks up only signals of disengagement needs to go further. He needs to see that the act of writing itself—even of writing ironically—is an act of commitment, that the true nihilist signifies himself only by his silence. He needs, in effect, to "reconstruct" what the ironist seems to be signifying about himself in order to see that the existence of the text itself negates the "literal" message. Even though Twain has Huck respond to Aunt Sally's "anybody hurt?" with "No'm. Killed a nigger," the thoughtful reader does not assume that the author sees slavery as an issue only to make jokes about any more than he assumes from the passage that Twain is racist. And even from the savagery of "A Modest Proposal," Swift sends out veiled signals of commitment to the welfare of the Irish whose children his narrator proposes to use for food. Only in what Booth calls "unstable" irony, the kind which is not reconstructable because the ironist himself occupies no solid ground of affirmation and invites the reader to occupy none, is there no yea-saying beneath the surface nays. And even here, Booth asserts, there is an oblique commitment to something besides complete negation:

> novelists, dramatists, and poets inevitably draw back from complete silence and in fact write works that embody their intentions and therefore have "meaning" of a kind—works of resignation, of lament, of complaint, of dark laughter at the chaos, of defiance, of pathos. And in doing so they usually provide—sometimes it seems almost with a sense of shame—some handle or other for interpreting their works at whatever level of instability or negation they have elected (245).

A second double sign the ironist transmits involves his relationship with his reader. On the surface level, the sign is a hostile one that seems to mock the reader. The ironist says what he does not mean, he talks out of both sides of his mouth at once, he is two-faced. He sets verbal traps for the reader to fall into; his indirection tempts the reader to risk foolish misreadings. There is a sense in which, as Northrop Frye tells us, the ironist "turns his back on his audience"[38] and there is a sense in which the ironist victimizes his reader: John B. McKee argues that the only constant in irony is the presence of a victim[39]—and that the victim is often the reader.

But that apparent hostility is undercut by the veiled signal the ironist sends out to his reader, a sign that tells him the writer has been growling bogus growls. The use of irony signifies a camaraderie with the reader that all the surface hostility cannot undo. The ironist flatters the reader by asking him to collaborate, to become a participant in the literary experience, what Coleridge called "an active creative being," rather than a mere spectator. Booth says that Swift pays us "the compliment of assuming that we can be trusted to work as a kind of assistant in building the final complex edifice" of "A Modest Proposal" (119). When rhetorical irony is at issue, the reader collaborates by the reconstruction process. With situational irony, the reader collaborates by bringing to the text information (in the case of dramatic irony) or the ability to see beyond conventional expectations produced by the ironic sign. The compliment the ironist pays the reader is reciprocated by the respect the *reader* pays by giving the ironist a fair hearing, by *not* assuming what he might assume if he were reading a text by, say, a student in Freshman English—that it's "odd, outlandish, or inept, or stupid." Thus, Booth argues, one of the effects of irony is

> the building of amiable communities. . . . Often the predominant emotion when reading stable ironies is that of joining, of finding and communing with kindred spirits. The author I infer behind the false words is my kind of man, because he enjoys playing with irony, because he assumes *my* capacity for dealing with it, and—most important—because he grants me a kind of wisdom; he assumes that he does not have to spell out the shared and secret truths on which my reconstruction is to be built (28).

By way of illustration, Booth reconstructs the irony of a friend who comes into a room dripping wet and asks "Think it'll rain?" What his friend really means, he decides, is

> "hello my good friend who understands me is it not a rainy day that we are enduring together by making something mildly humorous out of what might otherwise have been reason for grousing it is good to see you who thank God understand ironic joshing when you hear it and are not too critical even if it is rather stale and feeble" (12).

The effect of our collaboration is to make the communication both more economical—if the reader provides some of the message, the writer need provide less of it—and more forceful. Having collaborated in the meaning, we have a vested interest in it. Having earned our reading by working for it, we are more committed to it. Antony's Roman audience came away from his funeral oration with not just the message that the conspirators are ignoble, but with an appreciation for Antony's self-effacing skill in helping *them* arrive at *their* own conclusions. They are convinced by Antony's irony in a way that they would never have been had Antony used only straight language in its simple referential function.

Irony thus thought of demonstrates, if demonstrations are still needed, that the referential function is only one of the ways in which language works. Understanding the ironic sign forces us to realize, in Todorov's words, "the fragility of that conception according to which the signification of a discourse is constituted by its referent."[40] It forces us to remember again, if we are ever tempted to forget, that the only meaning a sign has is in the mind. Saying "the mind" obscures the complexity, implying as it does something monolithic. What we mean, of course, is that the various meanings a sign has exist only in the various minds that come in contact with it. We can stand with Booth in wonder that two or more minds ever get together about the ironic sign.

Notes

1. Edwin Arlington Robinson, "Pleasing Letter from Edwin Arlington Robinson Regarding the New England Sonnet," *The Gardiner Journal*, Feb. 14, 1924, p. 1.
2. "Nowadays," D. C. Muecke tells us, "only popular literature is predominantly non-ironical." D. C. Muecke, *The Compass of Irony* (London: Methuen, 1969), p. 10.
3. Jonathan Culler, "The Righting of the Reader," *Diacritics*, 5 (1975), p. 29.
4. Muecke, p. 3.
5. J. A. K. Thomson, *Irony, An Historical Introduction* (Cambridge, Mass.: Harvard University Press, 1927), p. 171.
6. A. E. Dyson, *The Crazy Fabric: Essays in Irony* (London: Macmillan, 1965), p. ix.
7. I. A. Richards, *Principles of Literary Criticism* (New York: Harcourt Brace Jovanovich, Inc., 1926), p. 250.
8. Cleanth Brooks and Robert Penn Warren, *Understanding Fiction* (New York: F. S. Crofts & Co., 1943), p. xvi.
9. Cleanth Brooks, "Irony and 'Ironic' Poetry," *College English*, 9 (February 1948), p. 232.
10. Wayne Booth reminds us that Wimsatt and Beardsley, who alerted us to the critical error of assuming that a work means what the author says was intended rather than what was written, "rule out only statements made by the author outside the work"; they did not mean to rule out intentions that may be inferred from *within* the work (Wayne Booth, *A Rhetoric of Irony*. [Chicago: University of Chicago Press, 1974], p. 126).
11. Muecke, pp. 56-57.
12. Muecke, p. 20.
13. Eleanor Newman Hutchens, *Irony in Tom Jones* (University, Ala.: University of Alabama Press, 1965), p. 13.
14. Muecke, p. 49.
15. Quoted by Terence Hawkes, *Structuralism and Semiotics* (Berkeley and Los Angeles: University of California Press, 1977), p. 141.
16. Tzvetan Todorov, *The Poetics of Prose*, trans. Richard Howard (Ithaca, N.Y.: Cornell University Press, 1977), p. 59.
17. Michael Riffaterre, *Semiotics of Poetry* (Bloomington: Indiana University Press, 1978), p. 65.
18. Boris Uspensky, *A Poetics of Composition: The Structure of the Artistic Text and Typology of a Compositional Form*, trans. from Russian by Valentina Zavarin and Susan Wittig (Berkeley: University of California Press, 1973), p. 103.
19. Cited by Muecke, p. 56, and Booth, p. 55.
20. Booth, p. 40; because *A Rhetoric of Irony* will be referred to so frequently, all subsequent quotations from it will be indicated by page numbers in parentheses immediately following the quotation in my text.

21. Jonathan Culler, *Structuralist Poetics* (Ithaca, N.Y.: Cornell University Press, 1975), p. 156.

22. Booth quotes the passage from Anatole France, *Penquin Island* (New York: J. Lane Co., 1908), Book 4, Chapter 4.

23. Culler, *Structuralist Poetics,* p. 154.

24. Culler, *Structuralist Poetics,* pp. 154-55.

25. David Worcester, *The Art of Satire* (Cambridge, Mass.: Harvard University Press, 1940), p. 78.

26. Quoted by Muecke, p. 15.

27. Quoted by Worcester, p. 90.

28. Worcester, p. 94. Those who have traced the history of irony tell us that Socrates was following the Old Comedy example of the mock-humble character called the *eiron,* the antagonist of the *alazon,* the braggart. By pretending to be less than he was (while the *alazon* was pretending to be more), the *eiron* was able to defeat his opponent. That sort of stock plot, Thomson tells us, began as a result of the Greek "doctrine of Divine jealousy" (Thomson, p. 9)—that is, the notion that the gods are angered when a mortal climbs too high, the result often being the hubris-nemesis sequence in Greek literature. So, Thomson says, the Greek, to avoid making the gods jealous, felt "it is best . . . to lie low, to 'escape his notice,' as the Greek word says. Pretend to be of no importance in . . . [the gods'] sight, and then perhaps you may have a little fun and prosperity" (Thomson, p. 8).

29. Quoted by Muecke, p. 108.

30. Wayne Booth, *The Rhetoric of Fiction* (Chicago: University of Chicago Press, 1961), p. 300.

31. From Anatole France, *Le Procurateur de Judée,* quoted by Muecke, p. 26.

32. A. R. Thompson, *The Dry Mock, A Study of Irony in Drama* (Berkeley: University of California Press, 1948), p. 59.

33. Raymond W. Barry and A. J. Wright, *Literary Terms: Definitions, Explanations, Examples* (San Francisco: Chandler Publishing Co., 1966), p. 47.

34. Dyson, p. xiii.

35. For a discussion of this danger, see May Sarton, "The Shield of Irony," *Nation,* 182 (April 14, 1956), pp. 314-16.

36. William Van O'Connor, *Sense and Sensibility in Modern Poetry* (Chicago: University of Chicago Press, 1948), p. 132.

37. Worcester, p. 142.

38. Quoted in Booth's *A Rhetoric of Irony,* p. x.

39. John B. McKee, *Literary Irony and the Literary Audience: Studies in the Victimization of the Reader in Augustan Fiction* (Amsterdam: Rodopi, 1974), p. 102.

40. Todorov, p. 59.

Bakhtin's Theory of the Utterance*

Tzvetan Todorov

Bakhtin formulates his theory of the utterance on two occasions: once during the late twenties, in the texts signed by Medvedev and especially by Voloshinov; and in several works published at the end of the fifties, some thirty years later. I will present these two syntheses separately, although there is no great difference between them (in fact, the only changes involve accentuations of various aspects of the utterance).

The first general formulations concerning the utterance are already to be found in *Freudism* (1927); one page of *The Formal Method in Literary Studies* (1928) evokes this problem from a similar viewpoint, with an insistence on the social rather than the individual nature of the utterance; but Bakhtin introduces here a new notion, which is not reiterated in subsequent writings: that of a discursive strategy.

> Discursive strategy plays a particularly significant role in daily verbal communication by determining its form as well as its organization. It gives form to everyday utterances by establishing both the style and the genre of the verbal expression. Strategy is to be understood here in a broad sense: politeness represents but one of its moments. This strategy can pursue different directions, moving, as it were, between two poles—the compliment and the insult. The strategy is determined by the set of all social inter-relations between the speakers, by their ideological horizons, and finally by the concrete situation of the discussion. Whatever may be its particular nature, such a strategy determines our every utterance. There is no discourse without strategical consciousness.[1]

In *Marxism and the Philosophy of Language* (1929), Bakhtin accomplishes a major step by forsaking his general theories to propose instead a detailed description of the utterance: this will constitute Chapter 3 of the second part, entitled "Verbal Interaction."

---

* This paper is an excerpt from an over-all presentation of Bakhtin's work. The Soviet scholar M. M. Bakhtin (1895-1975) has published under his name three books and a number of articles; three more books and other articles were written or inspired by him but published under the name of Medvedev or Voloshinov. I quote the Russian editions. In English translations, Bakhtin's name is sometimes spelled Baxtin.

One may recall the criticism which Bakhtin voiced about the "individualist subjectivism" school (Vossler and his disciples): although superior to that of Saussure insofar as it does not ignore the utterance, yet it mistakenly believes that this utterance is individual.

> Any moment of the expression-utterance one may observe will invariably be determined by the real conditions of the speech-act, primarily by the *nearest social situation.*[2] *Verbal communication will never be understood or explained without a reference to its link with the concrete situation.*[3]

In other words, the difference between an utterance and a proposition (or a sentence), a unity of language, is that the former is necessarily produced within a particular context which is always social. This sociality has a dual origin: first of all, the utterance is addressed to someone (this implies the existence of a micro-society comprising two people, the speaker and the addressee); secondly, the speaker himself is always a social being to begin with. These are two primary elements of the speech-act context which we need to consider in our interpretations of an utterance.

> Let us first observe the role of the addressee. The utterance is established between two socially organized people: should there be no real interlocutor, then he is presupposed, in a certain sense, as a normal representative of the social group to which the speaker belongs. *The discourse is oriented towards the interlocutor,* towards what the interlocutor *is.*[4]

Instead of the individual interlocutor we can thus imagine a certain type of addressee or, in other words, a certain horizon of reception; a notion we shall again encounter in an article published the following year (1930):

> From the daily primitive utterance to the achieved poetic utterance, each one invariably comprises, as a necessary ingredient, an "implied" extra-verbal horizon. We can analyze this living and concrete horizon in terms of three components: *spatial, semantic,* and *of values.* The *value horizon* assumes the most important role in the organization of a literary work, especially in its formal aspects.[5]

As we shall see, Bakhtin later returns to this question of values (although the suggestions formulated above will not be pursued).

The sociality of the speaker is equally important, albeit less evident.

After taking certain precautions (acts of acoustical phonation and perception are indeed individual but they do not concern the essential aspect of language: its significance; a biological and individual "I-experience" does indeed exist, however, unlike the "we-experience," it remains inaccessible), Bakhtin states that the expression of an individual is not individual in the least.

> There can exist no experience beyond its incarnation in signs. This immediately precludes the possible principle of any qualitative difference between interior and exterior. (. . .) Expression is not organized by experience, but on the contrary, experience is organized by expression which, for the first time, imbues this experience with form and direction.[6] Aside from material expression, there is no such thing as experience. Moreover, expression precedes experience; it is the cradle of experience.[7]

A footnote to the last sentence declares that this "assertion was in fact originally drawn from certain statements of Engels" which are to be found in *Ludwig Feuerbach;* beyond this, we can perhaps perceive a more distant and common source in the work of Humboldt (the inspiration for "individualist subjectivism"): an experience is pre-formed by the possibilities of its expression. Once we have located the formative traces of an expression at the very core of the expressible, then whatever its sources may be, there can no longer exist any sphere which is entirely devoid of sociality (since words and other linguistic forms do not belong to the individual).

> Only the inarticulate animal cry is truly organized within an individual physiological system. (. . .) But even the most primitive human utterance, produced by the individual organism, is already organized in external terms, through the inorganic conditions of a social milieu which shapes its content, significance, and meaning.[8] The very howls of an infant are "oriented" towards its mother.[9]

We might formulate this observation by saying that every utterance can be perceived as part of a dialogue, in the general sense of the word; only in his subsequent writings will Bakhtin define this more specifically (as a dialogue between discourses).

> Verbal interaction is the fundamental reality of language; and dialogue, in its narrow sense, is a single form, though clearly the most

important one, of verbal interaction. But dialogue can be interpreted in a much broader manner, as referring not only to the direct verbal communication which is voiced between interlocutors, but also encompassing every form of verbal communication.[10]

As a first important consequence of this new framework, we must radically distinguish between meaning in language from meaning in discourse or, to use the terminology adopted by Bakhtin at the time, to distinguish meaning from *theme*. In and of itself, this distinction is nothing very new; however, it will quickly become so, due to the increasing importance Bakhtin attaches to the theme. Indeed, the standard oppositions of that period between current and occasional meaning, between fundamental and marginal meaning, or between denotation and connotation, are equally fallacious in that they favor the first term, while in fact discursive meaning, or theme, is never marginal.

Thus we will strictly reserve the term "meaning" for language ("langue"); meaning is recorded by dictionaries, and any one meaning is always identical to itself (since it is merely potential): in other words, like all other linguistic elements, it can be repeated.

> Meaning in opposition to theme, will represent those moments of an utterance which *can be repeated* and yet *remain identical to themselves*.[11] Meaning actually signifies nothing except for the potentiality, the possibility of meaning within a concrete theme.[12]

In contrast, the theme—like the utterance as a whole—is unique and cannot be repeated, since it arises from the interaction of meaning with the equally unique context of the speech-act.

> Let us call the significance of an entire utterance its *theme*. (. . .) In fact, like the utterance itself, the theme is individual and cannot be repeated. It is an expression of the concrete historical situation which engendered the utterance. (. . .) It must then follow that the theme of an utterance is not only determined by the linguistic forms which compose it—words, morphological and syntactical forms, sounds, and intonation—but also by the extra-verbal aspects of the situation. And if we should lose these aspects, we will not be able to understand the utterance, as if we had lost the most important words themselves.[13]

One essential feature of a theme, and therefore of an utterance, is that it is endowed with *values* (in the broad sense of the term). Vice versa, meaning, and therefore language, do not share this relation with the world of values:

> Only an utterance can be beautiful, just as only an utterance can be sincere, delusive, courageous, or timid, etc. These value determinations are linked to the organization of utterances and literary works insofar as they involve the functions assumed by the latter within the unity of social existence and, above all, within the concrete unity of an ideological horizon.[14]

The idea of an evaluative dimension in the utterance is further pursued by the article already referred to, "On the Boundaries Between Poetics and Linguistics." Bakhtin investigates the possible formal embodiments of this value judgment; and first considers the use of non-linguistic means.

> Let us say that any evaluation which is incarnated through the (verbal) material is an *expression of values*. The human body itself will provide the original raw material for such an expression of values: *gesture* (the signifying movement of the body) and *voice* (outside of articulated language).[15]

Within language itself, phonetic means are naturally to be distinguished from semantic means; and somewhat more remarkably, these are classified according to a dichotomy between selection and combination; this division is familiar today, but was unpublished at the time (although one may seek its origin in the work of Kruszewski).

> We must distinguish two forms of *value expression* [in poetic creation]: 1) *phonic* and 2) *structural* [tektonicheskuju], whose functions can be separated into two groups: first, *elective* (selective), and secondly, *compositional* (organizational). The elective functions of the social evaluation emerge through the choice of lexical material (lexicology), the choice of epithets, metaphors, and other tropes (the entire range of poetical semantics), and finally, through the choice of a "content"). In this way, most stylistics and certain elements of thematics belong to the elective group.

> The compositional functions of the evaluation determine the level and hierarchical positioning of each verbal element in the work as a

whole; they also determine its general structure. This involves all problems of poetic syntax, of composition in its literal sense, and finally of *genre*.[16]

In the first book signed by Bakhtin himself, which is devoted to the work of Dostoevsky, the utterance will assume a new dimension, whose importance will steadily increase: every utterance can be linked to preceding utterances, thereby giving rise to intertextual relations. In this first edition, Bakhtin does not concern himself with general theories but rather with a typology of the utterance, thus he merely states:

> No member of the verbal community will ever discover any words in language which are totally neutral, devoid of another's aspiration and evaluations, or free of another's voice. No, a word is apprehended through the voice of another which will remain forever imbedded within it. A word reaches one context in terms of another context, penetrated by the intentions of another; its own intentionality encounters a word which is already inhabited.[17] (In the second edition of the work, 1963, the instances of "intention" will disappear to be replaced by *osmyslenie,* interpretation, and *mysl',* thought.)

In a previously cited article, signed by Voloshinov, these contentions, as well as several others, are paraphrased with one curious variation: "intonation" here replaces "intention":

> For the poet, language is permeated with living intonations; it is entirely contaminated by social considerations and by the embryonic phases of social orientations. The creative process must continually struggle with such elements; it is from among their midst that one must choose one linguistic form or another, one expression or another, etc. . . . An artist never receives any word in a linguistically virginal form; it has already been 'impregnated' by the practical circumstances and poetic contexts in which it is encountered. (. . .)

> This is why the work of a poet, like that of any artist, can only accomplish certain transvaluations, or certain displacements of intonation; these will be perceived by the artist as well as his public through the perspective of previous evaluations and intonations.[18]

Let us now turn to the second synthesis which appears in the notes written during the fifties, and published after Bakhtin's death, under the title "The Problem of the Text"; the "Methodological Remarks" of the second edition *Dostoevsky* presents a summary of these issues. The frame of reference is no longer sociology, as it was thirty years earlier, but now involves translinguistics, the new discipline Bakhtin intends to found, whose primary object will be the utterance. Three factors are immediately set forth to distinguish an utterance from a sentence: an utterance has a speaker and an object, moreover it partakes in a dialogue with previous utterances.

> The utterance is determined not only by its relation to the object and the speaking subject—the author (and by its relations to language as a system of potential possibilities, or givens) but, most importantly from our perspective, it is directly determined by other utterances within the framework of a certain field of communication.[19] In simpler terms: purely linguistic relations (that is to say the object of linguistics), comprise the relations between one sign and another, or several others (in other words all systematic or linear relations between signs). The relations an utterance may have with reality, the real speaking subject, and other real utterances, that is to say, those relations which render the utterance true, false, or beautiful, etc., can never become an object of linguistics.[20]

We must make a slight digression at this point concerning the speaking subject, the speaker. He is viewed as a constituent element of a speech-act and thus of an utterance; at the same time, one refers to the image of the author which is deduced from the utterance; and one naturally tends to project the second onto the first. However, a clear distinction between the two must be maintained. An author produces an entire utterance which does comprise the "image of the author" but he himself is a producer and never a product, *natura naturans* instead of *natura naturata*.

> Even if an author-creator could create the most truthful autobiography of confession, he would still remain excluded from the universe he has portrayed simply insofar as he has produced it. If I should recount (or write) an event I have just experienced, then the mere act of narrating (or writing) this event will place me outside the time-space in which it has occurred. It is impossible to be absolutely identified with one-self, to reconcile one's veritable "I" with the "I" of his narration, just as it is inconceivable to lift oneself up by his own hair. However realistic and authentic a represented universe may be,

yet it can never be chronotopically identical to the real representing universe in which the author-creator of the representation is located. For this reason, it seems to me that the term "author's image" is quite unfortunate: what has become an image of the work and thereby entered its chronotope, is a product, not a producer. "The author's image," when perceived as the image of the author-creator, is a *contradictio in adjecto;* each image represents something which has been produced and cannot be a producer.[21]

Let us return to the general scheme of the utterance. We have seen that language ("langue"), the speaker, the object, and other utterances are all to be taken into consideration; we must not forget the addressee.

Discourse (like any sign in general) is inter-individual. All that is said or expressed exists outside the "soul" of the speaker; it does not belong to him. Discourse cannot be attributed to the speaker alone. He clearly holds inalienable rights over the discourse, but the auditor has certain rights as well, as do those, whose voices reverberate in the words chosen by the author (since there are no words which do not belong to somebody). Discourse is a drama with a cast of three characters (not a duet, but a trio). It is performed outside the author, and one may not introject it (introjection) back into him.[22]

Meaning, a property of language, will be opposed here to significance; this more familiar term replaces *theme* and links the utterance to the world of values which language does not know.

Isolated signs, and linguistic or textual systems (insofar as they represent a unity of signs) can never be true, false, or beautiful, etc.[23] Only an utterance can be exact (or inexact), beautiful, just, etc.[24]

We can summarize the preceding observations by reconstituting a *communication model* according to Bakhtin, and by comparing it with the currently more familiar model which Roman Jakobson has presented in his article "Linguistics and Poetics."

	Bakhtin			*Jakobson*	
	object			context	
speaker	utterance	auditor	addresser	message	addressee
	intertext			contact	
	language			code	

Two kinds of differences are immediately apparent. Jakobson isolates "contact" as an independent factor. This is absent from the Bakhtinian model, yet the relation to other utterances (which I have designated here as the "intertext") is absent from Jakobson's schema. There are then a series of differences which would seem to involve minor questions or terminology. Jakobson uses rather general terms (semiotic as well as linguistic) and they reveal the influence of his frequent associations with communication engineers. "Context" and "object" both correspond to that which other language theorists would call the "referent."

But after a more careful scrutiny, it is clear that the differences are much more important, and that the terminological discrepancies betray a deeply-rooted opposition. Jakobson sets forth these notions as a description of "the constitutive factors in any speech event, in any act of verbal communication." While for Bakhtin, there exist two radically distinct events, so distinct that they necessitate the use of two independent disciplines, linguistics and translinguistics. In linguistics, words and grammar rules provide the initial basis for the formation of sentences; in translinguistics, one starts off with sentences and the speech-act context eventually to obtain utterances. From Bakhtin's point of view, any attempt to formulate a proposal concerning "any speech event," that is to say, of language as well as discourse, would be futile. In the very schema I have drawn above, the "language" factor is not to be considered on a par with the others.

Moreover, it is no accident that Bakhtin says "utterance" instead of "message," "language" rather than "code," etc.: he quite deliberately rejects the use of engineering language to speak of verbal communication. This language could all too easily lead us to perceive a linguistic exchange in terms of telegraphic work: in order to transmit a certain content, one telegrapher first encodes it with a key and then broadcasts it; once contact has been made, the other uses the same key to decode the message and recover the initial content. This image does not correspond to discursive reality: in fact, prior to the speech-act, the speaker and the addressee literally do not exist as such; it is only the discursive process which thus defines them in relation to each other. For this reason, language is not to be considered as a code; for this reason as well, Bakhtin cannot possibly isolate one "contact" factor amidst the others: the entire utterance is contact, but in a stronger sense of the word than the "contact" of radiotelegraphy or electric work.

It is quite curious to find a page in the book signed by Medvedev which criticized the Jakobsonian model of language, thirty years before it was actually formulated; however one must note that the critique was written as a reply to certain theories of the Formalist group—to which Jakobson belonged.

> That which is transmitted cannot be separated from the forms, the means, and the concrete conditions of the transmission; whereas the Formalist interpretations tacitly presuppose an entirely predetermined and immutable communication, as well as an equally immutable transmission. This might be explained schematically in the following manner: let us take two members of Society, A (the author), and B (the reader); for the time being, the social relations between them are unchangeable and immutable; we also have a prepared message X, which A must simply deliver to B. In this prepared message X, the "what" ("content") is distinct from the "how" ("form"), since literary discourse is characterized by the "set toward the expression" ("how") [this is a quotation from the first published text of Jakobson].
>
> (. . .)
>
> The schema set forth above is completely wrong. In actual fact, the relations between A and B are in a state of continual formation and transformation; they are further modified during the very process of communication itself. There is no prepared message X; it is established by the communicative process between A and B. Moreover, it is not transmitted from one to the other but is built between them like an ideological bridge through the process of their interaction.[25]

Thus, in 1928, we can discern a rather precise prefiguration of certain recent French language theories which are sometimes based on the work of Benveniste (for example those of Oswald Ducrot or François Flahault).

As we now turn from the model of the particular utterance to the set of utterances constituting the verbal life of a community, we should note the fact which would appear to be most striking in the eyes of Bakhtin: there exists a large, but nonetheless limited, number of utterance or discourse *types*. One must indeed beware of two possible extremes: first, to recognize the diversity of languages and ignore that of utterances; secondly, to consider this variety as being individual and therefore limitless. Besides which, Bakhtin accentuates difference rather than plurality (one need not attempt to conceive of any common denominator which would reconcile various discourses; the argument here runs counter to the idea of unification). To designate this irreducible diversity of discursive types, Bakhtin introduces a neologism, *raznorechie,* which I translate (literally but in Greek) as *heterology;* this term is flanked by two parallel neologisms, *raznojazychie,* heteroglossy, or diversity of languages, and *raznogolosie,* heterophony, or diversity of voices (individual).

We will recall that every utterance is oriented towards a social horizon which comprises semantic and value elements. The number of these verbal and ideological horizons is quite high but not unlimited; and every utterance necessarily falls within one or several of the discursive types determined by a horizon.

There are no longer any words or forms in language which are neutral and belong to no one: it appears that language has been pillaged, pierced through and through by intentions, and accentuated. For a consciousness which exists within language, it is not an abstract system of normative forms but a concrete heterological opinion of the world. Each word evokes a profession, a genre, a trend, a party, a particular work, a particular man, a generation, an age, a day and an hour. Each word evokes a context and the contexts within which it has experienced an intense social life; every word and every form is inhabited by intentions. Contextual harmonies found in a word (of the genre, of the trend, of the particular individual) are inevitable.[26]

Through the preceding enumerations we can already see that the stratification of language in discourse is not restricted to one dimension. In the course of the most detailed study which he devoted to heterology (in "Discourse in the Novel," text of 1934-35), Bakhtin discerns up to five types of stratification: genres, profession, social levels, ages and regions (dialects *strictu sensu*). Let us merely note that social class does not play a different role from that of profession or age group: it is simply one diversifying factor among several others.

In a certain sense, heterology is inherent to society; it is engendered spontaneously by social diversification. But just as the unique state attempts to contain this social diversity by means of its laws, so do the authorities fight the diversity of discourse by aspiring to a common language (or rather idiom).

> The category of common language is a theoretical expression of the historical processes of unification and centralization—an expression of the centripetal forces in language. A common language is not a given; in actual fact it is always ordered, and opposes genuine heterology at every instant throughout the life of a language. Yet at the same time, this common language is perfectly real when seen as a force which overcomes this heterology, constrains it within certain limitations, assures a maximum mutual comprehension, and is crystallized in the real, albeit relative, unity of literary and spoken (everyday) language, which is the "proper language."[27]

Bakhtin will refer, as one can see, to this tendency towards unification as a "centripetal force" and by the same token, to heterology as a "centrifugal force." Different types of discourse themselves favor one force over the other for varying reasons. For example, the novel (or what Bakhtin defines as such) reinforces heterology, while poetry does not; for heterology is linked to the representation of language, which is a characteristic feature of the novel.

> While the principal sorts of poetic genres develop within the flow of the centripetal unifying and centralizing forces which inform verbal and ideological existence, the novel, as well as other related genres of literary prose, emerged historically within the flow of decentralizing, centrifugal forces.[28]

Therefore, the high periods of the novel correspond to those which witnessed a weakening of centralized power.

> The embryonic forms of novelistic prose appear in the heteroglossic and heterological world of the Hellenistic epoch, in imperial Rome, also in the decomposition and decadence of the verbal and ideological centralism of the medieval church. Similarly, the period of fruition of the modern novel is always tied to a general decomposition of verbal and ideological systems, to a process of reinforcement and intensification which opposes linguistic heterology in the literary dialect but also outside it![29]

On the other hand, as Bakhtin remarks, the different theories or philosophies of language are always born in the wake of unifying movements; this moreover explains their helplessness when confronted by heterology. Thus, for example, the sad fate of stylistics when it tackles the novel: a "Ptolemaic" discipline cannot account for a "Galilean" genre.

> Traditional stylistics ignores the kind of combination whereby languages and styles merge in a superior unity; it has no means of approaching the particular social dialogue of languages within a novel. This is why stylistic analysis is not oriented towards the novel seen as a whole but only towards one or the other of its subordinate stylistic aspects. The specialist bypasses the distinctive characteristic of the novelistic genre; he transforms the object of his study, and instead of the novelistic style he in fact analyses something completely different. He transposes an orchestrated symphonic theme in the place of a piano.[30]

Bakhtin enumerates several other examples of such helplessness in the face of heterology:

> The poetics of Aristotle, the poetics of Augustine, Medieval religious poetics of the common language of truth, the Cartesian poetics of Neo-Classicism, the abstract grammatical universalism of Leibniz (the idea of universal grammar), the concrete ideologism of Humboldt—whatever may be the distinguishing nuances—these all express the same centripetal forces of sociolinguistic and ideological existence; they all serve the same objective: the centralization and unification of European languages.[31]

The rather surprising name in this roster is Humboldt, a distant source of inspiration for Bakhtin, as we know, and an advocate of linguistic diversity, that of languages as well as that of individuals (language expressing a national spirit, the utterance—an individual one). However, Humboldt forgets a crucial gap between these two: social diversity. Beyond the unicity of Classicism and the Romantic infinite variety, Bakhtin seeks a third path: that of typology.

Translated from French by Claudine Frank.

Notes

1. P. Medvedev, *Formal'nyi metod v literaturovedenii*, (Leningrad: Priboi, 1928), pp. 131-32. English translation, P. N. Medvedev/M. M. Bakhtin, *The Formal Method in Literary Scholarship* (Baltimore and London: The Johns Hopkins University Press, 1978).
2. V. Voloshinov, *Marksizm i filosofia iazyka* (Leningrad: Priboi, 1929). English translation, *Marxism and the Philosophy of Language* (New York and London: Seminar Press, 1973), p. 101.
3. *Marksizm*, p. 114.
4. *Marksizm*, p. 101.
5. V. Voloshinov, "O granizakh poetiki i lingvistiki," in *V bor'be za marksizm v literaturnoi nauke* (Leningrad: Priboi, 1930), p. 226.
6. *Marksizm*, p. 101.
7. "O granizakh poetiki," p. 229.
8. *Marksizm*, p. 111.
9. *Marksizm*, p. 104.
10. *Marksizm*, p. 113.
11. *Marksizm*, p. 120.
12. *Marksizm*, p. 122.
13. *Marksizm*, pp. 119-20.
14. Medvedev, p. 117.
15. "O granizakh poetiki," pp. 227-28.
16. "O granizakh poetiki," p. 232.
17. M. M. Bakhtin, *Problemy tvorchestva Dostoevskogo* (Leningrad: Priboi, 1929), pp. 370-71. English translation of the second edition, *Problems of Dostoevsky's Poetics* (Ann Arbor: Ardis, 1973).
18. "O granizakh poetiki," p. 231.
19. M. M. Bakhtin, "Problema teksta," *Voprosy literatury*, 10 (1976), pp. 144-45. Written in 1959-61.
20. "Problema teksta," p. 146.
21. M. M. Bakhtin, "Zakljuchitel'nye zamechanija" (to "Formy vremeni . . .", in *Voprosy literatury i estetiki* (Moscow: Khudozh. lit., 1975), p. 405. Written in 1973.
22. "Problema teksta," p. 144.
23. "Problema teksta," p. 146.
24. "Problema teksta," p. 145.
25. Medvedev, pp. 203-04.
26. M. M. Bakhtin, "Slovo v romane," in *Voprosy literatury i estetiki*, p. 106. Written in 1934-35.
27. "Slovo v romane," pp. 83-84.
28. "Slovo v romane," p. 86.
29. "Slovo v romane," p. 182.
30. "Slovo v romane," pp. 76-77.
31. "Slovo v romane," p. 84.

Prefigurements of Art*

Thomas A. Sebeok

0. Preliminaries.

That language is a biotic property specific to man is a truism even in the sense that no other species encountered so far is, in the technical acceptation of this term, language-endowed. Language is a cognitive structure which, like the behavioral extension of any organ of man's body, may be studied along several more or less agreed upon semiosic/ethological dimensions,[1] including the characters of its initial state (ontogenesis), mature state, and end-state (gradual breakdown, partial reconstitution, and eventual termination).[2] With regard to the phylogenesis of language, there has been much random conjecture and some empirical stumbling, but scarcely even translucent enlightenment so far. Verbal sign configurations have been elaborated throughout history into many complex forms of message oriented constructs, encompassing both spoken and literary genres, which are best called jointly—as I had suggested nearly a quarter of a century ago[3]—the "verbal art." Furthermore, language, being "absolutely distinct from any system of communication in other animals," and thus "also the most diagnostic single trait of man,"[4] has as its corollary, by definition as it were, the tautologic proposition that man has a monopoly on all manifestations of the verbal art. These statements and their implication, while hardly contestable, are surely trivial, owing to the equally unchallengeable fact that the communication system of every *other* species stamps it with a unique hallmark, much as language conspicuously segregates out our humanity.[5] They do, however, suggest one interesting question which I propose to explore, if tentatively, in what follows, namely, whether the optimal design of certain animal communication systems can allow, given certain contextual conditions, for a superimposed aesthetic function. In other words, how reasonable is it to search for prefigurements of aesthetically charged averbal sign configurations in man's animal ancestry? What, for instance, could Julian Huxley have meant when he asserted, in passing,

* The entire text, supported by 27 Figures, including nine color plates, has appeared in *Semiotica*, XXVII (1979), pp. 3-73; the definitive version is scheduled to be published as Ch. 9 in the author's forthcoming book, *The Play of Musement* (Bloomington: Indiana University Press, 1981).

during a Darwin Centennial panel discussion, that in the behavior of the
Satinbird (*Ptilonorhynchus violaceus*)—a remarkable bowerbird living in
the coastal forests of Eastern Australia, and a species certain members of
which paint the inside of their bower efficiently, even, to echo Huxley's
word, "deliberately"—there is "definitely the beginning of aesthetics"?[6]
This seemingly bizarre habit, Marshall surmised, "may be an aesthetic extension of a basic drive,"[7] namely, the birds' courtship feeding phenomenon—
or just the sort of displacement activity of sexual behavior that some
Freudians have posited in men. Gannon,[8] the discoverer of bower painting
in this species, also observed that the male appeared to employ a tool—a
wad of bark, like a brush or sponge, held in the tip of the bill—to apply
the paint, which is composed of saliva mixed by the bird with charcoal
dust, dark berries, or wood-pulp. It was subsequently noted that the paint,
washed away by the heavy tropical rains, is replaced daily during the height
of the sexual season and fibrous bark, often still saturated with charcoal
and saliva, is commonly to be found on the avenue floor between the two
painted walls and where fallen leaves are always quickly removed. This
bird, when constructing its social signals, exhibits a decided preference
for blue, less so for yellowish-green, shunning red altogether, a bias manifested, moreover, in such like-colored ornamental objects as feathers, flowers,
leaves, berries, snail shells, cicada integument, and, near human habitations,
pieces of blue-colored glass beads, strands of wool and tinsel.[9] Generalizing
about the entire family *Ptilorhynchidae,* of which about nineteen species
occur, Dobzhansky remarks that "it is impossible to deny that a well-
adorned bower may give the bird a pleasure which can only be called
aesthetic."[10]   Recall in this context Nicolas Poussin's maxim—a 17th
century evocation of the mediaeval doctrine of *delectatio* as a sign—that
"la fin de l'art est la délectation," apropos of which Panofsky insists that
"a work of art always *has* aesthetic significance,"[11] regardless of whether
it serves some practical—let me qualify: biological—purpose at bottom.
We must likewise concede the possibility that "animals perform some of
the behavior patterns we observe because they enjoy the resulting experience,"
regardless of whether such patterns are adaptive, or virtually so, "but result
in a pleasantly satisfying feeling" on the animal's part.[12] Whether or not
bowers are built, painted, and decorated for the makers' pleasure, the fact
remains that the constructions take place, as a rule, during the breeding
season and serve as the sites where territorial displays are performed. The

key issue, what the differential effect of the bowers may be on the females, remains unresolved, because this has not been systematically tested.[13]

Contrary to Barthes' contention, that the semiotician is entitled to treat writing and pictures in the same way because what he retains from them both is "qu'elles sont toutes deux des *signes*,"[14] in all living systems that I know of the characteristics of the signs employed are inseparably joined to the kind of information they carry. Similarly, the concept of "secondary modeling system,"[15] which is assuredly among the more salient features of Soviet semiotics, posits a superstructure that persistently confounds two diverse artistic realizations which, I would argue, demand radically different treatment: on the one side, the products of the verbal art and its derivatives, being inescapably built up from signs that are the operands of a natural language, plus certain traditional or newly invented rules for combining them in possible, impossible, contingent, or imperative ways to advance human cognition and communication; and, on the other side, the artistic products of averbal semiotic systems into which verbal signs may, to be sure, encroach in varying degree. The performances we call the verbal art and those that we call the averbal arts generate, respectively, in the dominant and the minor hemisphere, although the specializations normally have a complementary relationship. As Eccles has recently pointed out, "the minor hemisphere is specialized in relationship to pictures and patterns, and it is musical."[16] This separation of hemispheric functions, by the evidence to date, is genetically coded. The minor hemisphere is best envisaged as "a very superior animal brain,"[17] a conception which points precisely in the direction in which future researches are most likely to prove fruitful. The two repertoires of signs may, and often doubtless do, "enter into subtle semantic relationships," as Veltruský emphasizes,[18] the resulting meaning being compounded by a process called codified contiguity. This is achieved by the immense and incessant traffic in the corpus callosum linking the two cerebral hemispheres of the intact human brain, for "probably everything that happens in the minor hemisphere leads to a kind of reverberation in the major hemisphere."[19] There is, however, no ground that I know of for belief that would compel the conclusion that the interpretant of *every* artistic sign must have a verbal component; and should a semiotic system of the second kind be identified in the infrahuman biosphere, it would certainly be altogether delusive to postulate a verbal infrastructure for the sort of hemispheric specialization intimated is, after all, "unique to man."[20]

The authentic singularity of man consists of this, that he alone disposes over a *pair* of communicative codes: "along with our wholly new and wholly distinct system of true language,"[21] the verbal code, we retain an older system that, for want of a better name,[22] is frequently, contrastively, and hence negatively designated as a human manifestation of a cross-specific averbal code. The latter comprehends a trio of subcodes recently differentiated into separate categories by Uexküll:[23] first, endosemiotic averbal sign systems, or the metabolic code,[24] involving humoral and nervous factors that convey information within the bodies of all animals, including man;[25] second, somatosemiotic averbal sign systems, that function to compact the unity of every organism,[26] a notion kindred to Leibniz's concept of apperception (as expressed in his 1714 paper, *Principes de la nature et de la grâce, fondés en raison*), which is our conscious reflection of the inner state of the monad; and third, outspreading averbal sign systems, such as are used for communication between organisms and between any organism and its external environment. In man, the output of this entire array of subcodes, but particularly of the third kind, is exquisitely harmonized in performing with his outpouring of verbal messages, although the diverse repertories each serve separate ends substantially at variance one from the other—a point worth reemphasizing with Bateson,[27] who rather clearly saw how wrong it is to assume that, in hominid evolution, verbal semiosis has, in any sense, replaced "the cruder systems of the other animals,"[28] that is, averbal semiosis. Had this been the case, our averbal skills and the organs that execute them would inevitably have undergone conspicuous decay. Obviously, they have not; on the contrary, while the verbal art flourished, we have perfected our averbal arts as well—they too "have been elaborated into complex forms of art, music, ballet . . . and the like, and, even in everyday life, the intricacies of human kinesic communication, facial expression and vocal intonation far exceed anything that any other animal is known to produce."[29]

The ideal of semiosic analysis is to combine causal with functional explanation—to show how sign form interrelates dynamically with sign function, both in synchrony and in diachrony. But an evolutionary sequence is hard to come by in an area so complex and multiply amphibiological as art. Instances may be temporally ordered but are not necessarily in linked sequence. Guthrie offers some interesting ideas, in a semiotic frame, "about how some aspects of our aesthetic sense evolved,"[30] but the part he was concerned with was that which underlies our appreciation of human physical beauty, the valuation of which he traced to two major elements, copulatory lures and status badges. One perhaps insuperable difficulty all investigators have to face is to identify ineffable "signs of artistic enjoyment in other species,"[31] all of them being creatures that are speechless.

The only general survey I can find in the entire literature of the life sciences of basic aesthetic principles possibly shared by man with at least the higher animals was drafted in the late 1960s by another ethologist, Rensch, in an essay that was published only much later in the U.S. (1974) and Great Britain (1976).[32] This authoritative but still, unfortunately, all too inconclusive review, based in large part on the author's well-known experiments aimed to demonstrate the reality of protoaesthetic phenomena, the results of which were found to be in good conformity with those of psychologists[33] who studied the elements of aesthetic preferences in human subjects, is devoted in the main to scribblings and paintings by monkeys and apes, with but a laconic page on "auditive aesthetic sensations."[34] In 1958, Rensch had investigated the efficacy of aesthetic factors in vertebrates, testing preferences for different patterns in a jackdaw, a carrion crow, and six fishes. He showed that, while the fishes always preferred irregular patterns, both species of birds preferred the more regular, more symmetrical, and more rhythmical patterns, doing so in statistically significant numbers. In a color choice test, these birds exhibited a preference for gray and black, being the colors of their own plumage. However, "they preferred patterns with two or four different colours to simpler patterns of one colour or two colours respectively."[35] A student of his, Tigges,[36] later found that jackdaws preferred pure colors (red, blue, yellow, green) to equally bright mixed ones (orange, brown, violet, lilac).

Although painting experiments were conducted by N. N. Ladygin Kohts with a chimpanzee named Joni, in Moscow, as far back as 1913, and Shepherd[37] reported that a chimpanzee drew lines with a pencil, and many an anecdotal story found its way into the literature since then, there are only three serious studies of primate aesthetics: the series of papers by Rensch,[38] a posthumous publication by Schiller,[39] and the engaging book by Morris,[40] especially showing, on the basis of a detailed analysis of one young chimpanzee, Congo, that the splashes of paint or the pencil marks made by apes are not at all random. The immature Congo, given an incomplete pattern, often made marks which tended to complete it. Alpha, the first-born chimpanzee of the Yerkes Colony, if given a piece of paper, with a cross placed on three of the corners, would put a cross in the fourth corner: "she would also in her crude way try to complete designs and pictures which had been given to her deliberately unfinished or unbalanced."[41] One is thus forced to assume the presence, in advance, of a representation in the animal's nervous system that corresponds to the picture displayed.

The most recent survey of ape creativity may be found in the psychologist Andrew Whiten's excellent account.[42] Rensch, who had worked with a capuchin monkey and a green monkey as well as chimpanzees, observing their drawing or painting with pencil, colored chalk, or brush, professes to have been astonished "to find also aesthetic factors having a positive effect with apes, monkeys and [even] crows comparable with the effect in man."[43] He believes that our feelings of aesthetic pleasure, as we look at different black and white patterns are, in the main, attributable to three basic conditions: symmetry, rhythmic repetition of similar component parts, and consistency of curvatures. His results demonstrate that, with these animals, as with man, "the greater facility to apprehend a design, the details of which are rhythmically repeated or otherwise more easily apprehended, the 'complexibility' is connected with positive feelings and arouses aesthetic pleasure."[44] Rensch tells of incidents where "competent art experts, on being shown monkeys' paintings without being told who had painted them, sometimes enthusiastically praised the dynamism, rhythm and sense of balance."[45] In so doing they have not made fools of themselves, but simply confirmed what the experimental biologists had already also established.

Rensch further supposes that the tendency of apes, including orangutans and capuchin monkeys, to put scarves, ribbons, chains, and the like, around their neck, and to romp about with them on, is to be interpreted as enjoyment of dressing up; hence, in his view, aesthetic factors would be involved in this behavior as well. "It is even more likely," he adds, "that birds find aesthetic pleasure in repeating tunes they hear from other birds or from humans, and in 'composing' new melodies from phrases either learned or already known."[46]

*   *   *

Following these brief prefatory observations, I would like to reexamine in some detail the question of the putative aesthetic propensity of animals, with specific (although uneven) attention to four semiotic spheres: (1) kinesthetic signs, (2) musical signs, (3) pictorial signs, and (4) architectural signs. Sketchy as such a review must be, no such comprehensive literature survey has been attempted before, probably for several reasons. One of these may be due to the fact that cultural anthropologists who have sought to inquire into the biological roots of art have typically set out to do so with a preconception common to many members of the profession. Alland, for one, opens his chapter on "The Evolution of Art" with this uncompromising sentence: "The creation and appreciation of art in its many forms are uniquely human activities,"[47] adding, a few pages later: "True [*sic*] artistic behavior is seen in no species other than *Homo sapiens.* Not even a hint of it occurs in the natural behavior of other species."[48] His brief exploration of its origins, sensitive as it is, suggests that this lies in play as a biological property, leading him to a debatable definition of art as "play involving rules."[49] This same notion was earlier advanced by Ellen Eisenberg,[50] subsuming art in a more inclusive class of behavior patterns, one which includes all forms of exploration; and earlier still, by Dobzhansky, who felt that at least some forms of art "are related to play."[51] (The union of the play-impulse with aesthetic feelings and sentiments, as linked with superfluous activities and corresponding pleasures, was first propagated by Spencer eighty years ago;[52] he argued that the aesthetic sphere in general may be expected to occupy an increasing part in human life owing to greater economization of energy resulting from superiority of organization bringing a growing proportion of the aesthetic activities and gratifications.) Dobzhansky, however, perceived even in artistic activity an adaptive value, for he saw in it a wellspring of social cohesion, thus raising once again a utilitarian interpretation of the role of art. This viewpoint is most fruitfully developed by Jenkins, a thoroughgoing evolutionist for whom art has its "ultimate source in the human effort to adapt to the environment," and who insists, more generally, that any inquiry into the origins of art must move, as he emphatically puts it, *"toward an analysis of the adaptive situation."*[53] Klopfer, who means by aesthetic preferences simply "a liking for objects or activities because they produce or induce particular neural inputs or emotional states, independently of overt reinforcers," answers his own question, whether we can attribute aesthetic impulses to animals other than man, in the affirmative. The inquiry entails the belief that there must be a biological basis to aesthetics, and thus shifts to a search into the basis thereof: "what are the historical or ultimate reasons for the development of an aesthetic sense; by what mechanisms is the development of the species-characteristic preferences assumed?"[54] Klopfer, too, comes up against the predicament posed by the traditional view that aesthetic preferences are those for which no immediate functional advantage can be perceived; consequently, he strikes out in a different direction, seeking for guidance from sensory physiology, while also redefining play as a kind of exploratory activity by which the organism "tests" different proprioceptive patterns for the goodness of fit.[55]

When ethnologists search for the sources of art, they more often than not mean the verbal art; play thus comes to mean wordplay, which Alland, for one, connects with poetry,[56] and which must then be excluded *per definitionem* from the rest of the animal kingdom. Archaeologists tend especially to dwell on representative art; as Marshack puts it, "art and symbol are products that visualize and objectify aspects of culture. . . ."[57] Although, on balance, the neuroanatomist Young is undoubtedly right when he says, in the course of his synthesis tracing the sources of human activity from their biochemical basis to the highest levels of consciousness, that "there is no body of facts that yet enables us to understand the origins of aesthetic creation . . . ," [58] the issue remains a tantalizing one, for, as another distinguished biologist put it, "in some situations it becomes really difficult not to impute to animals some sort of aesthetics."[59] The dialectic seems to have begun between Darwin, whose theory of sexual selection is based on the assumption that female birds, for example, are able to appreciate the beauty of male plumage,[60] and his contemporary, Wallace, who disputed this view precisely in semiotic terms. Wallace argued that what is involved here is an instinctive interpretation of certain strings of signs emitted by the male. However this may be, it would be unreasonable to expect a perfunctory and iterative scrutiny of the literature of animal behavior to shed much illumination; a deeper search, on the other hand, might at least highlight some fundamental issues—such as the often misunderstood dichotomy of analogy *vs.* homology, and the even less understood distinction between phyletic homologies and homologies of tradition.

1. Kinesthetic signs.

The kinesthetic art—as the multisensory dance when viewed in a semiotic frame is sometimes reductively termed after its most distinctive feature, because in dance (contrasted, particularly, with mime) "movement is often an end in itself"[61]—is seldom alluded to in the context of animal behavior. Sachs adduced several striking cases of bird displays he and others in his field, including recently Royce,[62] explicitly dubbed "dancing." One of his examples is cited after Maclaren,[63] who witnessed this dance of the stilt birds, or cranes, in Cape York in Northeastern Australia:

> The birds . . . were long-legged creatures, tall almost as storks, and white and gray of feather; and the dance took place in the center of a broad, dry swamp. . . . There were some hundreds of them, and their dance was in the manner of a quadrille, but in the matter of rhythm and grace excelling any quadrille that ever was. In groups of a score or more they advanced and retreated, lifting high their long legs and standing on their toes, now and then bowing gracefully to one another, now and then one pair encircling with prancing daintiness a group whose heads moved upwards and downwards and sideways in time to the stepping of the pair. At times they formed into one great prancing mass, with their long necks thrust upward; and the wide swaying of their backs was like unto the swaying of the sea. Then, suddenly, as in response to an imperative command, they would sway apart, some of them to rise in low, encircling flight, and some to stand as in little gossiping groups; and presently they would form in pairs or sets of pairs, and the prancing and bowing, and advancing and retreating would begin all over again.[64]

His second example, which comes from British Guiana, cited after Appun, is, as Royce underlines, "even more interesting since it describes what is essentially a performer-spectator situation":[65]

> [A] group of some twenty mountain chickens of a brilliant orange-yellow color, gathered together in a kind of dance characteristic of these beautiful birds. In the center one of the cocks executed the dance-like movements, as he hopped about the open place with wings extended and tail outspread. On the branches of the bushes round about, the others sat and expressed their admiration of the dancer with the strangest sounds. As soon as one cock was exhausted, he

joined the spectators, uttering a peculiar cry, and another took his place.[66]

These parallels immediately raise several problems, the most obvious being whether the animal's behavior is "merely" analogous to man's, whether, that is, shifting to a more familiar parlance, the label "dance" is "just" a colorful and suggestive metaphor—as it must surely be in Frisch's designation of the kinetic component of the communication system of the honeybee as a "dance"[67]—or whether something deeper is implied, perhaps indeed a remote phyletic homology.[68] Even if only an analogy is meant, this is far from valueless, since its study would throw light upon "the laws of function that rule the evolution of a behavior pattern."[69] It is, in fact, highly productive to compare biological constructs with cultural ones if only to ascertain whether seemingly similar signifiers trigger comparable interpretants, in the sense that the wing of an insect (developed from an epidermal fold), the wing of a bird (developed from a vertebrate extremity), and a wing of an airplane (manufactured, say, of metal), are all shaped in response to the universal laws of aerodynamics. Armstrong, who devoted an entire chapter to drawing parallels between the dances of birds and men, feels that he is justified in employing the identical label for both sets of motor signs because of "a natural recognition of the remarkable similarities which actually exist between the dances of birds and men and the identity of the emotional sources from which both take their origin. The resemblances between avian and human dancing," he claims, "are the outcome of emotional drives which underlie the behaviour of all the higher animals; and the natural corollary is that we can use the terpsichorean activities of men to interpret those of birds, and vice versa. Let us not be scared," he concludes, "by the bogey of anthropomorphism into the arms of the spectre of Cartesian mechanism. It is not anthropomorphism to believe that man and the higher animals have much in common so far as instinct and emotion are concerned, but an acknowledgment of truth scientifically demonstrated."[70]

Sachs' questions, by distinguishing—to recast in modern ethological terminology what he says—phyletic homologies, or those that are transmitted via the genome, from homologies of tradition, that is, those that are passed on via memory, whether animals in fact do dance as man does. The traditional distinction between innate *vs.* acquired characteristics is not at all as clear-cut as Sachs implies, however, and becomes increasingly inappropriate when one considers the alloprimates. One reason for this is that, for research dealing with homologies, "it is only necessary that information emanating from one common source is passed on. It is not necessary for reproductive relationships to be involved."[71] What we know about dancing in apes is, while doubtless fascinating, unfortunately far from abundant, and even here a further discrimination demands to be promptly introduced, namely, as between studies of animals in captivity, some of which Sachs knew of, and observations of groups in the wild, which are of much more recent vintage. Both sets of data concern chimpanzees—the latter all but exclusively from the popular writings of Lawick-Goodall.[72]

Lawick-Goodall repeatedly refers to a display, which she reports having seen but three times in ten years, as a "rain dance." These group performances lasting almost half an hour, involved adult males—with females and youngsters in watchful attendance—although often individual males were also observed to "react to the start of heavy rain by performing a rain dance."[73] It is not at all clear from Lawick-Goodall's description of these spectacles what the chimpanzees' behavior pattern could possibly signify. In the human context, what is commonly called a rain dance is performed in many societies as a fertility rite in order to produce rain; it belongs to a class Royce calls metaphorical dances.[74] By contrast, feral chimpanzees, to all appearances, "dislike the rain," reminding the observer of "primitive men . . . defying the elements."[75] Their carnival display is in reaction to a sudden downpour. What we have here is a striking resemblance in form—sufficiently so, it seems, to account for the labeling— but a dearth of information about referential sign function, and therefore a gnawing question mark about the meaning of the convergence between man and chimpanzee in this arena of expressive movement.

Reports of chimpanzees dancing in the laboratory—including what Sachs claimed to be the "most valuable document"[76]—come from the psychologist Köhler, who was for six years in charge of a research establishment in Tenerife.[77] Köhler frequently observed couples moving in dance-like fashion. He depicted a particular configuration about which he remarked that "Die ähnlichkeit mit einem Tanz war besonders gross,"[78] a characterization Sachs wholly concurred with. Nor was this all. Stylized group dances took place, such as the following, which Sachs insisted "was a genuine round dance":

In mock fighting two of them drag each other about on the ground until they come near a post. Their frolicking and romping quiets down as they begin to circle about, using the post as a pivot. One after another the rest of the animals appear, join the circle, and finally the whole group, one behind another, is marching in orderly fashion around the post. Now their movements change quickly. They are no longer walking but trotting. Stamping with one foot and putting the other down lightly, they beat out what approaches a distinct rhythm, with each of them tending to keep step with the rest. When two posts or boxes stand close to each other, they like to use these as a center, and in this case the ring dance around both takes the form of an ellipse. In these dances the chimpanzee likes to bedeck his body with all sorts of things, especially strings, vines, and rags that dangle and swing in the air as he moves about.[79]

Sachs identifies here the prefigurements of a series of basic human dance motifs: "as forms, the circle and ellipse around the post, the forward and backward pace; as movements, hopping, rhythmical stamping, whirling, and even ornamentation for the dance."[80] Köhler further tells us that the sympathetic observer would gladly join in this dance, and that when he initiated the movement around the post "in der besonderen Schrittart, welche für die Tiere dazugehörte," he was immediately followed by a couple of chimpanzees; but when he quit, because of fatigue, his dancing companions would squat and sulk.[81] What Sachs is concerned with here ought to be taken very seriously, but remains as yet unresolved, for, as he summarizes: "If the dance, inherited from brutish ancestors, lives in all mankind as a necessary motor-rhythmic expression of excess energy and of the joy of living, then it is only of slight importance for anthropologists and social historians. If it is established, however, that an inherited predisposition develops in many ways in the different groups of man and if its force and direction is related to other phenomena of civilization, the history of the dance will then be of great importance for the study of mankind."[82]

If one defines dance, in the stark fashion of Boas, as "the rhythmic movements of any part of the body, swinging of the arms, movement of the trunk or head, or movements of the legs and feet,"[83] then clearly the chimpanzees' behavior can legitimately be bracketed with ours. It is plausible, moreover, to regard both underlying structures as homologous, implying that they owe their similarity to a common origin, much as laughter and smiling fit into the phyletic scale.[84] The postulation of a homologous relationship does not, however, necessarily imply a distinction between characteristics that are innate *vs.* those that may be acquired, for homologies may be passed on either via the genome or via memory, that is, by cultural or quasi-cultural mechanisms, in the manner, say, of song traditions in the parasitic weaver finches (*Viduinae*), which were discovered to even transgress species boundaries: these birds learn not only the songs but also the calls of their host species, and close mimicry of the vocalizations of the step-father results in parallel development which may, in turn, lead to eventual species genesis. Whether dance behavior is innate or acquired is not known, but it is important to be mindful that information may be communicated to a succeeding generation in several different ways, and therefore, since form depends on the function, convergence can hardly be excluded. In studies of expressive movements, the investigation is particularly complicated by the fact that the specific adaptations are not simply responsive to the environment, but involve subtle selective pressures which cannot yet be formulated in terms of physiological or biochemical correlates—for instance, a concept such as "aesthetic pleasure." Nonetheless, I find myself concurring with Griffin, when he exclaims that "this does not seem to [him] to be a sufficient reason for avoiding the concepts themselves, as though they were a dangerous plague."[85] This view, moreover, accords, I think, with the line taken by such specialists in the dance as Hanna, who, while she feels "that the configuration of human behaviour that is called dance is significantly different from the behaviour of other animals, including that which has also been labelled dance," at the same time affirms "that human dance has its roots in phylogenetic and ontogenetic evolution, firstly in predisposing psychobiological processes and secondly in social experience."[86]

2. *Musical signs.*

"Music," Merriam tells his readers, "is a uniquely human phenomenon . . ."[87]—but his generalization begs the very question that needs exploring. I would therefore prefer to start journeying backward in time from the Janus-like portal that is the sole rational means of access from nature to culture that Lévi-Strauss sagaciously threw open when befittingly noting that "la musique opère au moyen de deux grilles. L'une est physiologique, donc naturelle; son existence tient au fait que la musique exploite les rythmes organiques, et qu'elle rend ainsi pertinentes des discontinuités qui resteraient autrement à l'état latent, et comme noyées dans la durée. L'autre grille est culturelle; elle consiste dans une échelle de sons musicaux, dont le nombre et les écarts varient selon les cultures."[88]

Boas made two fundamental observations concerning music: first, that the only kind of music that occurs universally is song, "and the source of music must therefore be sought here;" and, second, that two elements, and only two, are common to all song: rhythm and fixed intervals.[89] It is in the class of birds that the rootstock lies to which these remarks must inevitably lead the unprejudiced investigator, fortified by the opinion of so experienced an ornithologist as Thorpe, who, in repudiation of a typically naive remark of Suzanne Langer's,[90] proclaims his own stand: ". . . increased familiarity, from long study, certainly for me, increases my conviction that our judgment that bird songs, in some instances and in some degree, represent music is not mistaken."[91]

Within the last decade, several competent and thoughtful studies have appeared appraising a field that in the course of its recent development has even won a name of its own: ornithomusicology.[92] One such survey, on the aesthetic content of bird song, was compiled by Hall-Craggs, a British ornithologist.[93] Another, a book-length global reinterpretation of bird song, was undertaken by Hartshorne, a prominent philosopher (perhaps best known to this readership as the senior editor of the *Collected Papers* of C. S. Peirce).[94] As for the controversial but hardly verifiable central thesis of ornithomusicology—an idea first articulated, I believe, by Montaigne— it is argued that birds evolved elaborate musical utterances long before the appearance of man, who may be supposed to have derived his primitive music under the instigation or, at any rate, influence of their song: men certainly heard it and some may have imitated it. (It should be mentioned here that man often mimics different aspects of animal behavior,[95] and particularly that the imitation of bird dances is quite widespread. One example from Europe is the incorporation of a figure, the *Nachsteigen,* from the behavior of the mountain cock, into the Bavarian *Schuhplatter*.)[96] The process of adoption would have been facilitated by the undeniable fact that man and bird share certain requisite physiological foundations: both of us sense the world most consequentially by optical means, and both of us address it most saliently by acoustic means.[97] Indeed, in a number of crucial respects, and particularly as to the predisposition of some song birds, manifesting critical periods in their lives for song-learning, to master certain sounds rather than others in a manner reminiscent of the kind of constraints on first language acquisition detectable in human children, and in several other important respects, "these birds are closer to man than any nonhuman primate. . . ."[98]

Were the ornithomusicologist's contentions demonstrable, then one could postulate a true homology of tradition, if not a phyletic one: human song would thus be as homologous to bird song as, say, a genetically unrelated second language acquired by a foreign speaker is homologous to the first language learned by a native speaker of that same language. Failing that, we must fall back on the principle of convergent evolution, justified by adequate evidence for formal correspondence. But Szöke's line of argumentation is by no means abrogated or contradicted by the prodigiously erudite Armstrong's chapter on "Bird Song as Art and Play," where this English life-long student of bird behavior repeatedly remarks that "As evidence increases it becomes more difficult to deny that birds possess some aesthetic sensitivity," and that, "whatever else our aesthetic taste may be, it is an extension and refinement of animal abilities." He quotes an apt observation by Paracelsus, the early 16th century physician and alchemist, who admonished: "Man need not be surprised that animals have animal instincts that are so much like his own. . . . Man may learn from the animals, for they are his parents."[99]

The most elusive problem in demonstrating "that birds have aesthetic taste is the difficulty of proving that any characteristic of bird song is non-utilitarian."[100] Hartshorne's book is in part addressed to this predicament, which he formulates thus: "To say 'aesthetic' is to say 'not merely or too directly utilitarian.' But we must be careful to balance this consideration against the seemingly contradictory one that unless an aesthetic activity has some connection with utility it will be unlikely to survive evolutionary change."[101] Hartshorne speculates that there may be an optimum here between irrelevance to survival needs of the species—notably, as an expression of its territorial requirements (the birds with the "best" songs are usually the ones with the most marked territorial behavior)—and too close or immediate a connection with such needs, as represented by the individual singer in a given context. He postulates "a safety factor," a sort of emergency valve for the outlet of surplus energy, a luxury activity that can always be nullified in exigent circumstances.

Rhythm is the basis of form in bird song, as in all music, much as symmetry is in space or equilibrium in matter. Hall-Craggs discusses its prevalence in some detail, as well as of the transposition of fixed intervals that Boas deemed the second all-important element of music, comparable with melody.[102] Armstrong remarked earlier that "it can hardly be fortuitous that some birds do sing and transpose in accordance with our musical scale."[103] An important series of experiments bearing on this point was carried out by Reinert with jackdaws (*Corvus monedula*).[104] After being conditioned to distinguish certain rhythmic acoustic signals, the jackdaws were able to identify them even when played by different instruments, that is, with a different timbre, or when the tempo, pitch, or interval are transposed. They could also distinguish between two-four time and three-four time. The birds could perceive acoustical patterns differing in intensity and duration of tone, and recognized a great many variations. In sum, they did not depend on absolute clues only but, as we ourselves do in the perception of phonemes, on relative ones. Ultimately, I suppose, this is a mathematical matter, and eventually Nelson, in fact, undertook a sophisticated quantitative comparative study of this kind, showing similarities of structuring in several taxa, including behavioral organization in bird and man, with respect to acoustic signals.[105]

Many birds, moreover, possess the ability to follow a train of changing pitches, as a scale, and to distinguish it from another train proceeding simultaneously but at a different speed or in a different direction. In other words, these birds appear to have solved what Cherry had designated in man as the "cocktail party problem,"[106] the essence of which I take to consist of the capacity to select one particular acoustic string, viz., a tune, out from its accompaniment or to distinguish it from another string proceeding at the same time (polyphony). A single individual veery (*Hylocichla fuscescens*) is, for example, able to produce complex polyphonic patternings; nor need there be, in this species, an interval between primary patterns, although it may be present in one voice but not in the other. "At the end of most songs, the two voices come together to cooperate in a characteristic extended trill of *overlapping arpeggios* (song *A*); sometimes this 'cadence' appears to be left to the lower voice alone (song *B*)."[107] Thorpe, on the basis of his distinguished fieldwork, supplemented by laboratory studies, has clearly confirmed the existence of "something like musical appreciation, albeit on an elementary scale, existing in a good many birds,"[108] derived, in part, from discoveries of antiphonal singing, especially in the compulsively duetting African shrike (*Laniarius aethiopicus*).[109] The notes of the duet constitute polyphonic singing, such that the pitch, timing, and phrasing can, to a large extent, be controlled very exactly, but can also be varied by the singers. Either sex can start and the other finish, either bird can sing the whole pattern alone if the partner is absent, and, when the partner returns, the two birds can either duplicate in perfect time or resume antiphonal singing.

The organized singing patterns of birds have long attracted our attention. In some, the singing is organized to conform with strict sequencing rules; the structure is hierarchical, the levels comparable with the build-up of the human mode of vocal display. Ethologists tend to interpret bird song in terms of the adaptive advantages it confers on the performers and their conspecific audience, while keeping an open mind on the ramifying consequences of the display, which may well surpass a single function and come to encompass the aesthetic dimension. To summarize: "That birds 'sing' is a notion applied popularly to vocal performances that people find aesthetically pleasing, but singing lacks a fully accepted and rigorous descriptive meaning in ethology."[110]

The ornithomusicological hypothesis becomes muddled when one considers that other animals than birds have variously been alleged to "sing": "Cicadas [i.e., locusts] are noisy, daytime musicians, the male alone singing. The sound is produced by snapping a special structure, the tymbal, with a muscle."[111] As with birds, singing is emulative, and this, as Darwin had noted, sometimes gives rise to antiphonic duets or trios.[112] This application of "song" is, however, likely to be metaphorical just like "dance" is in application to the honeybee. Then there is the California singing fish (*Porichthys notatus*), whose song, which varies in tone pitch and quality from specimen to specimen, produced under conditions of colonial activity, was carefully described by Greene.[113] The striking vocalizations of frogs and toads have also been termed "songs,"[114] often in reference to the existence of duetting throughout some nineteen genera, or more complex chorusing behavior, the biological function of which has hitherto eluded all investigators. The bellow of the alligator, assumed to convey an assertion of dominance and a challenge to other males within earshot, is likewise often called "song" in the reptile literature. I personally doubt if phenomena of this sort can be considered as prefigurements in any interesting sense. However, there are at least two groups of mammals in which singing has been reported, and these may be worthier of our regard.

First, there is the case of the humpback whale (*Megaptera novaengliae*), a species whose phonograph recordings have received considerable publicity in the media and on at least American college campuses during this decade; (George Crumb's exotic composition, "Vox Balaenae For Three Masked Players," was directly inspired by the voice of the whale). Mysticete sounds have for some decades been recognized to be varied and complex, but the humpback is the baleen whose rich sonic repertoire has been most thoroughly studied so far.[115] The animals certainly "emit a series of surprisingly beautiful sounds,"[116] including a long train, called a "song," that recurs in cycles lasting up to 30 minutes and perhaps longer. This song is often produced in continuous soliloquy, very loudly, by a single whale for a full eight minutes; there is no evidence of duetting. But its purpose is not really understood; "we can only guess what function this remarkable series of vocalizations serves."[117] This being so, no one can yet say whether the performance has, for the whale—in contrast to the human listener—any sort of aesthetic significance, and thus whether the designation "song" is biologically justified.

The climactic question whether song-like behavior has been observed in the order of Primates can be answered affirmatively, but, among the monkeys, it seems, only for some platyrrhine (New World) species, notably, *Callicebus moloch* (titi monkey). In the case of this monkey, Moynihan applies the term song "in a very broad and general sense, to include all series of notes uttered in more or less rapid and regular succession and distinctly set off, by relatively long pauses, from both preceding and succeeding notes."[118] Moynihan characterizes such passages as only moderately rapid throughout all or most of their length, and these he calls "ordinary" songs. He describes four or more other types and calls these "compound" songs. Among the ordinary songs, he identifies nineteen, but says that this list is certainly not exhaustive. He terms two of the most common compound sequences "full" songs; in these, the normal sequence of pitch is from higher to lower, irrespective of the actual notes involved.

In general, the vocalizations of catarrhine (Old World) monkeys, and especially those of tailless apes, deserve much closer study. Marler and Tenaza have recently stressed that "a comprehensive acoustical description" of the chimpanzee—which has been studied far more than any other ape—

"has yet to be published."[119] With respect to singing behavior, the gibbon may be the most interesting animal of all: as long ago as the 1890s, Blanford, a well-known authority on South Asian mammals, wrote about the hoolock (a species of gibbon found in Assam and Upper Burma), that its powerful voice, at a distance, "much resembles the human voice; [its song] is a peculiar wailing note, audible afar, and . . . one of the most familiar forest sounds. The calls commence at daybreak, . . . several of the flock joining in the cry, like hounds giving tongue . . . . [They] remain silent throughout the middle of the day, but recommence calling towards evening, though to a less extent than in the earlier part of the day."[120] This is an example of the diurnal rhythm that so frequently characterizes song displays. The same term, "song," is also used for the hoolock and several other varieties of gibbon by Marler and Tenaza, who distinguish three kinds of choruses based upon the sex of the singers: those consisting entirely of males singing; those consisting entirely of females singing; and those consisting of duets sung by mated pairs of gibbons.[121] They describe individuals engaged in dyadic countersinging with adjacent neighbors in several species. Predawn chorusing occurs very frequently, with choruses beginning as early as five hours before sunrise. This separates them temporally from dawn bird choruses, and it is assumed that the timing is an evolutionary consequence of interspecific competition for the auditory environment. "Captivity seems to have no effect upon the song structure or the nature of duetting in gibbons," according to these authors.[122] In conclusion, Marler and Tenaza supply a long list of unanswered questions about pongid signaling behavior, insisting that, "Above all, new approaches should be sought to characterize the *functions* of different vocalizations, so that more subtle interspecies comparisons of the proportions of a signal repertoire devoted to different kinds of adaptive tasks may be possible."[123] Considering, therefore, the uncertain state of knowledge about the biological uses of what is nevertheless persistently called "song" in the alloprimates, it seems premature to probe for its aesthetic function, if any.

In concluding this section, and before turning to the representational arts, I should mention that there are birds, among some sixty species of the family *Pipridae,* that *both* sing *and* dance, each species according to its own ritual. Even the earliest explorers of South and Central America noticed them because of their unique dances and the music connected with these dances, as in this entrancing description by Nutting (in 1884): "Upon a bare branch which overhung the trail at a distance of about four feet from the ground, two male 'Bailadors' were engaged in a 'song and dance' act that simply astounded me. The two birds were about a foot and a half apart, and were alternately jumping about two feet into the air and alighting exactly upon the spot whence they jumped. The time was as regular as clock-work, one bird jumping up the instant the other alighted, each bird accompanying himself to the tune of 'to-lé-do—to-lé-do—to-lé-do,' sounding the syllable 'to' as he crouched to spring, 'lé' while in the air, and 'do' as he alighted."[124] In Costa Rica, where this enchanting bird is known as *el toledo,* people tell the same story in almost exactly the same words while alternately raising each index finger to illustrate the quaintness of the performance. The bird is technically known as *Chiroxiphia linearis* (one of the four so-called Chorus species), or the Long-tailed Manakin, whose antics were recently described, with some variations, anew by Slud.[125] All observers agree that the males do dance and that the *tolédo* call is a constant accompanying feature, although their views differ as to some other details.

3. Pictorial signs.

You have already been introduced above to bowerbirds, a group about whose "artistic" productions no less a scientist than Karl von Frisch has said that it has "much similarity with human behavior in comparable situations: those who consider life on earth to be the result of a long evolutionary process will always search for the beginnings of thought processes and aesthetic feelings in animals, and I believe that significant traces can be found in the bowerbirds."[126] He goes on to quote a wondrous observation by the naturalist Heinz Sielmann about the decorating behavior of a New Guinea species, the Yellow breasted bowerbird (*Chlamydera lauterbachi*): "Every time the bird returns from one of his collecting forays, he studies the over-all color effect. He seems to wonder how he could improve on it and at once sets out to do so. He picks up a flower in his beak, places it into the mosaic, and retreats to an optimum viewing distance. He behaves exactly like a painter critically reviewing his own canvas. He paints with flowers; that is the only way I can put it. A yellow orchid does not seem to him to be in the right place. He moves it slightly to the left and puts it between some blue flowers. With his head on one side he then contemplates the general effect once more, and seems satisfied."[127] Even though Marshall, who, after more than two decades of study, became the foremost authority on bowerbirds, had indicated, or tried to, a utilitarian basis for all such seemingly artistic manifestations, he summed up his findings thus: ". . . I see no reason, provisionally, to deny that bower-birds possess an aesthetic sense although, it must be emphasized, we have as yet no concrete proof that such is the case. Some bowerbirds certainly select for their displays objects that are beautiful to *us*. Further, they discard flowers when they fade, fruit when it decays, and feathers when they become bedraggled and discoloured. . . . The fact that some bower-birds select objects that appeal to man's sense of beauty is no proof that such articles have a similar effect on the bird. If all bower-birds made collections of bleached bones, less would be written of aestheticism. Yet nobody would suggest that its pile of dry bones and dead snail-shells is less beautiful to [the Great Gray bowerbird] than is the 'beautiful' array of blue and red berries to [the Yellow-breasted variety]. It would, of course, be unthinkable to suggest that bowerbirds—or any birds for that matter—do not get pleasure from the vocal, architectural, and other activities they perform but whether such pleasure has much in common with that of Man, engaged in comparable pursuits, has yet to be proved."[128] At any rate, a scientist of the stature of Haldane was convinced that "a few animals, such as bowerbirds, show *sundaradharma,* behaviour satisfying aesthetic needs. This is most marked in the bowerbirds . . ."[129] Nor does it seem surprising, in the light of conclusions such as this, that Odoardo Beccari, the first naturalist to discover the display of a bowerbird, should have believed that he had stumbled upon a playhouse built by native children!

Over and over, we keep encountering the same pivotal aesthetic paradox: this emerges from a profound confusion about purpose; it drives us to compulsively ferret out any semblance of utility, usually defined as adaptive value.[130] We find it difficult to conceive of art as a coherent part of animal life and can scarcely imagine it as an adornment of their leisure. All researches in this field are stamped by a tension between a deeply felt conviction on the part of many distinguished and sensitive biologists that artistic activity indeed exists in the animal world and the inability to face its presumed lack of importance, even uselessness. More generally, Jenkins has argued that the position assigned to the aesthetic life in Western culture, from Plato onwards, is imbued by an uneasy fluctuation between these two attitudes, "that art is at once useless and fraught with significance, purposeless and yet important."[131] The two poles Jenkins speaks of are perhaps reconciled in a casual comment of Vygotsky's: "Apparently the possibility of releasing into art powerful passions which cannot find expression in normal everyday life is the biological basis of art."[132] Viewed thus, art becomes a kind of cybernetic device for keeping the organisms' *milieu intérieur,* or, to use Uexküll's corresponding concept, *Innenwelt,*[133] in balance with its surroundings (*milieu extérieur,* or *Umwelt*).

Art, in this homeostatic sense, is surely recognizable in many other biological systems than man. Birds that construct elaborate nests, such as the weavers, build improved nests in their second season, after having practiced during the previous one, now opting for habitations which are "better" in the sense of tidier, neater, more elegant, but not at all demonstrably more useful. One may well ask with the late Waddington, "is it then or is it not an aesthetic 'better'?" Spiders will repair damage made to their webs, but "it is debatable whether this repair is governed solely by utilitarian consideration." The webs of certain drunken or drugged spiders appear both, one assumes, to them, and certainly to us, very unappealing. And chimpanzees and gorillas, when offered the materials used by human artists, "which are obviously exceedingly unnatural and exotic in relation to a normal primate life, produce paintings and drawings in which some aesthetic qualities may perhaps be discernible."[134] This is the topic of a recent overview article by Whiten, himself a practicing painter.[135] Before, however, turning to ape aesthetics, I should at least mention Dücker's interesting work on color preferences of forty-two specimens of birds of different families, in eleven species, especially spotted weaver finches.[136] Animals have an innate positive and/or negative feeling-tone for particular colors or patterns; commonly this is related to species-characteristic signs that serve as releasers triggering their responses to each other.

Schiller's study of more than 200 of Alpha's drawings was a landmark among researches of visual composition in apes.[137] Her drawings, Schiller found, in no case yielded representations. He compared them, in this respect, to scribblings of the human infant from twelve to eighteen months. Nor did he find any evidence of imitative drawing.

Morris discusses the results obtained with Alpha, and compares them with those of his mascot Congo, the second ape artist to be studied in depth.[138] Congo's responses were found to be comparable, when given like tests, with those of Alpha; similar behavior has also been observed in other great apes, and in a capuchin monkey who drew lines on the floor of his cage when he was presented with color chalks.[139] Several gorillas, from Rotterdam and Basel to Palo Alto, have been known to draw and paint very successfully, as have occasional orangutans. In the mid-1950s, an ape known as Baltimore Betsy became famous from her fingerpaintings. Her work, and those of two other apes, were shown, without identification, to child psychiatrists. "One of the psychiatrists interpreted them as coming from an aggressive seven- or eight-year-old boy who had paranoid tendencies. Baltimore Betsy's drawings were said to be from a fiercely belligerent ten-year-old schizoid girl. A second picture by the same animal was also said to be by a ten-year-old girl who was paranoid and showed a strong father identification."[140] Eventually, twelve paintings by Betsy as well as twenty-four Congos were exhibited—and practically all sold—in London. Julian Huxley, who had opened the exhibition, later made the following comments: "The results show conclusively that chimpanzees do have artistic potentialities which can be brought to light by providing suitable opportunities. One of the great mysteries of human evolution is the sudden outburst of art of a very high quality in the upper Paleolithic period. This becomes more comprehensible if our apelike ancestors had these primitive aesthetic potentialities, to which was later added man's unique capacity for symbol-making."[141]

Morris recapitulates in his justly famous book half a century's picture-making with twenty-three chimpanzees, two gorillas, three orangutans and four capuchin monkeys. Alpha and Congo, who produced some 600 pictures in all, were studied most intensively. The principle that Morris stresses and elaborates is the fact that painting involves actions which are self-rewarding activities, that is, they "are performed for their own sake rather than to attain some basic biological goal. They are 'activities for activities' sake,' so to speak."[142] In human art, this sort of motivation has appeared in many guises. Jenkins' roll-call includes such celebrated aesthetic doctrines as "detachment, catharsis or purgation, isolation, objectification, emotion remembered in tranquility, psychic distance, self-surrender, passivity, pure perception, will-less knowing, reposefulness, equilibrium, synthesis, impersonalness, contemplativeness, empathy, pleasure objectified, disinterested pleasure, receptivity," and many others echoing the same meaning.[143] For Morris, the category of self-rewarding activities is essentially biological, of course: "Most of them are basically physical, meteoric outbursts and are fundamentally similar to human gymnastics and sports, except that they lack any ulterior motives such as the obtaining of health, money, or social standing. They may inadvertently keep the animal mentally and physically healthy and thus indirectly assist in its struggle for survival, but the actual driving force behind these self-rewarding activities appears to be simply the unleashing of surplus nervous energy."[144] This immediately suggests a central question: why, if they have such a strong picture-making potential, have apes neither developed nor utilized it in the wild? This question corresponds closely to a second one, far more widely debated these days: why if, as alleged, apes have the cognitive prerequisites for the acquisition of language competency haven't they elaborated it in nature? No satisfactory answer to the latter question has been put forward thus far; even the rankest activist hasn't proposed that they have done so, outside of science fiction of the likes of Jules Verne and on the planet of the apes. Morris' answer to the former rests on his claim that, as soon as man "had a real language which described objects as well as moods, the gateway was open to the pictorial representation of these objects,"[145] or, in other words, that the emergence of this averbal art required the antecedence of verbal signs. This suggestion may appear likely to some, although I personally doubt it and, in any case, it is entirely speculative.[146] More to the point, it sheds no light at all on the previous conundrum. The holistic interpretation of pictures is a function of the right hemisphere, an operation normally exercised in conjunction with the left hemisphere; but the minor hemisphere, which seems specialized for dealing with things all at once, has an extremely limited verbal capacity, even though its performance is said by Eccles to be "superior to that of the brains of the highest anthropoids,"[147] while the dominant hemisphere, which tends to deal with things in sequence, is "almost illiterate in respect to pictorial and pattern sense."[148]

Morris adduces five further biological principles of picture making beside the basic one, that the accomplishment is in and of itself rewarding. His second principle is that of compositional control, the power of which is illustrated by Alpha's and Congo's adherence to the simple rules of filling a space and keeping within it, balancing, and cadenced repetition. This was previously evidenced from Rensch's investigations with a capuchin and a guenon monkey, and found, as well, in jackdaws and crows. As Morris notes, the vital words here are: "steadiness—symmetry—repetition—rhythm."[149] His third principle, "calligraphic differentiation," is a developmental one, referring to a slow progress of pictorial growth, which, however, is less strikingly exhibited by apes than by children. It is closely related to the fourth principle, thematic variation, or, as we might say in semiotics, the concept of invariance with allowable reformulations.

Whiten rightly regards the last two principles—which the proponent himself had put forward merely as a working hypothesis—of dubious status: "optimum heterogeneity," Morris suggests, governs the composition and point of completion of each picture, meaning by this the stage at which the picture is considered to be finished. Congo, it seems, had a very distinct concept of when a drawing or painting of his came to an end. By contrast, Alpha continued to cover the whole sheet with scribble if the paper was not removed. "Universal imagery" is what gives ape pictures as a whole a recognizable character, Morris finally maintains, but the only image which seems to recur with any regularity (also in capuchin art) is the "fan."

Whiten moves beyond the problems of artistic creation[150] that had preoccupied Morris to those of aesthetic appreciation, relying in the main on several papers by Humphrey.[151] Humphrey's initial series of tests was designed to determine if monkeys had favorite colors and preferences for certain brightnesses. The four monkeys tested for color gave the same result: the order of preference in each case was blue, green, yellow, orange, and red. Brightness preference, which was tested by pairing the standard white slide with white slides of differing brightnesses, turned out to be monotonically related to brightness over the range used.

Next, Humphrey tested preferences for pictures, using thirty colored photographs classified as "men" (e.g., a portrait of the keeper), "monkeys" (two infants playing), "other animals" (cow), "foods" (banana), "flower" (daisy), "abstract painting" (a Mondrian). This order of preference turned out to be: other animals/monkeys/men/flowers/paintings/food.

One may well ask, with Whiten, "whether such preferences have anything at all to do with aesthetics."[152] Humphrey posits two different patterns which reflect a dichotomy as to the ways both we and monkeys may exploit our senses: we may, he affirms, look at a stimulus "purely for pleasure" or "purely for interest." The pleasure dimension, corresponding to a pure aesthetic, can be either positive or negative, but is little affected by novelty, whereas the curiosity dimension is positive and changes only toward indifference as the novelty of the stimulus wanes. In Humphrey's view, the two types of responses operate quite independently, although they often coalesce as to timing, in which case their combined effects will yield a summative expression of preference. Humphrey resumes his findings in five simple principles, to wit:

1. Two independent kinds of relationship obtain between the monkey and the stimulus, called 'interest' and 'pleasure/unpleasure.'

2. When there is a choice between two stimuli, the monkey ranks them according to their relative interestingness and relative pleasantness.

3. If one stimulus is 'appreciably more interesting' than the other, the probability that the monkey will prefer it is 1.

4. If one stimulus is 'appreciably more pleasant' than the other, the probability that he will prefer it is 1 unless the other stimulus is appreciably more interesting.

5. If neither stimulus is either appreciably more interesting or pleasant, the probability that he will prefer each is 1/2.

Unfortunately, these principles were derived from monkeys, not apes, but Humphrey was able to predict from his quantitative model with a high degree of accuracy preferences for a stimulus which combined the two distinctive features of interest and pleasure. Visual feedback, we may safely surmise, is an important part of painting for apes, but we can't be sure—and the question still abides why their desire to create visual art remains latent, to surface, if at all, only in captivity, whether spontaneously or under instigation.

Another puzzle which continues to perplex has been well posed by Whiten, who wonders, "why has nature equipped the chimp and the human with such ability? The interest or curiosity dimension of art can be seen as an offshoot, functionless in terms of survival value . . . But if a pure aesthetic sense is a functional offshoot of some other functional attribute, what is this?"[153] Humphrey has wrestled with this difficult question himself, and I find this animal behaviorist's suggestions particularly intriguing because he believes, as I do, "that a structuralist approach is the key to the science of aesthetics,"[154] and because he has so fruitfully employed semiotic concepts. Like Lévi-Strauss's, whom he cites, his starting point is a conceptualization of an artistic product as a system of signs, but from this obvious notion he goes on to ask how such works acquire their artistic charge. The answer he proposes is that, "considered as a biological phenomenon, aesthetic preferences stem from a predisposition among animals and men to seek out experiences through which they may *learn to classify* the objects in the world about them. Beautiful 'structures' in nature or in art are those which facilitate the task of classification by presenting evidence of the 'taxonomic' relations between things in a way which is informative and easy to grasp."[155] This argument, of course, presupposes that the capacity for effective classification is important for survival, perhaps on a par with eating and sex. If so, techniques of classification were bound to evolve so as to be a source of pleasure to the animal and thus to shape the nonrandom differential reproduction of its genes (natural selection). After all, as Humphrey remarks, both animals and men can be relied on to do best what they most enjoy doing. This point of view, coupled with the idea that no work of art is arbitrary, suggests where an animal's feeling of beauty may come from. In the terminology of René Thom, "the work of art acts like the germ of a virtual catastrophe in the mind of the beholder." In other words, although art is always unpredictable, "it appears to us to have been directed by some organizing center of large codimension, far from the normal structures of ordinary thought, but still in resonance with the main emotional or genetic structures underlying our conscious thought."[156]

Humphrey carries his taxonomic metaphor much farther, enriching it with the notion of rhyming, or, as I would prefer to denominate the phenomenon more generally, parallelism. He brings experimental evidence to bear from a rich array of studies of exploratory behavior, and from his own investigations of "stimulus novelty" in monkeys. Parallelism involves the psychological notion of "stimulus discrepancy," or, what in the early 1950's was called "discrepancy theory," ugly coinages for a fundamental concept with wide applications in the animal world and among human babies.

The propensity to classify seems to have acquired, through evolution, diminishing survival value, but then so did sex: humans can enjoy either, but most *tokens,* though pleasurable per se, are not biologically relevant. Only the *type* of activity has a clearcut biological function.

Finally, let it be noted that Humphrey's pleasure principle seems equivalent to Morris's principle of composition. Pleasure, more likely than curiosity, tends to motivate compositional control, but the reverse holds for calligraphic differentiation and thematic variation. To some extent, all of these principles are likely to involve both types of preferences; these components, acting together, may manifest themselves in a principle of optimum heterogeneity. The prefigurements of visual art in our species can thus be understood a little better against its simian backgrounds. This should surprise no one who is even superficially acquainted with D'Arcy Thompson's classic book, *On Growth and Form*,[157] where this great zoologist, so far ahead of his time, dealt with the basis for beauty in numberless exquisite structures produced by the plant and animal worlds, and showed that it is possible to construct an abstract, purely geometrical theory of morphogenesis, independent of the substrate of forms and the nature of the forces that create them.[158]

4. Architectural signs.

"A building is not only an object but also a sign," Bogatyrev noted in 1936,[159] and Jakobson later elaborated on this dictum by stressing that "[a]ny edifice is simultaneously some sort of refuge and a certain kind of message."[160] The utility—i.e., technological interest—of different architectural configurations is thus generally taken for granted. What remains in question is their correlation with the corresponding universe of signifieds, in particular as regards its aesthetic dimension, and the direction of the artistic movement: is it from external form, considered as a signifier, toward internal organization, which becomes the signified, or is it the converse? The architectural work of art, everyone seems to agree, is devoted to the realization of several ends. It stands at the confluence of multiple interests. Its character is syncretic *par excellence*.

In looking at the endlessly manifold abodes constructed by animals—that serve perhaps to trap prey, to protect or comfort the architect or its kind, especially the young, or to attract the attention of a potential mate—we must look for the artistic value that may be involved, although subordinated to the principal interest of the "survival machine," as Dawkins calls the temporary receptacles housing the colony of genes inhabiting every plant and animal.[161] If there is such a subsidiary purpose, falling passively under the sway of "mere" biological advantage, or supplementing it, an effort must be made to ferret out this aesthetic component. Such a quest is far from trivial, for, in the end, it is tantamount to asking: what is art?

The sources for the materials utilized by animals to erect their dwellings are twofold: either the substances are produced from within their own body, or they are assembled from the environment surrounding them. In the latter case, members of some species may exhibit subtle preferences, which may justly be termed aesthetic, in their very selection of particular habitats. Indeed, Klopfer even supposes that "the most convincing evidence for the existence of esthetic preferences come from the literature on habitat selection . . ."[162] This discerning ethologist has consistently allowed for constraints due to psychological factors, the most intriguing cases of which are posed by those situations in which the preferences cannot be related to physical abilities, "as when a particular color of flower or shape of leaf or complex of factors is preferred to any other."[163] It is difficult enough to isolate the relevant feature of a complex *Gestalt;* to provide an explanation for the underlying sensory or neural basis for preferences that are termed aesthetic remains generally a difficult research problem for the future.

In the process of building, animals employ essentially the same techniques that we do: digging, masonry, plaiting, weaving, and so on. For Vitruvius —the failed Augustinian architect and engineer later turned influential writer—the universal *homo faber* was the architect, to whom the Romans assigned the art of building as well as the craft of fabricating machinery (i.e., secondary tools).[164] Vitruvius, in spelling out what architecture is, maintained that "two considerations must be constantly kept in view" in the execution of his art and craft, "namely, the intention, and the matter used to express that intention. . . ."[165] Whatever one's opinion may be about the intrusion of intention, volitional control, or, more broadly, of teleological considerations, into the domain of semiotics,[166] there can scarcely be any doubt that man fully shares the second attribute mentioned by Vitruvius with the speechless creatures.

In respect to the concept of *animal laborans,* the animal "which labors and 'mixes with'," or "which with its body . . . nourishes life," but which "still remains the servant of nature and the earth,"[167] it is, in truth, hard to perceive essential differences among the species. Such discriminations as may exist must be sought in Arendt's redefined and refined view of the classic *homo faber,* an anthropocentrically utilitarian figure she nonetheless so insistently, although eloquently, opposed to *animal laborans—homo faber,* "who makes and literally 'works upon'," whose production is tantamount to what she calls reification, the creation, that is, of a uniquely human world in the face of nature. Only *homo faber,* she claims, "conducts himself as lord and master of the whole earth."[168] For her, *homo faber,* "in his highest capacity," assumes, of course, the functions "of the artist, of poets and historiographers, of monument-builders or writers, because without them the only product of their activity, the story they enact and tell, would not survive at all."[169] This bleak and in the end still narrowly parochial view implies that none of the works of nature, which manifestly come into being without man's intervention, let alone his midwifery, can have aesthetic or even economic value. As Karl Marx has put the same idea in *Das Kapital:* "Der Wasserfall, wie die Erde überhaupt, wie alle Naturkraft hat keinen Wert, weil er keine in ihm vergegenständlichte Arbeit darstellt."[170] This attitude to nature and to natural productions degrades objects into means, where animals are always presumed to be building something not for its own sake but for the sake of instrumentality, or expediency toward the realization of some putative biological end. The absurdity of this Sophistic devaluation of nature was despised by many Greeks, as Arendt noted,[171] and its inherent anthropocentrism perhaps most persuasively resolved in Plato's celebrated argument against Protagoras, whose subjective idealism fails to accord, as I have tried to show elsewhere,[172] with the most elementary lessons of the modern life science.

The field of "natural architecture" is exceptionally fortunate in that there exists a splendid recent book devoted to that subject in its entirety ranging from the invertebrates, particularly the arthropods, to the birds and on to the highest mammals, inclusive of apes. This compendium, which requires no specialized knowledge for its enjoyment, was written by Karl von Frisch,[173] in collaboration with his son, Otto. It bore the original title, *Tiere als Baumeister*—which translates into "Animals as Master Builders" —both more powerful and more suggestive, as well as less overburdened or presumptuous, than the English rendering on the title page.[174]

The architectural activity of animals is best regarded as a manifestation of tool-using behavior—a sophisticated way of manipulating objects and exploring their uses to adaptive advantage. According to Frisch, the use of tools that are not parts of their bodies is rare among animals: "They mostly use the organs of their bodies, chiefly their mouth parts and their legs."[175] Rare though the use of extrinsic artifacts may be over-all, statistically speaking, newly discovered instances continue to be published. A case in point is a learned behavioral sequence recently detected in Northern blue jays (*Cyanocitta cristata*), which involves tool-making, to wit, by the tearing and alteration of pages from a newspaper, and employing these as tools to rake in food pellets which otherwise lay out of reach.[176]

Even the larva of the green lacewing (*Chrysopa slossonae*) uses a tool in the climax of a complicated sequence that has been inelegantly dubbed "trash-carrying behavior."[177] This insect form disguises itself as, i.e., mimics, its own prey by plucking some of the waxy "wool" from the bodies of the alder aphids amidst colonies of which it lives and feeds, and then applies this material to its own back. The exogenous shield thus constructed protects the larva from assault by the ants that ordinarily "shepherd" the aphids.

Some social insects, notably, several species of *Aphaenogaster*—none of which are mentioned by Frisch, despite the relatively large amount of space he otherwise devotes to the constructions of eusocial insects[178]—use pieces of leaf, mud, and sand grains as tools for carrying soft foods from distant sources to the colony, a maximally efficient way of exploiting available resources.[179]

I recite these random examples of recently uncovered cases of tool-using activity to adumbrate my hunch that such forms of behavior anticipate the more advanced forms of animals' building activities. In ethological jargon, the question becomes: how does tool-using behavior become ritualized?[180] Or, in semiotic parlance: how does a tool, with a primary amplifying function, acquire a superimposed sign-function?[181] The answer to this question, at this stage in the development of both ethology and diachronic semiotics, is precisely the same as to the deceptively innocent one, "What passes in the mind of a bowerbird when he builds and decorates his bower?" Frisch replies, "Naturally, I cannot answer [my own] question. No one can." His denial notwithstanding, Frisch proceeds to declare his conviction that in these birds, no less than in chimpanzees, "not only insight into the consequences of their actions but also evidence of aesthetic feelings can be found."[182]

No purpose would be served by rehearsing here even a sampling from among the host of striking examples of exterior and interior designs masterfully adduced by Frisch. The multitalented bowerbirds figure prominently, as does a large variety of other kinds of birds, including those consummate nestbuilders, the weavers, and especially *Malimbus cassini,* noted for the care and precision of the working male, reminiscent in his technique of a human basket weaver or one with a loom. Among the many mammals whose imposing labors are illustrated, the impressively productive accomplishments of the beaver (*Castor fiber,* or the American kind, *C. canadensis*), however, do deserve to be singled out. The fantastic edifices of this "architectural mute"—the evocative epithet was coined, in 1868, by Lewis H. Morgan[183]—are exemplified by the construction of dams, lodges, burrows, and canals. The opinion that "there is no other animal that can by its labor transform the landscape in the same way as can the beaver and man"[184] is shared by all informed observers. This pre-eminent master builder, particularly busy in the mountains, checks turbulent brooks and, with its dams, protects the fields and pastures below from becoming silted up with sand and gravel. The artificial reservoirs thus created are soon stocked with trout and other fishes, and turned into a refuge for water birds. The very magnitude of some beaver projects is stupefying—the largest dam is that on the Jefferson River, near Three Forks, Montana: one can follow it for some 2,300 feet. Although the beavers' basic engineering skills are innate—"the principles of their art are theirs by inheritance"[185] —their brain is exceptionally well-developed in comparison with that of other rodents, and their correspondingly superior adaptability to changing ecological situations is emphasized by knowledgeable ethologists. Morgan even felt "at liberty to infer an intention on the part of the beaver,"[186] and others believe that beavers profit from example or experience.

By contrast, there is nothing remarkable about the building activities of the Great Apes. Adult chimpanzees, in some regions, are known to fashion fresh nests up in the trees nightly, as do orangutans and gorillas, although heavy males among the latter tend to sleep on the ground. Köhler's experiments with chimpanzees that solve the problem of getting fruit situated beyond the reach of their arms by manufacturing a suitable tool for bridging the distance from themselves to the food—by fitting two bamboo rods together, for instance, or by erecting a tower from packing cases—are widely known, although his interpretation is still debated. While the actions of Köhler's chimpanzees were portrayed as conveying an impression of deliberation and purpose, the animals seem to have but a very modest sense of either statics or balance.[188] Some never managed to solve the problem at all.

The penumbra of an absorbing lifelong research commitment is delineated in two arresting sentences at the end of Frisch's study: "The evolutionary roots of human behavior reach far back into the behavior patterns of animals. Those who are fascinated by these connections need only fasten on one such puzzle, the architecture of animals perhaps. . . ."[189] The prefigurements of architecture, however, are but one detail in the mosaic of the much vaster, much deeper, mystery of the precultural emergence of the averbal arts.

5. Concluding remarks.

At the outset of this essay, I drew a sharp distinction between the verbal art and the averbal arts, proclaiming my conviction that, while it seems unavailing to search for the prefigurements of language-based sign systems, a scrutiny of the roots of the four other semiotic spheres discussed might prove illuminating. Differences in the neurological processing of verbal vs. averbal patterns of input and output are solidly and rationally grounded in separate dominions of the human brain. The evolutionary antecedents are also assuming shape, although they remain blurred at the edges.

The late Bronowski wondered whether "any animal language [has] figures of speech,"[190] by which he appeared to question whether an animal ever uses the same sign-vehicle corresponding to two or more different significates. The answer to the latter must unequivocally be in the affirmative, since the context in which any gesture is delivered decisively shapes its "correct" interpretation. But Bronowski's "figures of speech," as he used the expression in his exploratory article on "Human and Animal Language," is itself merely a figure of speech—a rhetorical device of his own. It has little to do with verbal art. To be sure, it has been widely reported that the creation of signed metaphors as well as metonyms was recorded in different home-raised chimpanzees. In 1976, I recounted that both sorts of tropes were alleged to have occurred: "whereas Washoe created 'water-bird' for duck, a metonymic or indexical expression, being a sign in real reaction with the object noted . . . , Lucy generated 'candy fruit' for watermelon, a metaphoric or iconic term, possessing the qualities signified. . . ."[191] Lately, however, I—and others (e.g., Martin Gardner, personal communication)—have come to feel that such interpretations must be reviewed if not with suspicion at least with caution. Both chimpanzees were getting a steady stream of unconscious feedback from their trainers. Thus only her handler was present in the canoe when Washoe glimpsed her first duck and made a sign for "water" followed by a sign for "bird." There was no awareness of the possibility that Washoe, dragging her hand in the water, didn't sign "water," next noticed the bird, and only then signed "bird." The behavior of the trainer, who (for all we know) repeated the two signs, could easily have taught Washoe a new sign, namely, the "water-bird" sign which she would associate from then on with ducks. The circumstances were, *mutatis mutandis,* similarly indeterminate for Lucy's "candy fruit," "cry fruit" (for onion) and for every other such case that I am aware of. All of these are subject to other, less portentous, construals, the simplest among which is the pervasive emission of subthreshold involuntary cuing of the destination by the source, or the "Clever Hans" experience.[192] In sum, there is no hard evidence whatsoever for the existence of figures of speech, in the literal sense, among the speechless creatures—a prototypal *contradictio in adjecto!*

A second leitmotif of my article skirted the profound problem of aesthetic significance—particularly in opposition to or juxtaposition with utility—viz., purposiveness of directedness, tantamount, in some contexts, to the Aristotelian art of *chrēmastistikē*, or the amassment of wealth with no limit in respect of its end, but in this context simply to the preservation and improvement of the gene pool, or the long-term environment of the gene. The question whether animals are endowed with "consciousness" has remained wide open,[193] being no doubt poorly posed, but many distinguished life scientists concur that some animals on some occasions behave toward some objects *as if* the organisms were motivated by a recognizably aesthetic incentive. This much is clarion clear, for instance, as regards the bowerbirds.

The essence of the aesthetic impulse surely lies in the structures organisms extract and reconstruct from among salient features of their environment. Albrecht Dürer, among a host of commentators, believed this to be so; according to him, "Denn wahrhaftig steckt die Kunst in der Natur, wer sie heraus kann reissen, der hat sie."[194] Others make a separation between natural or organic beauty and artificial or aesthetic beauty, contrasting the realm of living things with that of "living" forms. But the two are obviously bonded, since all the percipients themselves are a part of nature. The spectacles through which we see the world are partly an apparatus for bringing into focus certain aspects of our existence (*Umwelt*), but they are, at the same time, a means for relating harmoniously varied facets of the universe to each other. To paraphrase a saying of Henri Poincaré, aesthetic sensibility plays the part of a delicate sieve. The challenge, of course, is to explicitly define what those relations—of balance and order that delight—are in the characteristic idiom of each art, as well as in the all-embracing architectonics of the living megacosm. The concept of delight thus undergoes a radical transmutation: it is elevated into a function that biologists can recognize, objectify, cope with in familiar terms. The "artistic animal" is not defined by a heightened sensitivity to movement,

sound, color, shape, but by its innate and/or learned capacity to elicit a
stable dynamic structure from the fluid environment, whether inorganic,
organic, or a subtle blend of both. The sign systems thus created, which
serve an underlying semantic function, take in time an aesthetic turn. How
this happens is magisterially brought out in an 1865 Platonic dialogue on
the origin of beauty that Gerard Manley Hopkins had composed for his
tutor at Oxford.

The dialogue between the Professor of the newly founded chair of
Aesthetics (no doubt Walter Pater) and a student takes place in the tranquil
setting of a college garden, and the dialectic "battledore" quickly comes to
concentrate on "one of the most finely foliaged of trees," the chestnut. The
Professor points to the leaves of the tree to illustrate the principle of symmetry, or, more generally, of the structural relations inherent in nature.
The Professor asks:

". . . now what is symmetry? Is it not regularity?"

"I should say, the greatest regularity. . . ."

"So it is. But is it not that sort of regularity which is measured by length
and breadth and thickness? Music for instance might be regular, but not
symmetrical ever; is it not so?"

"Quite so. . . ."

"Let us say regularity then."

The Professor next draws attention to the oak, "an unsymmetrical tree."

"Then beauty, you would say perhaps, is a mixture of regularity and
irregularity."

"Complex beauty, yes. But let us inquire a little further. What is regularity? Is it not obedience to law? And what is law? Does it not mean
that several things, or all the parts of one thing, are like each other?"

The Professor continues:

". . . regularity is likeness or agreement or consistency, and irregularity
is the opposite, that is difference or disagreement or change or variety."

But do these distinctions apply to all things? Beauty is certainly a relation, but *what* is this relation? The sense of beauty in fact is a comparison.
The conversation now moves on to the subject of poetry: rhythm, meter,
and rhyme.

"Now you remember I wished beauty to be considered as a regularity
or likeness tempered by irregularity or difference: the chestnut-fan was
one of my instances. In rhythm we have got the regularity, the likeness;

so my aim is, as rhythm is agreed to be beautiful, to find the disagreement, the difference in it. . . . Rhythm therefore is likeness tempered with difference. . . ."

"What is rhyme? . . . Is it not an agreement of sound—?"

"With a slight disagreement, yes. . . . In fact it seems to me rhyme is the epitome of [our] principle. All beauty may by a metaphor be called rhyme. . . ."[195]

If rhyme is taken as the poetic paradigm for beauty, consisting of comparison for likeness's sake (metaphor, simile) as well as for unlikeness's sake (antithesis, contrast), what is the convenient word which gives us the common principle for all such kinds of equations? Hopkins proffers *parallelism,* and moves on to analyze parallelism "both structural and unstructural," parallelism of expression and parallelism of sense, and finally to illustrate his dictum that "The structure of poetry is that of continuous parallelism."[196]

Now it is evident—to recapitulate briefly—that the conspicuous use of reiteration, of a statement of a theme with variations, of the creation of suspense and countervailing tension, of the arousal of expectation and its denial, in short, of parallelism, is also the pervasive pivotal device common to all manifestations of the art of animals discussed in this essay: what is criterial of their kinesthetic art is rhythmic somatic motion; at the heart of their music are "les rythmes organiques" and the transposition of fixed intervals; the cardinal substantives that characterize their picture making are "steadiness—symmetry—repetition—rhythm"; and the mark of their virtuoso architecture is surely geometrical symmetry—broken in multiform ways—that transmutes the ulterior modularity of physical reality into macroscopic projects of utility as well as beauty.

Hopkins' insight about the source of beauty was amplified by Humphrey a little over a century later. He asked: "What is the biological advantage of seeking out rhyming elements in the environment?" The answer he proposed was this: "Considered as a biological phenomenon, aesthetic preferences stem from a predisposition among animals and men to seek out experiences through which they may *learn to classify* the objects in the world about them. Beautiful 'structures' in nature or in art are those which facilitate the task of classification by presenting evidence of the 'taxonomic' relations between things in a way which is informative and easy to grasp."[197] This proposition demands a tripartite justification.

One must explain, to begin with, why the knack for classification should be important for biological survival. If the function of categorization is to sort out sensory experience—to identify, with essential economy, good, bad, and indifferent forms, or, in semiotic phrasing, to sift out the presence of such forms "endowed with signification" that trigger appropriate long-term releasers—then the evolution of efficient classificatory techniques is bound to be of survival value. Humphrey argues that "just as with eating or with sex, an activity as vital as classification was bound to evolve to be a *source of pleasure* to the animal. Both animals and men can, after all, be relied on to do best what they enjoy doing."[198]

Second, it is necessary to show why a maneuver such as Hopkins called parallelism should be optimally advantageous to the classificatory animal. It seems clear that the fundamental role of the central nervous system is precisely to provide the creature with a local map simulating its position in the environment, to enable it to sort out, among other vital intelligence, the images of biologically and/or socially important organisms, viz., to distinguish prey from predator. This is surely best accomplished by an arrangement of such images into a distinctive feature matrix, or in terms of "likeness tempered with difference." Parallelism is the organizing principle employed in many of the most successful taxonomical procedures, including the Linnaean; (more generally, it imbues set-theory). "If it is helpful for the taxonomist to look for 'rhymes' in his materials," Humphrey continues, "so it is helpful for the animal to do so. It is for this reason that we have evolved to respond to the relation of beauty which rhyme epitomises. At one level we take pleasure in the abstract structure of rhyme as a model of well-presented evidence, and at another we delight in particular examples of rhyme as sources of new insight into how things are related and divided."

The third step is to seek evidence, beyond the prevailing propensity of man and animals to classify their surroundings, for the surmise that animals also are attracted in particular to parallelism. To amass a modicum of such testimony was, in fact, the main objective of this study: to adduce instances of parallelism in the animal world that have no demonstrable natural value but which nevertheless give people as well as the animals involved something akin to aesthetic pleasure, even when the process or the product is disunited from its proper biological context.

The universal propensity to classify dictates that animals generate units of signification, or significata, by stipulating redundancies. Several arrangements are possible, such as non-dimensional (taxonomic) classification or dimensional (paradigmatic) classification, in both of which classes are formed by means of intersection.[199] When classes and sub-classes are created, they may be defined by features which are either inherent in nature as the sole feasible solution or, as in man and his tamed creatures, arrays that are arbitrary to a degree (cultural categories, individual idiosyncrasies). Yet even certain human populations may be "forced to meet nature on its own terms and to categorize those aspects of the natural environment which are relevant to it in a biologically realistic way."[200] The conception of class, whether based upon naturally imposed or arbitrarily chosen qualities, sometimes acquires a certain elegance and power elevating it beyond a mere organizational tool, and we can then say that the production carries an aesthetic charge.

Lévi-Strauss and Piaget have both been concerned with primordial questions of human classification. The inquiry of Lévi-Strauss, instigated by a linguistic model, postulates a proclivity in all of us to think in opposites and contrasts, to pry perceptual information from the environment constrained by certain predetermined structures, and to consolidate and combine these percepts in classifying, naming, and mythic systems. Through a series of ordered transformations, these systems relate themes and variations upon them that are effable, for instance, in artistic products which themselves are embodiments of mind.

Animals create a taxonomy appropriate to their species and ecological niche. Thus predators, for instance, distinguish different categories of prey—by size, appearance, odor, and other signifiers—thus forestalling wastefully indiscriminate attacks. *Vice versa,* many potential prey distinguish among different kinds of predators, as we observe from their use of sundry warning signs, variations in their flight-distances and flight-reactions, e.g., depending on whether the enemy is up in the air or down on the ground. It is less well known, however, that animals assign to one another and carry proper names,[201] which individuate each from every other. As Hediger, who devoted a perceptive and semiotically sensitive study to the use of proper names in the animal kingdom, pointed out: "Its proper name is part of its [the animal's] personality. Therefore it distinguishes between its own self and the nonself."[202] Hediger also pleads for research on the appearance of proper names in evolution, for this may "open a new door to the delicate problem of selfconsciousness in animals." Concern with naming, moreover, focuses attention on parallelism as a special case. Parallelism of this kind evokes a sort of pleasure familiar to all observers of children's behavior. Humphrey comments on this pronounced tendency in children, which is promoted, among other devices, through picture books designed especially for them. The passion for collecting, he feels, is yet another manifestation of the pleasure both mature children and men take in classification.[203] Among the animals, it is no accident that bowerbirds are among the most sedulous of collectors, each species according to its predilection. Thus the display-ground of the Great Gray "may contain an almost inconceivable accumulation of pale or reflective rubbish"—but sometimes also bright specimens of gold or pieces of precious opal—yet every bit of their harvest of treasure "is chosen with great discrimination."[204]

Piaget has demonstrated that young children are limited in performing internally consistent classificatory tasks. Shown an aggregate of diverse objects and asked to place together those that go together, the child will come up with a range of volatile groupings of phenomena that are not yoked by a simultaneous awareness of a whole and its parts, either physically or conceptually. A sense of hierarchy comes later, at a mature stage of operational intelligence; accordingly, sophisticated art usually emerges in human ontogeny as an accessory only to adult cognitive capacity. Comparisons of animal artistic productions with those by children were made as early as 1935, when Nadie Kohts juxtaposed drawings by her chimpanzee, Joni, with those by her son, Roody. She showed that early scribbles by Joni and early scribbles by Roody resembled each other greatly. However, while later drawings by Joni evidenced greater complexity but no imagery, those by Roody exhibited, in addition, mimetic qualities, to wit, the recognizable icon of a face.[205]

When Mukařovský delivered his seminal 1934 lecture, on "L'art comme fait sémiologique," he meant his study to underline and exemplify certain aspects of the dichotomy—which he never questioned—between the natural sciences and the humanities, as well as to bring out the importance of semiotic considerations for aesthetics and for the history of art.[206] Referring, in conclusion, to this programmatic paper, I should like to note the paradoxical aspect of the proposed enterprise: a consistently carried out characterization of every work of art as an autonomous sign composed of an artifact (the signifier), an aesthetic object (its signification), and an abstract, context-oriented relationship to the thing signified, tends precisely to obliterate the factitious schism it is supposed to uphold.

Notes

1. Thomas A. Sebeok, *The Sign & Its Masters* (Austin: University of Texas Press, 1979), Chapter 2.

2. Sebeok, *The Sign,* Chapter 4.

3. William R. Bascom, "Verbal Art," *Journal of American Folklore,* LXVIII (1955), p. 246, fn. 9; Richard Bauman, *Verbal Art as Performance* (Rowley, Mass.: Newbury House Publishers, 1977), pp. 4, 49, n.2.

4. George Gaylord Simpson, "The Biological Nature of Man," *Science,* CLII (1966), p. 476.

5. Thomas A. Sebeok, "Talking with the Body," *Times Literary Supplement,* January 27, 1978, p. 84.

6. Sol Tax and Charles Callender, eds., *Issues in Evolution* (Chicago: University of Chicago Press, 1960), p. 195.

7. Alexander J. Marshall, *Bower-Birds: Their Displays and Breeding Cycles* (Oxford: Clarendon Press, 1954), p. 65.

8. Gilbert R. Gannon, "Observations on the Satin Bower Bird with Regard to the Material Used by It in Painting Its Bower," *Emu* XXX (1930), p. 39.

9. Karl von Frisch, *Animal Architecture* (New York: Harcourt Brace Jovanovich, 1974), pp. 238-39.

10. Theodosius Dobzhansky, *Mankind Evolving: The Evolution of the Human Species* (New Haven: Yale University Press, 1962), p. 215.

11. Erwin Panofsky, *Meaning in the Visual Arts: Papers In and On Art History* (Garden City: Doubleday, 1955), pp. 10-11.

12. Donald R. Griffin, *The Question of Animal Awareness: Evolutionary Continuity of Mental Experience* (New York: Rockefeller University Press, 1976), p. 78.

13. Even these remarks may need to be modified in the light of such casual but expert observations as S. Dillon Ripley's (in John F. Eisenberg and Wilton S. Dillon, *Man and Beast: Comparative Social Behavior* [Washington: Smithsonian Institution Press, 1971], pp. 8-9), concerning a species of Gardner bowerbird (*Amblyornis*), in New Guinea.

14. Roland Barthes, *Mythologies* (Paris: Seuil, 1957), p. 222.

15. Jury M. Lotman, "Tezisy k probleme 'Iskusstvo v rjadu modeliruiushchikh sistem'," *Trudy po znakovym sistemam,* III (1967), pp. 180-81.

16. Karl R. Popper and John C. Eccles, *The Self and Its Brain* (Berlin: Springer, 1977), pp. 351-52.

17. Thomas A. Sebeok, ed., *How Animals Communicate* (Bloomington: Indiana University Press, 1977), p. 1070.

18. Ladislav Matejka and Irwin R. Titunik, eds., *Semiotics of Art: Prague School Contributions* (Cambridge, Mass.: MIT Press, 1976), p. 254.

19. Popper, in Popper and Eccles, p. 482.

20. Popper and Eccles, p. 353.

21. Simpson, p. 476.

22. Thomas A. Sebeok, *Contributions to the Doctrine of Signs* (Lisse: Peter de Ridder Press, 1976), pp. 155-62; and *Animals,* pp. 1063-67.

23. Thure von Uexküll, "Positionspapier über das Thema 'Semiotik der Angst'" (forthcoming).

24. Sebeok, *The Sign,* Chapter 1.

25. Cf. Hansjochem Autrum, "The Communications Network of the Human Body," in *Man and Animal: Studies in Behaviour,* ed. Heinz Friedrich (London: MacGibbon & Kee, 1972), pp. 77-81.

26. Cf. Autrum, Appendix I.

27. Gregory Bateson, "Redundancy and Coding," in: *Animal Communication: Tech-*

niques of Study and Results of Research, ed. by Thomas A. Sebeok (Bloomington: Indiana University Press, 1968), p. 615.

28. Bateson, p. 614.

29. Bateson, p. 614.

30. R. Dale Guthrie, *Body Hot Spots: The Anatomy of Human Social Organs and Behavior* (New York: D. Van Nostrand Co., 1976), Chapter 9, and p. 73.

31. Guthrie, p. 73.

32. Bernhard Rensch, "Basic Aesthetic Principles in Man and Animals," in *The Nature of Human Behaviour,* ed. by Gunther Altner (London: Allen and Unwin, 1976), pp. 322-45, 445-47.

33. Cf. Rudolf Arnheim, *Art and Visual Experience* (Berkeley: University of California Press, 1954).

34. Rensch, "Basic," p. 345.

35. Rensch, "Die Wirksamkeit ästhetischer Faktoren bei Wirbeltieren," *Zeitschrift für Tierpsychologie,* XV (1958), p. 461.

36. Margarete Tigges, "Muster- und Farbebevorzugung bei Fischen und Vögeln," *Zeitschrift für Tierpsychologie,* XX (1963), pp. 129-42.

37. William T. Sheperd, "Some Observations on the Intelligence of the Chimpanzee," *Journal of Animal Behavior,* V (1915), pp. 391-96.

38. See especially "Malversuche mit Affen," (*Zeitschrift für Tierpsychologie,* XVIII [1961], pp. 347-64) on drawings and paintings as perhaps prestages of copying.

39. Paul Schiller, "Figural Preferences in the Drawings of a Chimpanzee," *Journal of Comparative Physiological Psychology,* XLIV (1951), pp. 101-11.

40. Desmond Morris, *The Biology of Art: A Study of the Picture-Making Behaviour of the Great Apes and Its Relationship to Human Art* (New York: Alfred A. Knopf, 1962).

41. Geoffrey H. Bourne, *The Ape People* (New York: G. P. Putnam's Sons, 1971), p. 216.

42. Don R. Brothwell, ed., *Beyond Aesthetics: Investigations into the Nature of Visual Art* (London: Thames and Hudson, 1976), pp. 18-40.

43. Bernhard Rensch, *Homo Sapiens from Man to Demigod* (New York: Columbia University Press, 1972), p. 90.

44. Rensch, *Homo Sapiens,* p. 91.

45. Rensch, "Basic," p. 342.

46. Rensch, *Homo Sapiens,* p. 91.

47. Alexander Alland, Jr., *The Artistic Animal: An Inquiry into the Biological Roots of Art* (Garden City: Anchor Press/Doubleday, 1977), Chapter 2.

48. Alland, p. 24.

49. Alland, p. 30. For a semiotic interpretation of play in vertebrates, cf. Sebeok, *Contributions,* p. 139.

50. Cf. John E. Pfeiffer, *The Emergence of Man* (New York: Harper & Row, 1969), p. 434.

51. Dobzhansky, p. 217.

52. Herbert Spencer, *The Principles of Psychology* (New York: D. Appleton, 1897), II, pp. 627, 647.

53. Iredell Jenkins, *Art and the Human Enterprise* (Cambridge, Mass.: Harvard University Press, 1958), p. 14 and passim.

54. Peter H. Klopfer, "Sensory Physiology and Esthetics," *American Scientist,* LVIII (1970), p. 399.

55. Klopfer, p. 400.

56. Alland, p. 27.

57. Alexander Marshack, *The Roots of Civilization: The Cognitive Beginnings of Man's First Art, Symbol and Notation* (New York: McGraw-Hill, 1972), p. 275.

58. John Z. Young, *An Introduction to the Study of Man* (Oxford: Clarendon, 1971), p. 519.

59. Dobzhansky, p. 215.

60. Cf. George John Romanes, *Darwin, and After Darwin: An Exposition of the Darwinian Theory and a Discussion of Post-Darwinian Questions* (Chicago: Open Court, 1892), pp. 380-85.

61. Anya Peterson Royce, *The Anthropology of Dance* (Bloomington: Indiana University Press, 1977), p. 197.

62. Royce, pp. 3-4.

63. Jack Maclaren, *My Crowded Solitude* (New York: R. M. McBride & Co., 1926).
64. Curt Sachs, *World History of the Dance* (New York: Norton, 1937), p. 10.
65. Royce, p. 4.
66. Karl Appun, *Unter den Tropen* (Jena: H. Costenoble, 1871), pp. 468-69.
67. Karl von Frisch, *The Dancing Bees* (London: Methuen, 1954), and *The Dance Language and Orientation of Bees* (Cambridge, Mass.: Harvard University Press, 1967).
68. I am not, of course, concerned here with spectacles, like circus acts, where animals have purportedly been trained by dint of a trans-species operation to "dance" in exhibitions. Hanna observes: "It is true that a human can dance mechanically or perform a dance pattern conceptualized and created by someone else, in the same way that a nonhuman can be trained to perform a dance by a human. We have all seen 'dancing' chimpanzees, horses, dogs, bears, parrots, or elephants." (Judith L. Hanna, "To Dance is Human: Some Psycho-biological Bases of an Expressive Form," in *The Anthropology of the Body,* ed. by John Blacking [London: Academic Press, 1977], p. 212). The latter, however, are only skillfully induced semiotic illusions. The animals' biologically appropriate movements are accompanied by the contrived music, not the other way about.
69. Irenäus Eibl-Eibesfeldt, *Ethology: The Biology of Behavior* (New York: Holt, Rinehart and Winston, 1975), p. 233.
70. Edward A. Armstrong, *A Study of Bird Song* (London: Oxford University Press, 1963), Chapter 15, and p. 195.
71. Eibl-Eibesfeldt, p. 233.
72. For her dramatic descriptions, see, e.g., Jane von Lawick-Goodall, *My Friends the Wild Chimpanzees* (Washington: National Geographic Society, 1967), pp. 75-77; *In the Shadow of Man* (Boston: Houghton-Mifflin, 1971), pp. 52-54. Henry W. Nissen, whose fieldwork was conducted during the dry season, occasionally alludes, nevertheless, to wild chimpanzees performing in parties, in "A Field Study of the Chimpanzee: Observations of Chimpanzee Behavior and Environment in Western French Guinea," *Comparative Psychology Monographs* 8, XXXVI (1932), pp. 1-222.
73. Lawick-Goodall, *Shadow,* p. 54.
74. Royce, p. 207.
75. Lawick-Goodall, *Friends,* pp. 74, 77.
76. Sachs, p. 10.
77. Wolfgang Köhler, "Zur Psychologie des Schimpansen," *Psychologische Forschung* I (1922), pp. 33-35; cf. his *The Mentality of Apes* (London: Routledge and Kegan Paul, 1925), pp. 314-15.
78. Köhler, "Psychologie," p. 33.
79. Sachs, p. 10.
80. Sachs, p. 11.
81. Köhler, "Psychologie," p. 34.
82. Sachs, p. 12.
83. Franz Boas, *Primitive Art* (New York: Dover, 1955 [1927]), p. 344.
84. Cf. Sebeok, *The Sign,* Chapter 1.
85. Griffin, *Animal Awareness,* p. 78. (See footnote 12).
86. Hanna, "To Dance," p. 211. (See footnote 68).
87. Alan P. Merriam, *The Anthropology of Music* (Evanston: Northwestern University Press, 1964), p. 27.
88. Claude Lévi-Strauss, *Le cru et le cuit* (Paris: Plon, 1964), p. 24.
89. Boas, p. 340.
90. Thorpe dismisses Langer's absurd view that the singing of birds, being "unconscious," is not art. For a critical consideration of her writings on music, see further Paul Henle, ed., *Language, Thought & Culture* (Ann Arbor: University of Michigan Press, 1958), pp. 202-20.
91. William H. Thorpe, *Animal Nature and Human Nature* (Garden City: Anchor Press/Doubleday, 1974), p. 307.
92. Peter Szőke, "Ornithomuzikológia," *Magyar Tudomány* IX (1963), pp. 592-607.
93. Joan Hall-Craggs, "The Aesthetic Content of Bird Song," in *Bird Vocalizations: Their Relations to Current Problems in Biology and Psychology,* ed. by Robert A. Hinde (Cambridge: Cambridge University Press, 1969), pp. 367-81.
94. Charles Hartshorne, *Born to Sing: An Interpretation and World Survey of Bird Song* (Bloomington: Indiana University Press, 1973).
95. Linguists will recognize this observation as a generalization of the so-called "bow-

wow theory" of the origin of speech, supposed to have arisen as a consequence of onomatopoeia.

96. See further, Edward A. Armstrong, *Bird Display and Behaviour: An Introduction to the Study of Bird Psychology* (New York: Dover, 1965), pp. 209 ff.

97. This notwithstanding, there are also profound differences, since song birds possess twin sound-producing organs—one in each bronchus—whereas in man, as indeed in all mammals, there is but a single vocal source. Our understanding of the acoustical and physiological processes involved in the singing of birds is as yet very far from satisfactory. For details, see the excellent but neglected work of Crawford H. Greenewalt, *Bird Song: Acoustics and Physiology* (Washington: Smithsonian Institution Press, 1968).

98. Peter Marler and Andrew Gordon, "The Social Environment of Infant Macaques," in *Biology and Behavior: Environmental Influences*, ed. by David C. Glass (New York: Rockefeller University Press, 1968), p. 128. Cf. Nottebohm's remark that "The gap separating human vocal exploits from those of other primates is enormous." (Fernando Nottebohm, "The Origins of Vocal Learning," *The American Naturalist*, CVI [1972] p. 133). The same investigator is principally responsible for the dramatic discovery of lateralization of vocal control in several song birds, notably the canary, in the brain of which localization of vocal control was found with an overlying left hemispheric dominance (Nottebohm, Tegner M. Stokes, and Christina M. Leonard, "Central Control of Song in the Canary, *Serinus Canarius*," *Journal of Comparative Neurology* CLXV [1976], pp. 457-86).

99. Armstrong, *Bird Song*, p. 235. Cf. also the comment of two anthropologists, cited in Roger W. Wescott, ed., *Language Origins* (Silver Springs: Linstok, 1974), p. 288, "emphasizing bird-song both as an analog to and a model for human song. . ."

100. Armstrong, *Bird Song*, p. 244.

101. Hartshorne, Chapters 2 and 3, and p. 53.

102. Hall-Craggs, pp. 311 ff.

103. Armstrong, *Bird Song*, p. 244.

104. Jürgen Reinert, "Takt- und Rhythmusunterscheidung bei Dohlen," *Zeitschrift für Tierpsychologie*, XXII (1965), pp. 223-71.

105. Keith Nelson, "Does the Holistic Study of Behavior Have a Future?" in *Perspectives in Ethology*, ed. by Paul P. G. Bateson and Peter H. Klopfer (New York: Putnam, 1973).

106. Colin Cherry, *On Human Communication: A Review, a Survey, and a Criticism* (Cambridge, Mass.: MIT Press, 1978), pp. 279-82.

107. Nelson, pp. 288-89.

108. Thorpe, *Animal Nature*, p. 205.

109. William H. Thorpe, *Duetting and Antiphonal Song in Birds: Its Extent and Significance. Behaviour* (Monograph Supplement 18) (Leiden: Brill, 1972).

110. W. John Smith, *The Behavior of Communicating: An Ethological Approach* (Cambridge, Mass.: Harvard University Press, 1977), p. 56.

111. Hubert Frings and Mabel Frings, *Animal Communication* (Norman: University of Oklahoma Press, 1977), p. 79.

112. Charles Darwin, *The Descent of Man* (London: John Murray, 1901 [1874]), p. 434.

113. Charles W. Greene, "Physiological Reactions and Structure of the Vocal Apparatus of the California Singing Fish," *American Journal of Physiology*, LXX (1924), pp. 496-99.

114. Frings and Frings, p. 179.

115. Roger S. Payne and Scott McVay, "Songs of the Humpback Whales," *Science*, CLXXIII (1971), pp. 587-97.

116. Payne and McVay, p. 587.

117. Payne and McVay, p. 597.

118. Martin Moynihan, "Communication in the Titi Monkey, Callicebus," *Journal of Zoology*, CL (1966), p. 119.

119. Marler and Tenaza in Sebeok, *How Animals Communicate*, p. 970.

120. William T. Blanford, *The Fauna of British India: Mammalia* (London: Taylor and Francis, 1888-1891), p. 7.

121. Marler and Tenaza, pp. 1001-09.

122. Marler and Tenaza, p. 1008.

123. Marler and Tenaza, p. 1029.

124. From Paul Slud, "The Song and Dance of the Long-Tailed Manakin, *Chiroxiphia Linearis*," *The Auk: A Quarterly Journal of Ornithology*, LXXIV (1957), p. 333.

125. Slud, pp. 333-39.

126. von Frisch, *Animal Architecture*, p. 244.

127. von Frisch, *Animal Architecture*, pp. 243-44.
128. Marshall, *Bower-Birds*, pp. 185-86.
129. J. B. S. Haldane, "The Argument from Animals to Men: An Examination of Its Validity for Anthropology," *The Journal of the Royal Anthropological Institute of Great Britain and Ireland*, LXXXVI, 2 (1965), p. 11.
130. So already in Romanes, *Darwin*, p. 410: "All cases where beauty can be pointed to in organic nature are seemingly due . . . to utility."
131. Jenkins, *Art*, p. 130.
132. Lev Semenovich Vygotsky, *The Psychology of Art* (Cambridge, Mass.: MIT Press, 1971), p. 246.
133. Sebeok, *The Sign*, Chapter 10.
134. In Brothwell, *Beyond Aesthetics*, p. 8.
135. In Brothwell, Chapter 2.
136. Gerti Dücker, "Spontane Bevorzügung arteigener Farben bei Vögeln," *Zeitschrift für Tierpsychologie*, XX (1963), pp. 43-65.
137. Schiller, "Figural Preferences," published posthumously, reported by K. S. Lashley.
138. Morris, *Biology of Art*.
139. Bourne, *Ape People*, p. 222; Rensch, "Basic Aesthetic Principles," p. 339.
140. Morris, p. 25; Bourne, p. 224.
141. From Morris, p. 27. The animal paintings at Lascaux, Altamira, and other famous decorated caves of the Upper Paleolithic (c. 35,000 to 10,000 B.C.) do not seem to me directly related to the issues discussed here. The prehistoric art forms of the last Ice Age—which, it is now known, include remarkably life-like engraved "portraits" of men and women, as well as elaborate musical instruments, such as a percussion orchestra of six pieces and the six-stop flutes excavated one at a Ukrainian site and another, dating from the same period, in France—are far too sophisticated to be productively compared with ape art.
142. Morris, pp. 144 ff.
143. Jenkins, *Art*, pp. 126-27.
144. Morris, pp. 144 ff.
145. Morris, p. 146.
146. Eugene S. Ferguson in "The Mind's Eye: Nonverbal Thought in Technology," *Science*, CXCVII (1977), pp. 827-36, has recently documented convincingly that much of the creative thought of the designers of our technology is nonverbal, nor is it easily reducible to words. The importance of his article lies in the fact that the origins of this component of technology lie not in science but in art. David McNeill, "Sentence Structure in Chimpanzee Communication," in *The Growth of Competence*, ed. by Kevin Connolly and Jerome Bruner (New York: Academic Press, 1973), p. 91, has cogently remarked that even if free-ranging chimpanzees had indeed evolved a capacity for language-like communication, "we should not expect it to resemble human language. . . ." This view accords with the opinion of Sherwood L. Washburn, "Human Behavior and the Behavior of Other Animals," *American Psychologist*, XXXIII (1978), p. 410, about apes in general, that "the structure of their natural communications will be like that of monkeys."
147. Popper and Eccles, p. 328.
148. Popper and Eccles, p. 251.
149. Morris, p. 161.
150. Brothwell, *Beyond Aesthetics*, pp. 32-40.
151. Nicholas K. Humphrey, "Colour and Brightness Preferences in Monkeys," *Nature*, CCXXIX (1971), pp. 615-17; and, "Interest and Pleasure: Two Determinants of a Monkey's Visual Preference," *Perception*, I (1972), pp. 395-416.
152. Brothwell, p. 27.
153. Brothwell, p. 39.
154. Nicholas K. Humphrey, "The Illusion of Beauty," *Perception*, II (1973), p. 430.
155. Humphrey, p. 432.
156. René Thom, *Structural Stability and Morphogenesis: An Outline of a General Theory of Models* (Reading: W. A. Benjamin, 1975), p. 316.
157. D'Arcy Wentworth Thompson, *On Growth and Form* (Cambridge: Cambridge University Press, 1945).
158. Thorpe, *Animal Nature*, p. 302; Thom, *Structural Stability*, p. 8.
159. In Matejka and Titunik, *Semiotics of Art*, p. 18.
160. Roman Jakobson, *Selected Writings II: Word and Language* (The Hague: Mouton, 1971), p. 703.

161. Richard Dawkins, *The Selfish Gene* (New York: Oxford University Press, 1978), pp. 21, 25.

162. Klopfer, "Sensory Physiology," p. 400.

163. Peter H. Klopfer, *Habitats and Territories: A Study of the Use of Space by Animals* (New York: Basic Books, 1969), pp. 57-58.

164. Thomas A. Sebeok, *Perspectives in Zoosemiotics* (The Hague: Mouton, 1972), p. 85.

165. Marcus Vitruvius Pollio, *The Architecture of Marcus Vitruvius Pollio, in Ten Books,* trans. by Joseph Gwilt (London: Priestly and Weale, 1826), p. 3.

166. I have previously alluded to these issues, and some of their implications, in Sebeok, *Contributions,* p. 35 (fn. 65), and 127, discriminating sharply between subjective and objective varieties of teleology. I was therefore surprised that several reviewers of my book, notably V. V. Martynov, "Review of Sebeok, *Contributions,*" *Literatury i iazyka,* XXXVII/2 (1978), p. 178, took exception to my strictures, introducing, in the process, several levels of confusion into the argument. Martynov also regrets that I failed to cite the well-known book by Russell L. Ackoff and Fred E. Emery, *On Purposeful Systems* (Chicago: Aldine-Atherton, 1972), who devote their Chs. 10 and 11 to semiotics, but they simply rehearse notions already dealt with much better in various writings of Charles Morris. Matters of artistic intent are obviously pertinent to the subjects dealt with here, but space precludes the possibility of their detailed consideration. Concisely put, in my view, intention had best be regarded as a convention, and the intent of any sign simply its use.

167. Hannah Arendt, *The Human Condition* (Chicago: University of Chicago Press, 1958), pp. 136, 139.

168. Arendt, p. 139.

169. Arendt, p. 173.

170. Karl Marx, *Das Kapital. Marx-Engels Gesamtausgabe,* Part II (Zurich: Ring-Vlg., 1933), III, p. 698.

171. Arendt, p. 157.

172. Sebeok, *The Sign,* Chapter 1.

173. von Frisch, *Animal Architecture.*

174. Perhaps this obvious translation was avoided because it would have echoed the title of another book, *Master Builders of the Animal World,* published at about the same time: David M. Hancocks, *Master Builders of the Animal World* (New York: Harper & Row, 1973). The author of this book is an architect.

175. von Frisch, *Animal Architecture,* p. 22. For a first approach to a semiotic typology of organismal vs. artifactual human and animal sign systems, see Sebeok, *Contributions,* pp. 30, 32. For further references to the use of tools by birds, see Thony B. Jones and Alan C. Kamil, "Tool-Making and Tool-Using in the Northern Blue Jay," *Science,* CLXXX (1973), pp. 1076-78. George M. Guilmet, "The Evolution of Tool-Using and Tool-Making Behaviour," *Man,* XII (1977), pp. 33-47, is concerned with reconstructing the behavioral context which coevolved with tool-using and tool-making in the hominid lineage. He argues that the method of socialization practiced by a tool-making group would affect the degree of formal standardization presented by the tools themselves.

176. Jones and Kamil, "Tool-Making."

177. Thomas Eisner, Karen Hicks, Maria Eisner, and Douglas S. Robson, " 'Wolf-in-Sheep's-Clothing' Strategy of a Predatious Insect Larva," *Science,* CXCIX (1978), pp. 790-94.

178. von Frisch, *Animal Architecture,* pp. 72-150.

179. Joan H. Fellers and Gary M. Fellers, "Tool Use in a Social Insect and Its Implications for Competitive Interactions," *Science,* CXCII (1976), pp. 70-72.

180. Sebeok, *The Sign,* Chapter 2.

181. Sebeok, *Contributions,* p. 30.

182. von Frisch, *Animal Architecture,* pp. 244-45.

183. Lewis H. Morgan, *The American Beaver and His Works* (New York: Burt Franklin, 1970 [1868]), p. 101.

184. Lars Wilsson, *My Beaver Colony* (London: Souvenir, 1969), p. 1.

185. von Frisch, *Animal Architecture,* p. 278.

186. Morgan, p. 99.

187. Köhler, *Apes,* especially Chapter V, on "Building."

188. Köhler, pp. 161, 163-64.

189. von Frisch, *Animal Architecture,* p. 286.

190. Jacob Bronowski, *A Sense of the Future: Essays in Natural Philosophy* (Cambridge, Mass.: MIT Press, 1977), p. 112. Cf. Sebeok, *Contributions,* p. 119.

191. Sebeok, *The Sign,* Chapter 6.

192. Sebeok, *The Sign,* Chapters 4 and 5. See now Thomas A. Sebeok and Jean Umiker-Sebeok, *Speaking of Apes* (New York: Plenum Publishing Corporation, 1980), esp. Ch. 1, "Questioning Apes," where this and related issues are discussed in detail.

193. Griffin, *Animal Awareness.*

194. William M. Conway, *Literary Remains of Albrecht Dürer* (New York: Cambridge University Press, 1889), p. 182.

195. Humphry House and Graham Storey, *The Journals and Papers of Gerard Manley Hopkins* (London: Oxford University Press, 1959), pp. 86-114.

196. House and Storey, p. 84. For an elaboration and application of Hopkins' path-breaking studies to grammatical parallelism by a modern master, see Roman Jakobson, "Grammatical Parallelism and its Russian Facet," *Language,* XLII (1966), pp. 399-429.

197. Nicholas K. Humphrey, "The Illusion of Beauty," *Perception,* II (1973), p. 432.

198. Humphrey, p. 433.

199. Robert C. Dunnell, *Systematics in Prehistory* (New York: The Free Press, 1971), pp. 44-45.

200. Ralph Bulmer, "Which Came First, the Chicken or the Egg-Head?" in *Echanges et Communications,* II, ed. Jean Pouillon and Pierre Maranda (The Hague: Mouton, 1970), p. 1082.

201. Sebeok, *Contributions,* pp. 138-40.

202. Heini Hediger, "Proper Names in the Animal Kingdom," *Experientia,* XXXII (1976), p. 1357. On the notion of the "Semiotic Self," see Sebeok, *The Sign,* Appendix I.

203. Humphrey, "Illusion," pp. 435-36.

204. Marshall, *Bower-Birds,* p. 92.

205. Cf. Fig. 3, in Brothwell, *Beyond Aesthetics,* p. 21.

206. Jan Mukařovský, "Art as Semiotic Fact," in Matejka and Titunik, *Semiotics of Art,* p. 8.

General Semiotics and Biosemiotics

Rudolf Jander

Semiotics, in its widest sense, comprises all explicit and implicit knowledge about signs and users of signs (semiotic systems) as accumulated and transmitted to us since the time of ancient philosophy. Some of this history is reviewed in Percival's contribution to this volume (pp. 1-132). In this essay, only incidental references are being made to the historical origins and transformations of ideas discussed.

Given the plain fact that absolutely all human knowledge is stored, transmitted and processed by means of signs, one would expect semiotic theory to be well-developed and to pervade all the sciences and the humanities as a unifying set of concepts and laws. Quite surprisingly, this expectation is still nothing but a vision, and as such, frequently expressed by competent writers and thinkers, such as John Locke, Charles S. Peirce, Charles W. Morris and Thomas A. Sebeok. Having studied some semiotics, I not only share these visions but am fully convinced that, ultimately semioticians are able to develop their theory toward a state that can be called scientific and encyclopedic. By the latter, I mean the capability of linking up and penetrating all disciplines of human knowledge. To forestall possible misunderstandings, being all-pervasive in this sense does not imply being all-encompassing. Given the deplorable fact that as of today no such theoretical semiotic foundation exists,[1] it will take multiple efforts, countless discussions and years of time to reach this visionary goal.

In the body of this essay I advance the outline of a scientific semiotic theory which is to constitute some first step toward the goal mentioned. In order to endow this theory with clarity and rigor, I merge elementary set-theoretical and information-theoretical ideas with semiotic reasoning. All fundamental and crucial concepts are italicized at passages that contribute to their definition and clarification. Some of these concepts are newly conceived, some of them will be highly abstract, but all of them are presented in their simplest adequate form, to minimize potential errors in factual representation, deductive arguments and in communication.

Semiotic laws, deduced from central and fundamental concepts, and factual knowledge constitute the core of the proposed scientific theory. These laws shall serve several eminently important purposes. First, they are to establish the scientific nature of the theory. Second, they are to inter-connect rigorously the fundamental concepts, thus clarifying their mutual relations and thereby strengthening the coherence of the whole. Third, and most important, they are to serve as powerful mental tools for discriminating between truth and falsehood in semiotic reasoning by ruling what infer-ences are possible or impossible, necessary or unnecessary, and sufficient or insufficient. Thus, skillful use of semiotic laws shall streamline and econo-mize semiotic reasoning. To give an example of this claim: Once a thinker absorbed the Fourth Semiotic Law, he would no longer waste his time puzzling over "knowledge *a priori*" because such genuine knowledge is absolutely impossible, in principle, according to this semiotic law.

Despite its potential universal importance, semiotics is still not widely acknowledged or even known among scholars. Among the various ex-planations for this, two are prominent. First, there are the charlatans who pretend to command deep insight by employing fuzzy, seemingly learned semiotic concepts, which, moreover, they do not even bother to define. More concretely, for instance, absolutely no new insight is gained, or any purpose served, if someone sees similarities of any kind between two other-wise different cultural creations, two novels for instance, and then simply relabels such similarities pretentiously as semiotic relations. On the other hand, if critically designated semiotic concepts were used to gain access to semiotic laws which, in turn, would allow new inferences or insights, then the cause of semiotics would be well served.

Second, a detrimental historical accident occurred when Morris in his still much too influential book married semiotics with behavioristic doc-trine, thus excluding all references to mental systems, references that are essential for the construction of any semiotic theory of true depth.[2] Fortu-nately, increasing numbers of psychologists turn away from radical be-havioristic doctrine, and some already have no qualms studying mental processes even in animals within the framework of cognitive theories.[3] Given this about-face, resistance should not be too great if progressive semioticians reintroduce references to mental systems of animals and man into their theories and reasoning, which is done below.

Modern semiotics comprises a vast body of knowledge which I propose to organize conceptually into four major categories. *General Semiotics* deals with fundamental concepts, generally applicable theories, and laws which all confer unity and coherence to semiotics as a whole. *Biosemiotics* is concerned with living semiotic systems. *Cultural Semiotics* is largely restricted to the semiotics of human social interactions, and has been singled out from biosemiotics because of its volume and specific concern to all of us. Finally, there is a newly emerging field of endeavor, artificial intelligence, which may also be referred to as *Computer Semiotics*.

This essay, in view of these four categories, is mainly concerned with general semiotics. Added to this is a brief introduction into biosemiotics.

A. *GENERAL SEMIOTICS*

I. Monosigns, Polysigns and Semiotic Systems

Sign is the central and crucial concept in semiotics and therefore requires thorough definition and analysis. Loosely and vaguely first, a sign is something that stands for something else. More precision is gained if we introduce set-theoretical concepts as mental tools. In this framework we define "sign" as a *discriminatory subset* that has to be explained. "Subset" implies the existence of a whole set, the *object set,* which is identical to the "object" or the "signified" in traditional semiotic terminology.

An object set may be realized by any circumscribed collection of absolutely any types of identifiable items, ranging from concrete objects to abstract ideas, or from permanent states to fast operations; even collections of signs are potential object sets. Except for the instance of a single object set, subsets that function as *proper signs* have to be discriminatory, that is, have to be peculiar to their particular object set. A given object set may be labeled by any one of several such discriminatory subsets. Supersets of mutually indiscriminate object sets, or several object sets that need not be discriminated, but belong to one class, may be labeled by a *generic sign*. The relationship between a generic sign and its superset is the same as that between the proper sign and the object set.

Signification is the deterministic process that changes a subset into a sign. Signification is always necessary since no subset has sign properties all by itself. The following two sets of numbers will help to clarify the important distinction between *passive, active* and *mixed signification:*

$$[2, 3, 6] \qquad [1, 4, 6]$$

If the respective second two elements in these two sets are thought to be kept out of sight, the respective first elements still distinctly identify or signify each individual set. The respective third numbers, however, could not serve this function. Recognizing such passive signification is of universal importance for the survival of all living organisms.

On the other hand, we humans may actively assign the given object sets some arbitrary labels, such as calling them "first set" and "second set." Such active signification is of crucial importance in the process of building a language. Finally, in a mixed process of signification, two numbers within each set may be combined by some logical operation. For instance, multiplying the respective first two above numbers produces two new distinctive signs; summing, however, would fail to do so.

For any rigorous semiotic analysis it is also necessary to discriminate between *inclusive* and *exclusive signification*. If we see a familiar face (sign), we consider it as an inseparable part of the whole person (object set) that it signifies. Contrary to such inclusive significations which are characteristic for the interpretation of *natural signs, conventional signs* typically are generated by exclusive signification. Thus, a word and its meaning (the idea behind it) are two nonintersecting, complementary subsets. In such instances of exclusive signification, I reserve the term "object set" to the set complementing the sign rather than to the overall set which includes the sign.

Signification is a relation or function of the type "many-to-one," as follows directly from the definition of signs as subsets (parts of wholes). In concrete reality, all such functions have to manifest themselves as some physical process, from which, however, the semiotician normally abstracts without loss of semiotic understanding in most instances. More specifically, physical signification is a causal process that somehow reduces complexity within a physical system; conceptually (abstractly), signification can be viewed as a nontautological (proper) logical operation. In this sense, any sign is the result of either a causal or a proper logical process depending on the level of abstraction. At the abstract level, any simple or complex logical operation produces a sign or signs. Abstraction, obviously, always produces signs. Thus, universals are signs for universes.

Signals are signs that have been generated by the physical separation (in space or time or both) of the sign (subset) from its original context (object set) for the purpose of long distance communication. This definition leads to a paradox which is the source of much confusion. Semiotically, a signal (as a sign) is part of a conceptual whole, comprising a subset and a complementary set; physically, the two sets are spaced apart. How is this paradox to be solved?

There are two directly incompatible *modes of reasoning,* in both of which, and in their mutual translation, semioticians have to be well versed. *Physical (causal) reasoning* takes time and space fully into account, and *nonphysical reasoning* is abstracting both from time and from space. Blind mixing of both these modes is bound to result in nonsense. Whenever we switch between these two modes, time and space has to be properly reintroduced or abstracted, if paradoxical results are to be avoided. More on these two modes of reasoning will be found in a later section.

Signification as a many-to-one central semiotic process is embedded into higher order and lower order semiotic processes which share some properties with it and which are of equal general importance. The higher order process shall be referred to as "symbolization" and the lower order process as "specification." Both are explained in turn.

Symbolization is a process akin to signification, except that it is many-to-few instead of many-to-one. In other words, an act of symbolization can always be decomposed into several acts of signification. Thus, symbolization is polysignification and its product is the *polysign*. Polysigns are sufficiently different from signs proper or *monosigns*. The following comparison will demonstrate the justification of this distinction.

Monosigns are semantic atoms; that is, they are the smallest subunits of sign-systems that can be associated with object sets and thus "carry" meaning. The internal structure of a monosign tells us absolutely nothing about the object set it stands for. In virtue of this property, all monosigns are potentially arbitrary; that is, a specific monosign could be replaced by any other similar structure irrespective of what the referred-to object set (meaning) is like. Semantically equivalent signs (synonyms) that are at least partially the product of some chance events, like biological evolution or cultural tradition, therefore greatly differ from one another, whenever they have been created independently, as is the case with bird songs or human languages. The linguistic monosign is the morpheme which frequently constitutes a single word. Some words, like "metaphysics," are polysigns, being composed of several morphemes, in this case "meta" and "physics."

Polysigns differ from monosigns in the important attribute that their internal structure represents some features of the internal structure of the super-object-set they stand for. This representation is nonarbitrarily defined by the objects for a given collection of signs. Polysigns, in contrast to monosigns, mimic, simulate or model aspects of the reality they represent. Spoken sentences, written mathematical expressions, photographs or the communication dances of the honey bees are some arbitrary examples of polysigns. The proposed distinction between monosigns and polysigns is of such fundamental importance because we, as humans, as any other semiotic system, can learn something new only by polysigns because individual monosigns are either meaningless or represent knowledge we already have, due to some pre-instruction with polysigns (the term "pre-instruction" is further explained below). Any polysign can be substituted by a monosign once it has served its instructive function; e.g., "semiotics" stands for everything we have been pre-instructed in by polysigns on the pertinent subject matter.

Peirce, around the turn of the century, already felt the need to label a concept closely related to that of the polysign. His label was "icon." Whereas in Peirce's system, the "icon" is one of several coordinated categories, the polysign in this new theory is a specific concept to which related concepts are subordinated.

Specification in the semiotic process takes place at the subsemantic level and is responsible for the specific substructure of monosigns. Linguists call "phonemes" the structural elements that constitute monosigns (morphemes). By analogy, I propose "signeme" as the general term for all elements that constitute monosigns of any type.

In summary, the three functional hierarchic levels discussed are organized in such a way that specification is a constituent of signification and signification a constituent of symbolization. All three are necessary components of any semiotic process. In complex semiotic systems each one of these functional levels is further highly organized in itself. This interesting topic, however, is beyond the scope of this brief essay.

At this point it is expedient for a discussion of more complex semiotic processes to introduce a symbolic notation for the process of symbolization. Let "s" stand for any many-to-few functions, no matter how simple or complex it is. The many-to-one function should be included. Similarly, "S" shall stand for mono- or polysigns, and "O" for the object to be signified. Symbolization and signification can then be represented by the expression

$$S = s(O).$$

Several acts of symbolization may be concatenated. For two we have $S = s_2(s_1(O))$. This takes us straight to the still valid Aristotelian triad (Percival, p. 2-3).

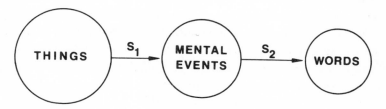

Things (O) of the outside world are symbolically represented (s_1) as mental events which are in turn represented (s_2) as words (S). The possible number of links in such a chain of symbolizations is only limited by the complexity of the original object and the degree of simplification per step. Several such chains may join.

One-to-one transformations or *isomorphic transformations* are common semiotic processes. Because of their theoretical simplicity not much need be said about them. Dissemination and conservation of collections of signs require one-to-one processes like replication, transliteration, literal translation, and transduction. The latter is the change of the physical substrate or vehicle that carries signs. When we speak, our brain produces nerve impulses that are transduced into muscle contractions which are in turn transduced into soundwaves and so on. In such a chain of transductions no signification or symbolization takes place. Signs and symbols maintain their identity as signs despite radical physical transmutations.

Prior to discussing few-to-many semiotic functions, I have to confess to a trick I used in order to simplify the line of arguments. Signs and polysigns after their emergence due to symbolization are not proper signs and polysigns (potential ones, only) unless there is a *receiver* or interpreter. To get around this fundamental requirement, I simply took advantage of the fact that you, the reader, function as an unwitting perfect receiver.

Now we have to introduce the receiver as an object of our discussion. This is done by means of a definition. A *semiotic system* is a system that is capable of receiving, processing and emitting signs and polysigns. There are different types of semiotic systems that differ markedly in complexity. I call these different types *species of semiotic systems.* Each individual of a species semiotically interacts at least with its heterospecific environment but there is also intraspecific interaction or communication. Such intraspecific communication establishes *semiotic hypersystems,* a prime example of which is human culture.

Once a sign or a polysign is received by a semiotic system, the system finds out its *meaning,* that is, interprets it. *Interpretation* is nothing but the inverse function of symbolization, that is, a *few-to-many semiotic function.* Remembering the definition of a sign as a subset of the original object set, inverse symbolization is finding the complement (meaning) to the subset, so that the original set can be restored.[4]

Semiosis can now be defined with the concepts at hand: It is the sequential linkage between symbolization and inverse symbolization, or, .in set theoretical terminology, the linkage between decomplementation and recomplementation of a subset (S). If we label the two terminal sets object sets (O) and symbolization and inverse symbolization "s" and "s⁻", respectively, a simple diagram illustrates the idea of semiosis.

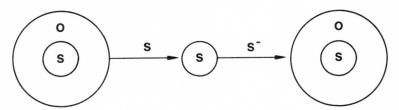

If semiosis is perfect, the two terminal sets are identical sets because a function and its inverse restore, by definition, the original state. In reality, however, we expect semiotic systems, acting as receivers, to be only partially capable of complementation or inverse symbolization, with the result that the meaning or restored set in the receiver is only a homomorphic model (instead of an isomorphic one) of the original set.

The *semiotic triad* (not to be confused with the Aristotelian triad), the original set, the symbolizing subset, and the terminal set (Figure 2), is the source of the *central conceptual dilemma* of traditional semiotics: What in the final analysis is a sign in itself? Disregarding time and space, it is nothing in itself but a subset. This is relatively unproblematical. In reality, however, a sign is an isolated entity that travels in space and time. It has no physical identity as sign since the physical vehicle can change (transduction), yet the sign maintains its identity. Only in sloppy language do we say that the sign conveys or carries meaning. Strictly, "meaning" is added by the receiver (complementation), and the sign itself is completely devoid of meaning (of which we are fully aware when listening to a speaker of an unknown language). Thus we conclude: the sign is a nonphysical and meaningless entity; a nothingness? Yet, after all, it must have some reality!

Before we discuss the kind of nonphysical reality to be attributed to a sign in scientific semiotics, let us see how other semioticians approached this dilemma. Peirce, as I understand it, negated the independent existence of signs and made them integral constituents of the semiotic triads which he considered as indecomposable "thirdness."[5] Morris avoided the issue by explicitly not defining "sign."[6] Saussure, I have the impression, just labeled the physical carriers of signs without concern about the abstract nature of a sign independent of its carrier.

The main topic of this section was to develop an understanding of the *central semiotic concepts*—sign, polysign, semiotic system, and semiosis—as clearly as possible with the help of set-theoretical concepts. Against this background, *semiotics* is defined as the science of signs and semiotic systems. The intriguing question, what the nature of the nonphysical reality is, with which semiotics deals, was left open and shall be investigated in the following section. With the central concepts now established, we have to turn to the fundamental concepts and/or premises on which scientific semiotics is to be grounded. Fundamental and central concepts together are the conceptual framework within which general semiotic laws can then be formulated.

Special attention has to be drawn to the fact that I introduced the central concepts of general semiotics by purposely ignoring one extraordinarily important aspect of absolutely all real semiotic processes: None of them are neatly and fully deterministic as presented, but they are all disturbed throughout by chance events. The degree of such disturbance varies from barely visible to magnitudes that destroy any order, thus generating pure noise or chaos. It is only by taking the interplay of chance and necessity into account that is is possible to gain a deep and useful understanding of semiotic systems and processes. In the following three sections, such interplay is taken into account.

II. Communication and Information

The starting point in this section is the simplest conceivable semiotic hypersystem, one semiotic system (SS) communicating with another one.

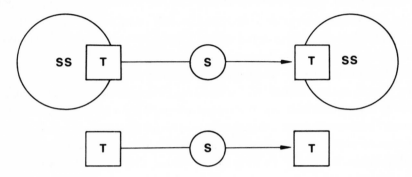

You can think in this context of two human minds. In order to communicate, the two semiotic systems have to have a *communication channel* which has as its basic constituents two transducers (T) and the channel proper or transmission line. The function of the transducers is simply to "load" signs on physical carriers so that they can travel as *signals* through the channel. Air is the channel when we talk, a wire is the channel for the telephone. Whereas the complex events inside the two semiotic systems are still largely a mystery and inaccessible when we are dealing with human brains, the communication channel is fully open to scientific investigation. We dissect the channel out of the semiotic hypersystem (as in Figure 3), study it in isolation, and forget, for the time being, everything about semiosis.

The theory of the communication channel has been developed over the past decades by communication scientists and engineers. The culmination point is Shannon's *Mathematical Theory of Communication*[7] which every serious semiotician has to understand at least intuitively. The following is an attempt to provide you with such an understanding (largely nonmathematical, intuitive). The necessary reasoning is highly abstract, and considerable effort is necessary to understand the basic terms in such a depth that they can be easily and correctly applied in all relevant contexts.

What is it that is carried through the communication channel that is the leftover of the message from which the meaning has been stripped? Shannon calls it *information,* and it will be this term that shall occupy our attention through the following pages.

"Information" is the most fundamental concept of semiotics if not of human knowledge in general. This fact rules out a definition, and it is only by examples that the contents and uses of this eminently important concept can be developed.

A salient aspect is quantification. Shannon's central question was how much information can be transmitted through a given channel. If the signals are words, you might propose: count the number of words in the string of signals. This is too simple, though. If the same sentence is said twice, the repetition definitely is without information content. This leads to our first rough definition: We quantify information by determining the minimal number of words that are necessary for the unambiguous representation of a given passage (string of words). Even though this measure roughly grows with "H," (which is the symbol that stands for Shannon's exact measure for amount of information), general application of this prescription is hampered by the arbitrary use of a given alphabet. Shannon eliminated this arbitrariness in his *theory of information* (which is the core of the theory of communication) by resorting to the simplest possible alphabet, that of two letters, or binary digits which, in principle, can be rendered in any form: $(0,1)$, $(+, -)$, (yes, no), and so on. We will stay with the first form in the following. Taking notice of the fact that absolutely any well described sign or polysign can—in principle—be coded into binary digits, the amount of information (H) within one symbol is exactly equal to the minimal number of binary digits that are necessary to code that symbol. This number is referred to as the *information content in bits*. Finding such a minimal number and designing the proper binary code frequently poses formidable mathematical problems that need not concern us here. Some simple aspects will be discussed below.

Next we will increase our intuitive understanding of "information contents" by comparing this concept with other concepts. It is fairly easy to see that the information content (H) of a system of signs increases with the complexity of that system. Therefore H is a useful measure for "complexity." Next suppose we managed to write down a string of the minimal number of binary digits necessary to code a system of signs; then a surprising discovery can be made: The digits in the string follow each other randomly; that is, completely disordered or unpredictable. It is easy to understand this. If there were some order left such as repetition of the same sequence, further condensation would be necessary in order to meet the above requirement for a minimal number of binary digits. From this the important conclusion follows: Information content is also a measure of *disorder, randomness,* or *unpredictability,* which all mean the same. The converse is also exactly true: The greater the disorder in a system, the greater its information content. At first this appears counterintuitive, but makes sense if you ponder a bit. If the same message keeps coming to you over and over again, you have the intuitive feeling that no new information is arriving, redundant information is the same information, and only the unpredictable, the nonordered, is truly new information.

From above we also have the impression that "information" grows with "uncertainty," which in turn is related to "disorder" but has a somewhat different meaning. Three simple coding examples shall clarify this point and a few additional ones:

I)	II)	III)
1-0	1-00	1-000
2-1	2-01	2-001
	3-10	3-010
	4-11	4-011
		5-100
		6-101
		7-110
		8-111

Here we coded the decimal digits 1-2, 1-4, and 1-8 with the help of binary digits (bits). In each of the three examples the information content of the decimal digits and that of the binary digit is exactly the same and equal to the number of binary digits necessary for coding. In the three examples the information content of one decimal digit is one, two and three, respectively. Much can be learned from these three examples. Notice that the decimal digits are monosigns; that is, their internal structure is arbitrary, stands for nothing and, therefore, need not be coded specifically as it would be necessary if the digits were polysigns. What we are coding here are not the *intrinsic* but the *extrinsic informational quantities.* What is immediately obvious is the fact that the more signs there are for us to choose from, the greater is the information content of the individual sign. If we assume for the sake of simplicity that in each of the three cases the decimal digits are used with equal frequency in some relevant context, then the relationship between the number (N) of signs to be chosen from and their individual or extrinsic information content (H) is particularly simple. For our three selections of N decimal digits, N can be expressed with exponents:

I) $N = 2 = 2^1$ II) $N = 2 \times 2 = 2^2$ III) $N = 2 \times 2 \times 2 = 2^3$

This demonstrates that if we express the number (N) of digits from which we select as powers of base two, then the exponent is the information content in bits: $N = 2^H$. If we solve this equation for H, we have

$$H = \log_2 N.$$

In words: The information content of a sign is equal to the logarithm (base 2) of the number of signs within the collection of signs under consideration.

N, the number of signs, acquires interesting meaning if we generate information, that is, a random sequence of these N different signs. Then N stands for the *uncertainty* that one particular of these signs will occur as we scan the sequence. Going back to the equation above, we can see that information content H is a logarithmic function of uncertainty. Uncertainty (U), in turn, is the reciprocal of *probability* (P) $U = 1/P$. Thus the concept of information is also linked up with the concept of probability. All this again makes good intuitive sense: The greater the uncertainty of an event and the smaller its probability, the more informative it is. Conversely, highly certain and probable events are not very informative, hardly ever draw our attention.

The conceptual relationships between *information and logic* play an important role in semiotic theory and semiotic reasoning. It was probably MacKay who first pointed out that the binary choice, which is equivalent to one bit of information, is also equivalent to what can be called a logical quantum, the most elementary logical operation, such as the yes-or-no or the true-or-false decision.[8] This relationship can be used in interesting ways. For instance, if a semiotic system creates a certain pattern of a definable information content (complexity), then this content allows inferences about the number of decisions that went into this production.

A convenient property of quantities-of-information is their additivity. Add up the minimal number of digits necessary for coding and you quantified the information content of some string of signs. However, finding this minimal code is frequently difficult, as mentioned above. Fortunately for many semiotic arguments, it is not necessary to calculate exact information contents; simple ranking is frequently sufficient. For instance, if you add a second nonrepetitive sentence to a first one, then you can be sure that the total information content roughly doubled, and you can be absolutely sure that you have more information than before.

Additivity of information contents is a highly useful property, and the concept has been designed specifically for this purpose. For the informationally naive, "additivity" is thoroughly counterintuitive and easily a source of confusion. Common sense, and specifically the Gestalt psychologists, keep telling us that the whole, like a piece of art, a perceptual impression, or an organism, is more than the sum of its parts. How then is *wholeness* related to information content? Knowing the fact that the information measure has purposely been made additive, we can utilize this insight in order to quantify wholeness; that is, find out exactly how much more "wholeness" is than the sum-of-its-parts.

We conceive of "wholeness" as a property of a system in which all the parts are interacting with each other or are in some way related. The total number of ways this is possible defines wholeness. In other words, in order to quantify wholeness of a given system, we have to find out how many alternative systems of equal complexity could be thought of. Information (H) quantifies complexity. Knowing H, we calculate the number N of alternatives with the formula explained above, $N = 2^H$. In words: Wholeness grows as an exponential function of H which in turn grows with the sum-of-parts; or shorter: Wholeness grows exponentially with the sum-of-its-parts. Such growth is so phenomenal that intuition certainly is satisfied with this measure. Note, with a complexity of merely 20 bits, wholeness, thus quantified, already amounts to more than one million.

III. Informational and Causal Reasoning

This is the point to take up again the two basic modes of reasoning mentioned in a previous section: reasoning in physical terms, in time and space, or in brief, causal reasoning; and abstract reasoning, after elimination of time and space. This nonspatial and nontemporal reasoning can now be characterized and defined as *informational reasoning*. Information is the "stuff" we are processing in informational reasoning, and information is the nonphysical "stuff" signs and polysigns are made of. Thus, informational reasoning resolves the central dilemma of traditional semiotic reasoning when combined with causal reasoning. Signs and polysigns, divorced in time and space from the sets to which they belong, are pieces of quantifiable information.

The recognition of the need and usefulness of the distinction between causal and informational reasoning is by no means novel. It is as old as human thinking. A few examples shall illustrate this. Aristotle, in his famous classification of causes drew a conceptual line between causal reasoning (*causa materialis* and *causa efficiens*) and informational reasoning (*causa formalis* and *causa finalis*). With the advent of modern philosophy came Descartes' consequential dichotomy between *res extensa* and *res cogitans*. The notion of the *res extensa* explicitly refers to the dimensions of time and space which are absent in the *res cogitans,* a concept which refers to what we now call semiotic systems and information. Unfortunately, Descartes failed to recognize that *res cogitans* are constituents of all living systems, not just of human systems. Much of modern humanistic reasoning and teaching is still based on this fundamental misconception of Descartes. Even before modern information theory became known, philosophizing scientists also felt the need to refer to what we now call information. Schrödinger refers to it as "aperiodicity,"[9] and Simpson refers to informational reasoning as "compositionism."[10]

Next, by combining informational and causal reasoning, we are defining some further concepts that are crucial for the semiotic theory and semiotic argumentation. Imagine two signals that are occupying different places in space and in time such as the signal entering and the one leaving a communication channel, or two books, or the following example of two pieces of information:

I) SMETSYS CITOIMES ERA SMETSYS GNIVIL LLA
II) SMETSYS CITOIMES ERA SNAMUH YLNO

Vertical comparison shows that these two pieces of information partially share information content. If this is to be visualized as the information at the input and the output of some *communication channel,* the shared information is the information correctly transmitted, and it is therefore called *transinformation.* If you think of the two pieces of information above as occupying different places in space at the same or different moments in time, then, abstracting time, the shared information is referred to as *syninformation.* Two copies of a particular book contain the *same information* in purely informational terms, and they contain syninformation in the combined informational and physical terms. Copying amplifies information but does not increase it. Our knowledge about all life contains syninformation. This syninformation defines our general notion of life. There is more syninformation between man and the great African apes (chimpanzee and gorilla) than between man and any other group of animals. Syninformation thus establishes biological relationships. Syninformation is invariant under transcoding. A book and its correct translation essentially contain syninformation. Semiosis, by definition, implies and establishes syninformation. Discovering the style of a piece of art is finding syninformation, and in general, art criticism, such as literary criticism, is the discovery of syninformation between a piece of creation and the rest of the world.

After this brief introduction into information-theoretical thinking, we return to semiotic systems and semiosis. Factual knowledge together with the concepts so far developed will be utilized to formulate *basic semiotic laws* and a series of useful, derived concepts.

IV. The Basic Semiotic Laws

It is a peculiarity of semiotic systems and the very reason for their existence, that they accumulate *knowledge* about their environment and also some about themselves. Knowledge is syninformation that is the same information that has been amplified, and then resides at different locations in space and time. The information storing capacity of all semiotic systems is finite, yet the information content of their environment is infinite. From this, we deduce the first semiotic law:

FIRST LAW: All knowledge about the world contained in semiotic systems is symbolic knowledge.

It is easy to see that a semiotic system as part of the universe cannot be as complex (remember: complexity = information content) as the whole universe. Yet, could it be that a minute section of the universe is nonsymbolical, that is fully known? Can there truly be exact syninformation? Informational reasoning proves this impossible. Take, for instance, the width of this paper. You can measure it in centimeters, or in millimeters, or in tenths of millimeters, etc., without any theoretical limit. And as the number of digits grows with the refinement of measurement, so does the information content of this string of numbers *ad infinitum*. In general, everything there is in time and space does contain an infinite amount of information, hence knowing something about some real thing always has to be a many-to-few relation which has been defined as symbolization.

Given the fact that there is always a limit of refinement in the knowledge a semiotic system contains, we can formulate the second semiotic law:

SECOND SEMIOTIC LAW: All knowledge in any semiotic system is ultimately discrete, that is, composed of signs that cannot be further decomposed.

The second law thus establishes theoretical or *logical atomism,* which we have to distinguish sharply from physical atomism. The atomism the ancient philosophers Leucippus and Democritus propounded was logical (metaphysical), not physical atomism because relevant physical facts were not known to them. It is a common mistake not to recognize this. The physical fact more relevant to logical atomism is reflected in Heisenberg's uncertainty principle which he derived from quantum physics and not from atomic physics. This principle sets an absolute and exact limit to the accuracy with which we can collect physical information.

Knowledge in a semiotic system can be true or false and therefore a semiotic definition of *truth* is needed. By definition, all semiotic systems are informationally connected with their environment. Incoming streams of signals are compared (correlated) with stored signs. If there is a correlation (matching), similarity, or syninformation between the incoming and the stored signs, truth is established, and the stored signs can be used to predict what kinds of future signals will come in. Existence of correlation entails order. And this leads us to the third semiotic law:

THIRD SEMIOTIC LAW: Any semiotic system has true knowledge about something only to the degree that there is order. Acquiring knowledge implies being able to discover order.

This third semiotic law has many interesting implications. One applies to Kant's philosophy (*Critique of Pure Reason*). Is it possible for a semiotic system to have knowledge *a priori,* that is, prior to any experience? Kant and many of his followers to this day naively affirmed this question and wasted much time, even on follow-up questions, such as whether synthetic *a priori* knowledge is possible. There is absolutely no way any semiotic system can have any knowledge about its outside but through experience. A semiotic system, all by itself, cannot even know whether or not knowledge is possible. In a world totally chaotic in space and time, having knowledge of any type is impossible. Without experience, no semiotic system can ever know whether the world has some order or not. Therefore:

FOURTH SEMIOTIC LAW: No semiotic system has knowledge a priori.

K. Lorenz made the proposal that Kant's so-called knowledge *a priori* might in reality be innate (instinctive) knowledge.[11] It has to be pointed out, however, that this interpretation in no way rules out experience in a more general sense. It substitutes individual experience with evolutionary experience, and this is definitely not what Kant had in mind. The problem of innate knowledge belongs to biosemiotics and not to general semiotics.

The above statement, that finding true knowledge implies the ability to discover order, raises two important questions. How much do or can we (as semiotic systems) know about the orderliness in the world outside, and second, what kind of knowledge do semiotic systems have to have in order to find order.

Experience tells us that there is at least some order outside ourselves. But could it be that the world is fully ordered or predetermined as Leibnitz proposed in his vision of a pre-established harmony in the world, thus permitting Pascal's demon to predict everything in the future from knowing the exact present? We have to be careful not to confuse wishful thinking with actual experience. As semiotic systems we have to be biased toward seeing order in the world in order to find order (that is then true knowledge). Is is a common experience of psychologists that we frequently see order where in fact there is none. Psychological tests, like the Rorschach test, take advantage of this propensity. Scientists, the professional seekers for order, are frequently inclined to consider the world fully determined. As "reductionists" they want to find a causal explanation for everything. Einstein reputedly said: God is not throwing dice. Is this realistic? Without going into further details, finding out whether the world is fully determined or not would entail an infinite amount of information which no conceivable semiotic system can process. Therefore:

FIFTH SEMIOTIC LAW: It is impossible for any semiotic system to find out whether the world in which it exists is fully ordered (fully determined).

In brief, discovering absolute or full truth about the world is impossible. How is it possible for semiotic systems to discover order in the barrage of incoming signals? We defined "having true knowledge" means to be able to match successfully future real signals with future anticipated signals. Let us call these matches touchpoints with reality. But what happens in the intervals between touchpoints? A simple example will clarify. A pigeon in a Skinner box is fed with some grain every two minutes. Soon the pigeon discovers the order in time and approaches the food dispenser shortly before the food actually appears. Now the pigeon has true knowledge; but what happens between touchpoints with reality which are spaced in intervals of two minutes? The pigeon has to have some internal timer for measuring intervals and with this timer a hypothesis is established: Food appears whenever the timer approaches a certain point. There is no need and no likelihood that the mechanism of the pigeon's timer matches that of the apparatus. Thus hypothetical knowledge is useful and necessary knowledge, but in its internal structure it is most likely not true. Let us call the body of such hypotheses which includes much of what we call scientific hypotheses and theories *hypophysics*. For hypophysical knowledge Occam's razor has to be applied: It should never contain more information than absolutely necessary to interconnect the touchpoints with reality. In conclusion:

SIXTH SEMIOTIC LAW: In order to establish knowledge about the outside world it is necessary for any semiotic system to develop a hypophysical system that interconnects the touchpoints with reality.

This new insight calls for a new classification of knowledge. Traditionally, and since Aristotle, philosophers discriminate between physics and metaphysics. In this theory we discriminate between straight sensory experience; hypophysics, the minimal knowledge necessary to interconnect experience; and metaphysics, which is all other knowledge that transcends the first two categories. This raises immediately the question, where does hypophysical and metaphysical knowledge (information) come from? Or more generally, what are all the sources of information available to a semiotic system? First, sensory input processes. This is unproblematical. How about logical processes? Think of any one logical operation. It will maintain the information content whenever it is tautological or else it will reduce information. From premises you can derive a conclusion, but from a conclusion you can never reconstitute all the premises. In general:

SEVENTH SEMIOTIC LAW: Intrinsic deterministic processes, like logi-

cal operations, never increase the internal information content (knowledge) of semiotic systems, and usually reduce it.

If deterministic processes are ruled out as sources of new internal information, what is left? It can only be random or chance events. Hence:

EIGHTH SEMIOTIC LAW: Any semiotic system can internally increase its knowledge or information content exclusively by means of chance events.

For the semiotically naive this law appears counterintuitive. Don't we have intuition, inspiration, sudden flashes of apparently novel insight? Yes, but this is deceptive. Much of what happens in the human brain is independent of our conscious experience, but nevertheless has to comply with all semiotic laws just as our conscious experiences have to. It is easy to see how the semiotically inexperienced can honestly believe in supernatural inspiration when the nonconscious part of the brain communicates with the consciousness. Seemingly something comes out of nothing, like a miracle.

The probability that chance events generate true knowledge about the world decreases with the total amount of information thus accumulated. Hence:

NINTH SEMIOTIC LAW: If a semiotic system autonomously develops a new body of "knowledge," the probability that this knowledge is false increases with the complexity (information content) of this knowledge.

This law rules out Leibnitz' *monads.*

Someone might object, by pointing to the impressive body of mathematical truths. However, this is fallacious. There are two types of truth between which we have to discriminate sharply: *truth proper,* or truth about the world as discussed before; and *self-truth,* or consistency within a system of signs. Pure mathematics is only concerned with self-truth, as is pure philosophy.

Important new insight is gained by applying semiotic laws to semiosis. Symbolization and signification are both true logical or deterministic operations that eliminate large chunks of information (complementary information). How can this information be reconstituted by the inverse process? Strictly speaking, it cannot. Semiosis as defined at the outset cannot function by itself. Whenever a sign or a polysign travels from some origin to some destination, origin and destination are required to share all complementary information, to have syninformation. This syninformation must have been imparted by some common source prior to semiosis. Hence:

TENTH SEMIOTIC LAW: All semiosis requires pre-instruction, the setting up of syninformation (shared knowledge) about all signs and their complements.

Pre-instruction need not pass through the same channel as used by semiosis and always predates semiosis. Thus, a double link or *semiotic loop* is established between origin and destination of signals. Honey bees, for example, innately understand their dance language. The semiotic loop between two individuals is thus formed by a genetic communication channel and a behavioral one.

Finally, we have to come back to the problem of self knowledge, the knowledge a semiotic system can have about itself. Is it possible that a semiotic system has complete knowledge about itself? In an absolute sense this is of course impossible as discussed in the context of the first semiotic law. A more modest self knowledge down to the smallest functional unit, down to logical atoms, would still satisfy anyone. In order to succeed even in this modest sense we have to violate informational laws. Such knowledge would entail that we load all information about ourselves into our memory for inspection. A memory, however, is only part of a whole system and no part of a system can be as complex (contain as much information) as the whole system. This establishes the

ELEVENTH SEMIOTIC LAW: It is impossible for any semiotic system to have complete functional knowledge about itself.

This last semiotic law is a simplified and special version of the much more general incompleteness theorem of Gödel (1931) which was first established for mathematical systems and then generalized around 1965 by Chaitin with the help of information-theoretical arguments.[12] This theorem implies that, for finding out how complex a given system is, you always need another system that is more complex than the one under study.

B. *BIOSEMIOTICS*

Biosemiotics is the application of general semiotics to living systems. All living systems or organisms are capable of responding to signs in their environment. From this fact we infer that they all contain semiotic systems that mediate the observed semiosis. A seedling responds to gravity as a sign, "knows" to grow downward with its roots, in order to find soil and moisture, and upward with its shoot to find light. A chicken flies into a tree on hearing another one giving the alarm call for a terrestrial predator.

Living systems are more than just semiotic systems. All the subsystems that one can identify within an organism can be subdivided into two classes: semiotic subsystems or informational subsystems, and trophic subsystems. The latter handle materials and energy and are disregarded. Semiotic laws tell us that for semiosis to occur we need pre-instruction, a learning process that establishes the information to be used to complement the information from incoming signs. There are two major semiotic systems in living organisms that we can discriminate by this criterion: the *genetic subsystem* and the *mental subsystem*. The learning process of the genetic system is usually called *"evolution"* and is very slow. That of the mental one we can call "behavioral learning," and it is fast.

Before discussing evolutionary learning, it is best to understand how evolutionary or genetic knowledge is stored symbolically in genetic systems. This storage system is fairly well known, down to the molecular level. By contrast, the storage mechanism for mental information is still virtually unknown. The genetic storage of information on linear macromolecules is surprisingly similar to information storage in human spoken language. It is because of this similarity (syninformation) that we can talk about a *genetic language*.

Exactly four types of molecular subunits (A, G, C, T) are comparable to the phonemes that constitute words. Like phonemes, these subunits have no meaning in themselves. Always three of the subunits (say A, G, T) make a genetic word, a *triplet,* which is the smallest unit that has meaning, hence a sign. The meaning of a word is one particular amino acid which is a molecular constituent of a protein. Among the triplets there are many synonyms, that is, different triplets that stand for the same type of amino acid. Analogous to human language, the formation of the genetic words is arbitrary. There is no chemical or biological reason why any particular triplet should stand for a particular amino acid; any other would function equally well. A chain of several hundred triplets makes a "sentence" which is normally the next higher functional unit, the *gen*. A genetic sentence stands for particular protein. Sometimes genetic sentences are subdivided into phrases that stand for subunits of protein molecules that are later linked up. Genetic sentences are combined into still larger functional units which are not discussed. The way genetic information is realized (epigenetics), is more of chemical than semiotic concern and need not be discussed. The replication (informational amplification) is semiotically interesting. It is a process comparable, in principle, to printing of books, or better still, printing of photographs: a negative copies a positive, a positive a negative, and so on. A surprising feature of the genetic system is its fundamental identity in all living organisms from bacteria to man. From this syninformation we conclude that this language and this semiotic system are as old as life, that is, some 3.5 billion years.

As already mentioned, the mechanism by which genetic systems acquire new meaningful information closely resembles learning, as Pringle originally recognized.[13] First, for a change to be made, an organism has to die and a new one has to be born. Thereby random processes (mutations)—analogous to creative behavioral learning—produce a new genetic information (say, a new word at a particular place). Another source of novel genetic information is due to sexual processes which establish new genetic combinations. All novel genetic information will then be tested by a process comparable to induction: The more accurate the interpretation of signs from the outside world by genetically providing the appropriate complementary information to the signs, the greater the reproductive success. And so evolution carries on.

Much of what *nervous systems* of animals do in organizing their behavior is still due to implemented genetic information. Such nonlearned behavior is called instinctive. Man still has instinctive behavioral knowledge. Exactly how much is hard to determine and therefore sometimes hotly debated, especially when the question comes to the ratio between genetic and nongenetic specification of intelligence.

A truly new semiotic system develops with the ability of individuals to learn. I call this newly emerging semiotic system mental because it developed gradually into the human *mental system*. The learning abilities of most insects are modest with the exception of a few, like bees. Some birds and mammals have learning (mental) capabilities of surprising complexity. The raven, for instance, has been shown to learn and use *abstract numbers* between one and seven. The experiment goes like this: If the raven sees three objects of any kind, he goes to the box with three points and finds food. If he sees seven objects, he goes to the box with seven points, etc.

And not surprisingly, the great apes learn to solve more complex problems than any other animal, even the making and using of simple tools.

One of the most difficult problems the genetic system had to solve in gradually evolving the genetic blueprint for a mental system was not only learning *per se,* having a memory and a logical operator, but taking care that from all that could be learned the right things are learned. This problem has been solved by building a positive and negative reward system into the semiotic system which learns.

What is biologically useful, like nutritious food and reproduction, is made pleasant. What is biologically deleterious is made unpleasant or painful. Experiences of this rewarding and punishing type would not make any sense in an organism incapable of learning. Yet there are many learning problems that cannot be solved with reward systems of the simple type mentioned above. A mouse, exposed to a cat, has not enough time to learn the shortest path to its mouse hole. A satiated ape is well advised to search and learn where to find more food in anticipation of future hunger. Indeed, learning for its own sake, or anticipatory learning which may or may not be useful later, is widespread among higher animals. Such learning appears to be self-rewarding in both higher animals and man. *Novelty* is a strong eliciting stimulus for it. It appears that much of what we call human values is based on our genetically determined reward system that encourages biologically useful learning.[14]

Mental semiotic systems finally develop into semiotic hypersystems. The most impressive examples from animals are the *dance language of the honey bee* and communication between apes and their human keeper by means of sign language.

Honey bees communicate in their dances the location of some resources such as nectar, water or a nesting site.[15] Places are specified by polar co-ordinates: direction and distance. The knowledgeable bee performs a figure-eight dance on the comb (see diagram).

The sign for distance is the speed of the dance. The greater the distance, the slower the dance. If, for instance, the food is one kilometer away, it takes three seconds to complete one circle of the figure-eight. For four kilometers, it takes six seconds.

The direction is indicated according to the following key: If the food is in the direction of the sun, then the straight section of the dance points vertically up. If the food is away from the sun, then the straight section

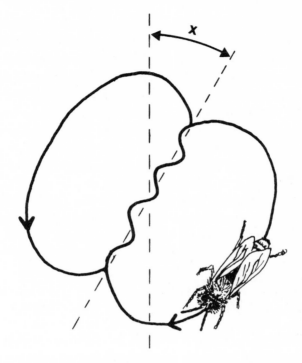

of the dance points vertically down. If the food is some angle to the right of the sun, say 30°, then the bee dances with the straight section 30° to the right of the vertical (x in Figure 4), and so on for all angles to the right of the sun, and it all holds, respectively, for angles to the left of the sun.

Now to the apes. Their mental abilities are of particular interest to us because of our close biological relationship to them. Moreover, the evolution of life from its beginning to the level of the apes took 3.5 billion years. The evolution from ape to man was completed in less than 10 million years and most likely in only three million years. In this period, the brain approximately tripled its weight. Since the genetic changes that are possible in such a relatively short evolutionary time cannot be very complex, one can suspect that the differences between man and ape are more quantitative than qualitative. Hence the question, is an ape smart enough to communicate with us if properly taught? All attempts to teach apes spoken human language have failed. Yet both gorillas and chimpanzees have been trained in the use of American Sign Language (ASL) of the deaf mute. These apes can learn to use correctly more than a hundred different signs to name objects and compose simple sentences of the type: "give apple," "open door." They answer questions of the type: "? color apple," with "red color apple." Exposed to the first cucumber in her life, a chimpanzee labeled it "banana with green." Koko, a gorilla, is the most "brilliant" one known. He masters more than 400 signs (ASL), it is said. Very little is known about how apes intercommunicate in the wild.[16]

Notes

1. This has been pointed out recently also by T. A. Sebeok, *Contributions to the Doctrine of Signs* (Lisse: Peter de Ridder Press, 1976).

2. C. W. Morris, *Signs, Language and Behavior* (New York: Braziller, 1946).

3. S. H. Hulse, H. Fowler, and W. K. Honig, eds., *Cognitive Processes in Animal Behavior* (Hillsdale, N.J.: Lawrence Erlbaum Associates, 1978).

4. In set theory the whole set is the union of a subset and the complement of the subset.

5. C. S. Peirce, "Logic as Semiotic: the Theory of Signs" (1895-1910), reprinted in *Philosophical Writings of Peirce*, J. Buchler, ed. (New York: Dover, 1955).

6. C. W. Morris, *Writings on the General Theory of Signs* (The Hague: Mouton, 1971).

7. C. E. Shannon and W. Weaver, *The Mathematical Theory of Communication* (Urbana: University of Illinois Press, 1949).

8. D. M. McKay, *Information, Mechanism and Meaning* (Cambridge, Mass.: MIT Press, 1969).

9. E. Schrödinger, *What is Life? The Physical Aspects of the Living Cell* (Cambridge: University Press, 1945).

10. G. G. Simpson, *The View of Life* (New York: Harcourt, Brace and World, 1964).

11. K. Lorenz, "Kant's Lehre vom Apriorischen im Lichte gegenwartiger Philosophie," *Blätter für Deutsche Philosophie*, XV (1941), pp. 14-25; English translation in *General Systems* VII, Bertalanffy-Rapaport, eds. (Ann Arbor: Society for General Systems Research, 1962), pp. 37-56.

12. G. J. Chaitin, "Randomness and Mathematical Proof," *Scientific American*, CCLII (May, 1975), pp. 47-52.

13. J. W. S. Pringle, "On the Parallel between Learning and Evolution," *Behaviour*, III (1951), pp. 174-215.

14. Recent summaries, in which such issues are discussed, are by E. O. Wilson, *On Human Nature* (Cambridge, Mass.: Harvard University Press, 1978), and G. E. Pugh, *The Biological Origin of Human Values* (New York: Basic Books, 1977).

15. K. von Frisch, *The Dance Language and Orientation of Bees* (Cambridge, Mass.: Harvard University Press, 1967).

16. For further information on animal communication, see F. Davis, *Eloquent Animals: A Study in Animal Communication* (New York: Coward, McCann and Geoghegan, 1978); D. Premack, *Intelligence in Ape and Man* (New York: Halsted Press, 1976); T. A. Sebeok, ed., *How Animals Communicate* (Bloomington: Indiana University Press, 1977); W. J. Smith, *The Behavior of Communicating: An Ethological Approach* (Cambridge, Mass.: Harvard University Press, 1977).

The Cybernetics of Cultural Communication

F. Allan Hanson and Louise Hanson

This essay is an investigation of the applicability of semiotics in anthropology. Specifically, we are concerned with the relation between the world and people's culturally derived perceptions of the world. While semiotics is an essential part of our investigation of this problem, it is not the only part. The communication of world-view does not appear amenable to analysis in terms of any single approach. We will attempt to demonstrate the crucial role that semiotics, in conjunction with other theoretical orientations, may play in the elucidation of one vexing set of issues in anthropology.

The Mind-Affected World

Several years ago one of the authors set out to discuss the German philosopher Wilhelm Dilthey's distinction between the natural and the "mind-affected" world in a seminar, and he wanted to show the class an example of each. To find a representative of the mind-affected world was simple: for the sake of drama he chose a Yanomamo arrow point which a friend had recently brought back from Brazil. Its sharp point, shiny coat of curare poison and deep incisions where it would break and splinter upon impact all eloquently testified to its lethal purpose. To find something from the natural world was far more difficult. Nothing in the house would possibly do—everything there was either man-made or else an *objêt trouvé* like a piece of driftwood, brought in for some decorative purpose. Even on the mile or so walk from our house to the university finding an authentic example of the natural world proved troublesome. "Stones" turned out to be chunks of concrete, or to have been artificially broken by quarrying and then transported to their present site for use as borders for flower beds or in paving someone's driveway. Blades of grass were special lawn strains developed and modified by human intervention. Finally he settled for an irregularly shaped piece of walnut bark pilfered from the yard of a philosophy professor. But probably even that was hedging, for doubtless the tree from which the bark had come had been planted by someone (or at least not cut down because it did not conflict with the functional or aesthetic landscaping design), and for all we know the black walnut species may have been brought to eastern Kansas by human beings, or perhaps modified by long cohabitation with and use by humans.

By now, what Dilthey meant by the mind-affected world is obvious. He was referring to those material objects which, being made or modified by humans to serve certain purposes, have intentions or meanings fixed in them by design. Innumerable cultural artifacts that populate the mind-affected world immediately spring to mind: the meanings built into the shape of chairs, coffee cup handles, airplane wings, automobile bodies, pencil sharpeners, gilded picture frames, and so on *ad infinitum*. Dilthey also recognized the *arrangement* of objects as part of the mind-affected world. "Every square planted with trees, every room in which seats are arranged, is intelligible to us . . . because human planning, arranging and valuing— common to us all—have assigned its place to every square and every object in the room."[1]

What is truly remarkable, when one stops to consider it, is the degree to which the environment in which we spend our lives is dominated by the mind-affected world. Inside any building, or in any city, literally everything we see, hear, touch, taste or smell except the air itself (considering air-conditioning or pollution, that too) is part of the mind-affected world. We humans have gone so far that even extremely "natural" environments like Capability Brown's design for Blenheim Park at Woodstock, or Japanese gardens, are highly contrived.

Dilthey's concept of the mind-affected world should be extended far beyond material objects and their arrangements. Ritual and magic also mold reality. As Mary Douglas has demonstrated, these are human means of shaping things that actually happen so as to make them more consonant with things as they should happen, according to the expectations of culture. So, among the Dinka, peace-making rituals include denials that the quarrels being reconciled ever took place, and the sacrifice to atone for incest involves the negation of kinship between the guilty parties. Rites like these shape experience in accordance with a culturally-defined image of reality. Events which do not conform to that image are ritually redefined or simply negated.[2]

Nor should the extension of the concept of the mind-affected world stop here. Every person's environment contains other people organized by mind-affected categories of kinship, friendship, economic or political ties. It is, moreover, an environment defined by and constructed in accordance with innumerable beliefs, values and symbols. In other words, the mind-affected world is a concept closely allied to what anthropologists call culture. We have, of course, long been accustomed to thinking about the world as mind-affected in the relatively weak sense that culture grafts meaning onto independently-existing reality. The Maoris, for example, designated New Zealand's North Island as Maui's fish (Te Ika a Maui); their myth recounts how the culture hero Maui drew it up from the depths of the ocean. Other myths account for the movements and present location of major mountains according to their attractions and antipathies for each other, while a myriad of place names denominates locations according to mythical or historical events which occurred there. New Zealand itself thus became a *paysage moralisé,* a mind-affected world thick with human significance.[3] The particular advantage of juxtaposing Dilthey's concept of mind-affected world with the anthropological concept of culture, however, is that it enables us also to conceive of culture in the far stronger sense as something that, to a degree which is astonishing the first time one realizes it, actually *creates* the ideological, social, architectural and even geographical environments that people inhabit. To the very considerable extent to which our world is mind-affected, we may assertively (but justifiably) contend that *reality as experienced is a cultural artifact.*[4]

Yet to speak of the world as mind-affected is to tell only half the story. The world is also mind-affect*ing*. This becomes obvious as soon as one asks how it is that people come to know about the world they live in. It is, of course, via learning. And the learning process can be understood in terms of the repeated exposure of the learner to reality. Thus, the individual's experience of reality (nature, architecture, other people, things they say and do, etc.) repeatedly takes certain forms. That experience leads the individual to develop certain expectations about the world, to organize his activities accordingly, and these expectations and actions are reinforced by subsequent experience.

Consequently, reality as experienced is both mind-affected and mind-affecting. We made the world according to our image of reality; we learn our image of reality from our experience of the world that we (especially our predecessors and contemporaries) have made. It is a cybernetic process, in which the reality people actually experience is linked in a feedback loop with the culturally derived *image* of reality in their minds. This essay will suggest a model for how the process works.

Consequential and Semiotic Relationships

In what follows, any bit of human behavior which is conventional or patterned will be called a cultural component. This includes stock greetings like "how are you?", customs such as tipping the waiter or producing a healthy belch to show your host that you enjoyed the meal, beliefs such as that the earth orbits the sun or that long hair wastes the body's finite store of vital energy, attitudes about higher education or about people from other races, forms and styles in art and architecture, and so on through the interminable list of conventions that mold the behavior of people in society. Cultural components are leveled phenomena, so that the American family or legal system may be seen as higher-order components composed of numerous more specific components such as conventions of behavior between husband and wife, mother and daughter, or between lawyers representing opposed clients, judge and defendant, and the like.

From the characterization just given, as well as from common knowledge about human culture, it becomes clear that cultural components do not occur in piecemeal fashion but are systematically related. At least two major classes of relationships among components are discernible—consequential and semiotic—and each of these can be further divided into two sub-types. Our model of the cybernetic process linking (1) reality as a cultural artifact experienced by people with (2) people's culturally derived mental image of reality, depends on the clear recognition of the differences among these kinds of relatedness.

Consequential relationships are those for which it is possible to distinguish independent and dependent variables, such that the dependent variable in some sense is a result or consequence of the independent variable. One variety of consequential relationship is causal. This occurs when the independent variable physically renders the dependent variable necessary or highly probable. A causal relationship among cultural components exists where, for example, in arid conditions such as the Kalahari or Central Australia, a hunting and gathering technology taken as the independent variable may be said to cause the dependent variable of a nomadic way of life.[5]

The other variety of consequential relationship is termed logical. This occurs when the independent variable is an idea or belief. We place this in a category separate from the causal because, while it is not universally accepted that ideas may *cause* actions or institutions, there is little argument that ideas are often reasons for them.[6] A logical consequential relationship is demonstrated by the belief that a source of illness is an excess of blood as the independent variable and the use of leeches or blood-letting in therapy as the dependent variable.[7]

Semiotic relations are those for which it is not possible to establish dependent and independent variables. In this case one item is not a consequence of the other; instead, their relationship is one of signification. It may be that one member of the relationship signifies another, so that we may speak of signifier and signified (as in the relationship between a family and its coat of arms). Or two or more items may be related because they are signifiers of the same thing (as in the relationships among a coat of arms, a name, a hereditary title and a hereditary estate, all of which may be signifiers of a family).

Again it is convenient to divide semiotic relationships into two categories. This may be done on the basis of Hume's distinction between ideas associated by resemblance and contiguity.[8] Semioticians have recently produced a number of variations and elaborations on this contrast, distinguishing between syntagm and association, syntagm and paradigm, syntagm and system, or metonymy and metaphor.[9] Here, however, we will continue to use Hume's simpler terminology. Things are related by contiguity if they commonly appear together, or if one is part of the other. Hence the relationship mentioned above among a family, its coat of arms, its name, its title and its estate is contiguous. A contiguous part-for-whole relationship (synecdoche) may be found in the nickname of the jazz drummer Nesbert Hooper, otherwise known as "Sticks" Hooper.

The other category of semiotic relationship is resemblance. Here things are related because of some kind of similarity between them. Depending on the context, it may be similarity of color, shape, odor, sound, use, or anything else. Most of the transformations or homologies upon which Lévi-Strauss' perceptive analyses rest are semiotic relationships based on resemblance, where the similarity is in structure or form. Indeed, while we will not pursue the issue here, Lévi-Strauss' work is valuable for its demonstration that systematic contrast is a sub-category of resemblance. His analyses of Northwest Coast masks and the relation between totemism and caste indicate that *reversal* of form can link institutions as effectively as similarity.[10]

Resemblance and contiguity cannot be completely separated. In fact, they are in a fundamental sense mutually dependent, in that each provides a necessary context for the other. This point becomes clear if we consider a common means of distinguishing between the closely allied concepts of syntagm and paradigm: the different elements in a conventional sequence or constellation are linked syntagmatically, while possible replacements for any one of those elements are related paradigmatically. Thus the words in the sentence "I want to buy a car" are related to each other syntagmatically or by contiguity, while "car" is related paradigmatically or by resemblance to other words that could replace it in the sentence, such as "doll," "dog," or "house." Again, soup, salad, beef, potatoes, green beans and. pie are related contiguously or syntagmatically as items that typically make up an American meal, while a paradigmatic or resemblance relation exists between beef and its possible replacements, like pork, chicken, or fish. Notice that resemblance relationships exist in the context of particular relationships of contiguity. Beef is replaceable by fish in the context of a meal but not in other syntagmatic or contiguous contexts, such as the treatment of a black eye. Similarly, contiguity is grounded in resemblance. It is no immutable law of nature that a meal consists of soup, salad, and the other foods listed above. That is a matter of social convention which is that way largely because it has been that way for some time: meals of soup, salad, and the rest have been served in the United States for years. The reason those foods are contiguously related to form a meal is largely due to the conventional repetition of their conjunction. And these reiterated repasts are related to each other by resemblance: they are similar to each other. Indeed, it is only on the basis of their similarity that we can recognize them as related. So, while it is helpful to distinguish between resemblance and contiguity, it is important also to recognize their fundamental interdependence.[11]

How Minds Affect the World

The distinctions that have been drawn are helpful in modeling the cybernetic process whereby the world is both mind-affected and mind-affecting. Briefly, our claim is that, in general, minds affect the world by consequential relationships while the world affects minds via semiotic

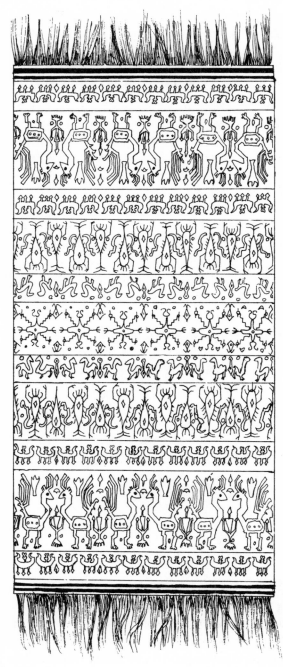

Figure 1. Sumbanese decorated men's textile, from Adams (1973:267). Drawing prepared by Myra Colbert.

relationships. This can be demonstrated most clearly by means of an example. Marie Jeanne Adams has postulated a common form for several cultural components on the Indonesian island of Sumba. She terms this form the "dyadic-triadic set." It consists of two symmetrical, opposed poles and, between them, a central element which has the same relationship to either pole. Decorated men's textiles are an example (See Fig. 1). These handsome rectangular cloths are worn or flown as banners on various ritual occasions. Their design consists of an odd number of bands which form a dyadic-triadic set in that the bands on either side of the central one form two symmetrical end fields reflecting each other across the central, bifacial band. The dyadic-triadic set is recapitulated in village lay-out, where two equally-ranked warrior clans reside at the ends and the center is occupied by priestly clans which mediate disputes between the warrior clans and serve them equally in religious matters. Formal negotiations also manifest the dyadic-triadic form with the two parties grouped on either side of a hall and, between them on a mat, speakers for each side who both make points for their own group and relay points made by the other side to their group.[12]

We can diagram the relation between the structural principle and three of its manifestations as follows:

I. Dyadic-triadic organization

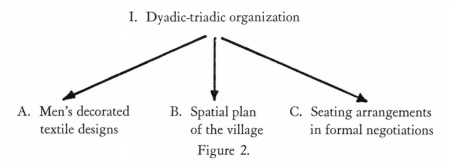

A. Men's decorated   B. Spatial plan   C. Seating arrangements
    textile designs   of the village   in formal negotiations

Figure 2.

A, B, and C are examples of cultural components: artistic style, use of space, and conventions of inter-group behavior. They are parts of the real world as it is experienced by the Sumbanese. And they are logical consequences of the cultural presupposition of dyadic-triadic organization. Hence we suggest that a major way in which minds affect the world is that the components which represent reality as experienced are logical consequences of cultural principles. Innumerable examples are at hand:

religious symbols, objects and practices are logical consequences of theological postulates; good manners are logical consequences of canons of proper and graceful social interaction; conventional behavior patterns among various types of relatives, friends, acquaintances and adversaries are logical consequences of principles of social organization; musical compositions and performances, paintings and sculpture are logical consequences of canons of style.

How the World Affects Minds

If A, B, and C in our example are each a logical consequence of I, their relationship *to each other* is semiotic. Sumbanese textile designs, formal negotiations, and village lay-out are similar in form, and are thus related by resemblance. Our claim is that the world affects minds through such semiotic relationships. The distinctive feature of semiotic relations is that they communicate messages by means of signs. This is why semiotic relationships participate in the character of the world as mind-affecting— because that process is one of people learning about the world, and *that* requires the communication of messages from the world to people. The concepts of information and redundancy, as these have been developed in information theory, can elucidate how this communication process works.

The technical sense of "information" is quite different from its ordinary meaning. In information (or communication) theory, information is the measure of the unpredictability in a message, while redundancy is a measure of its predictability. Hence, information and redundancy are related inversely. For example, the stock message, "I'm fine" in response to the inquiry "How are you?" is predictable and thus has a high degree of redundancy and a correspondingly low degree of information. "I have a bad earache" in response to the same question is far less predictable and hence the message has much more information (and much less redundancy) than the first.

Perhaps the simplest way to state the relationship between the technical and ordinary senses of information is to say that the greater the information (technical sense) in a message, the greater its *potential* to convey information (ordinary sense).[13] Obviously one does not *learn* much from a message which one could have predicted in the first place, while one can gain a good deal of information (ordinary sense) from a message which one could not have predicted. But this holds only to a point. To learn anything from a message one must understand it, and some messages may be so rich in information as to be unintelligible. "Much everything for conclusions awake story McGovern" is a group of words chosen randomly from a book. It is very high in information in that, given any part of it, it is extremely difficult to make any prediction regarding the rest. About the only redundancy in it rests in the fact that all its signs belong to the English language. And yet one derives no information (ordinary sense) at all from this message, because it is unintelligible. Redundancy renders messages intelligible, and hence natural communication systems have a great deal of it. Redundancy, for example, is what enables us to understand messages like those outside Owl's door in *Winnie the Pooh*:

> Underneath the knocker there was a notice which said:
> PLES RING IF AN ANSER IS REQIRD.

> Underneath the bell-pull was a notice which said:
> PLEZ CKNOKE IF AN RNSR IS NOT REQID.[14]

Messages which communicate successfully have enough information for the receiver to learn something from them and enough redundancy to be intelligible.

Now let us apply the concepts of information and redundancy to semiotic relations. Resemblance, as stated earlier, refers to relationships in which the relata are linked by similarity of some sort. It seems fair to say that the degree of similarity between relata is the redundancy of resemblance relations, in that the intelligibility of the message communicated by the relationship depends on that similarity. That is, the message of a relationship can be intelligible only if the relata are perceived *as related,* and in the case of resemblance relationships that is a function of the similarity between the relata. Because information is inversely proportional to redundancy, we could then state that the information in a resemblance relationship is the degree of difference among the relata. Coleridge's famous simile, for example, holds the Ancient Mariner's becalmed ship to be:

> As idle as a painted ship
> Upon a painted ocean.

The meaning is immediately grasped because of its high degree of redundancy: the obvious similarity between a painted ship on a painted ocean and a real ship on a real ocean. The information in the simile—what we *learn* from it—is in the differences between these relata. Our conception of the absolute stillness of the ship, so complete that time itself seems to have stopped, is enhanced by the comparison to a painted ship.

The simile at the beginning of T. S. Eliot's "The Love Song of J. Alfred Prufrock" is somewhat more difficult:

> Let us go then, you and I,
> When the evening is spread out against the sky
> Like a patient etherized upon a table.

This relationship is less readily grasped than Coleridge's because it has less redundancy: the similarity between an evening and an anesthesized patient is not so immediately apparent as that between a ship and the picture of a ship. Because the differences between relata are greater, Eliot's comparison has more information: as one ponders it one gains an increasingly vivid image of a peculiarly pallid evening, and in this way the simile effectively sets the stage for the anemic, flaccid tone of the poem.

In relationships of contiguity we take the redundancy—that which enables one to perceive the relata as related, and therefore renders the message intelligible—to be the degree to which the relata naturally (or, far more likely, conventionally) *belong* together. Conversely, the information in the relationship is the degree to which the juxtaposition is unanticipated. The room in which these lines are written, for example, contains a writing table, bookshelves, typewriter, and a globe. By convention these objects occur together very commonly, and hence the message conveyed by their juxtaposition is highly redundant and therefore readily intelligible. The room fairly shouts: "This is a study." In contrast, some friends had a room which they termed the "Gold Room." It was rather small, with yellowish walls, one of which supported shelves for a larder of canned foods while, opposite, there stood a toilet. These associations are quite unanticipated. The denomination "Gold Room" leads one to expect a spacious and richly furnished manor house drawing room, shelves of canned goods put one in mind of a pantry, while a toilet belongs in a bathroom. The contiguity relationships in this particular room were so rich in information (unpredictability), and conversely so low in redundancy, as to render the room essentially unintelligible. Ushered into the Gold Room, one looks around and wonders "What kind of place *is* this?" A contiguity relation with more information than our study but less information than the Gold Room is found in the sculpture "Et toujours et jamais" by Pierre-

Eugène-Émile Hébert that stands in the Spencer Museum of Art at the University of Kansas. It depicts a voluptuous nude in the embrace of a shrouded figure. The redundancy lies in the fact that pairs of human figures are commonly joined in embraces, while the information is found in the unanticipated fact that in this case one of the figures is a skeleton.

Now let us apply these concepts to our example from Sumba. Textile design, village lay-out, and formal negotiations are related by resemblance in that they share a common dyadic-triadic form. That similarity establishes the redundancy among the relata. What of the information? This consists in the *differences* among the relata. There are doubtless several, such as the fact that the dyadic-triadic form is more systematically presented in textiles than in village lay-out. One important difference is the obvious one that the relata are themselves quite different phenomena: designs in textiles, seating patterns in meetings, arrangement of houses. That is, the semiotic relationship Adams has postulated has more information than would have been the case had the relata been confined to different examples of decorated men's textiles. There is more difference between textiles and village lay-out than between two or more examples of textiles, and hence more information in the relationship among them.

Our claim has been that semiotic relationships communicate messages. What, then, is the message in this case? It is, we maintain, precisely a message about the original principle (I on the accompanying diagram): that an important and widespread structural form of reality is the dyadic-triadic set. In other words, the message communicated by the semiotic relationship among A, B, and C closes the feedback loop in the cybernetic process.

Now we are in a position to specify the cybernetic process whereby the world as experienced is both mind-affected and mind-affecting. Minds affect the world via the logical consequential connections between cultural principles and the components derived from them. The world in turn affects minds by communicating messages to people about those cultural principles, such messages being communicated by the semiotic relationships among the components.[15]

One might note in this model that the connection proceeding from A, B, and C to I is different from the links passing from I to A, B, and C. Why could messages about I not be transmitted simply by retracing, in reverse, the logical consequential routes from I to A, B, and C—in effect permit-

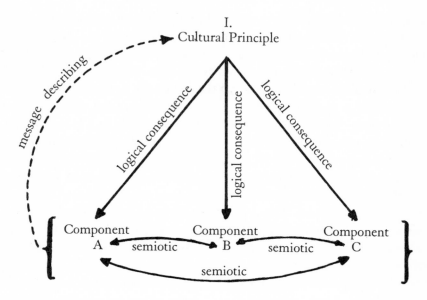

Figure 3

ting the arrows to point in both directions? Our response is that this procedure would not yield intelligible messages about I. The reason is that the logical consequential relationships I→A, I→B, I→C are independent of each other. (That is, the fact that textile design is a logical consequence of I is not linked directly with the fact that village lay-out is a logical consequence of I. Either could exist without the other.) None of these relationships can communicate a message because it has no redundancy and, as we have seen, redundancy is necessary if the message is to be rendered intelligible. To achieve the necessary redundancy we need to look elsewhere than to the independent logical consequential relationship between I and A, or B, or C. We must look instead at the relationship which directly connects A, B, and C. But that, as has been seen, is a different kind of relationship. It is a semiotic relationship (in this case, of resemblance). The similarity between A, B, and C, on the basis of which we may claim that a resemblance relationship exists among them, is simultaneously the redundancy which enables that relationship to communicate an intelligible message. Hence if the *communicative* element of the cybernetic process is to be realized—if the world is to be mind-affecting—it is necessary that a semiotic relationship be present in the process.

To illustrate this point, consider the circumstances under which many societies were introduced to firearms. European explorers would arrive, find themselves threatened by the people they met, and would shoot one or more of them. Typically the witnesses to such an event were completely bewildered. The causal link between the firing of a gun and the wounding or killing of a man was not apparent to them on the basis of just one event. It was perceived only after several demonstrations of the power of guns. Nor was this conclusion reached by mentally retracing, in reverse, the causal route from the firing of a gun to the impact of a bullet. Instead, the semiotic relationship between those events (one stemming from their resemblance) communicated the message to them (led them to get the idea) that the firing of a gun and the impact of a bullet are causally linked. The message was not successfully communicated until more than one episode had occurred, because it became intelligible only after repetition endowed it with redundancy.

Although it involves a digression from the main line of argument, it is perhaps of some interest to indicate the relevance of these remarks to the process of hypothesis formation in science. Bochenski's claim is that this process, which he labels "regressive reduction," entails the movement of thought from a known consequent (an observation) to an unknown antecedent (the hypothesis from which the observed phenomenon is logically derivable).[16] His diagram of the process shows arrows passing directly from observation statements to hypotheses. We maintain that the path of thought in regressive reduction is more accurately depicted by the diagram presented above when I is considered as the hypothesis and A, B, and C as observation statements. That is, thought moves not directly from observation statements taken individually to the hypothesis, but from a semiotic relationship among several observation statements to the hypothesis. This point is very much in line with philosophers of science such as Mary Hesse and Rom Harré who hold that analogy is a major conceptual tool in scientific hypothesis formation and theory building.[17] Scientific thinking, they claim, often proceeds by the notion that if a relatively unknown phenomenon is similar to a better known phenomenon in some ways (molecules and billiard balls, the flow of electricity and the flow of water), then it may be fruitful to pursue the possibility that they are similar in other ways also. This is closely allied to the picture of scientific thinking given here, in that recognition of an analogy between phenomena such as molecules

and billiard balls is nothing other than the recognition of a semiotic relationship (in this case resemblance) between them. Hypotheses are then
formed on the basis of messages communicated by those semiotic relationships. Returning now to the main thread of the argument, the same
processes are at work in human culture. People learn about the presuppo-
sitions of their culture from semiotic relationships among institutions, and
in this way the mind-affected world affects people's minds.

The Message is the Thing

The primary mandate for research from the perspective of these remarks
is of course to ascertain what the messages communicated by semiotic
relationships are, what they mean. Herein lies a caution and admonition
for those who would concern themselves with semiotic relationships. One
of course cannot even begin semiotic analysis without identifying what the
relevant signs are. But the message may be quite different from the signs.
So if investigation exhausts itself in the intricacies of resemblance and
contiguity, or in refinements on the taxonomy of icons, indices, and symbols,
then the forest may be obscured by the trees. Homeric scholars for example,
have detected a semiotic relationship between eighth century B.C. Greek
ceramics and epics of the same period. Cedric Whitman argues that the
Iliad has a symmetrical structure or "ring composition." Of the epic's
twenty-four books, the events of Book I correspond with those of Book
XXIV; Book II with Book XXIII, and so on (with varying degrees of
precision) throughout the entire poem. Reflective symmetry is also evident
in the designs on ceramics of the Geometric Period, especially the Dipylon
ware of eighth century Athens. (See Fig. 4.) Lines of inward-facing figures
flanking a central scene on ceramics can readily be seen as a visual homology
of the ring composition of the Iliad.[18] But the *message* communicated by
this resemblance between pottery and poetry is not just about ring composition or symmetry. For Whitman, the significance of symmetry of design
in eighth century Greece was a "rational concern with total patterns . . .
total design, not particularly of motif, is the end in view."[19] And this
artistic concern was part of the ascent of Greek civilization toward its
classical period: "it was a symptom of the spirit of the age which saw the
rise of the city state, and the foundation of those principles of rational order
which the Greeks imposed upon themselves."[20] Thus the interpretation of
semiotic messages often involves going well beyond the identification of

Figure 4: Detail from an Attic Geometric (Dipylon) amphora, mid 8th century B. C. National Museum, Athens. Drawing prepared by Myra Colbert.

the signs and the nature of their relationships. Perhaps this is what Geertz had in mind when, with reference to a semiotics of art, he wrote:

> Semiotics must move beyond the consideration of signs as a means of communication, code to be deciphered, to a consideration of them as modes of thought, idiom to be interpreted. It is not a new cryptography that we need, especially when it consists of replacing one cipher by another less intelligible, but a new diagnostics, a science which can determine the meaning of things for the life that surrounds them.[21]

Testing Semiotic Relationships

Any mode of analysis which claims to be objective or scientific requires some means of corroborating or falsifying its hypotheses. That is, if we are to claim that certain institutions are related in particular fashions, we need some way of testing our claim. The matter is relatively straightforward in the case of consequential relationships. There we can follow the procedures of natural science (which has traditionally also been concerned with consequential—specifically causal—relationships.) We interfere with the independent variable and then observe whether the dependent variable is affected in the predicted way. (E.g., if the belief that an excess of blood causes disease is discredited, bloodletting in therapy will be discarded.) Of course, in social science such testing procedures may be difficult to carry out practically, due to ethical, political and other constraints on experimentation with human subjects. This is why cross-cultural comparison and social change are of such methodological significance to social science: they often provide us with ready-made experimental conditions. But whatever the practical complexities, at least the logic of testing hypotheses about consequential relationships is clear.

It is very different in the case of semiotic relationships. Indeed, uncertainty about means of testing semiotic relationships is a major reason why, in American anthropology at least, the last few years have witnessed a regretable turning away from the once immensely influential structuralism of Lévi-Strauss. Although many of his postulated transformations are brilliantly insightful, if means are lacking to *test* whether the hypothesized relationships are true of the culture under study, there is little people can do with them other than to acknowledge and appreciate a certain genius in the mind which came up with them and then turn their attention to more objective ways of doing anthropology. This situation is unfortunate, particularly for studies that concentrate on world view, because semiotic relationships are of primary importance in the establishment of cultural constructions of reality. They are, as we have seen, a major means whereby knowledge of the world as it is construed in a particular culture is communicated to the members of society.

If, however, one examines the question of testing hypotheses about semiotic relationships from the perspective of the model developed above, it becomes much less problematic. For one thing, that model specifies what semiotic relationships *do* in culture, and, for another, it shows how they do it in conjunction with consequential relationships. Both factors are relevant to testing procedures.

Semiotic relationships, as has been maintained, communicate information about the world to members of society. Care has been taken to point out that the intelligibility of messages communicated in any natural language is directly proportional to their redundancy. One important means of testing hypotheses about semiotic relationships is to check for redundancy. If that is not found, it is unlikely that a semiotic relationship has in fact been discovered because, lacking redundancy, it could not effectively communicate messages to members of society. As an example, consider again the hypothesized link between the Iliad and Dipylon vases. Certainly this is a curious *similarity* among elements of ancient Greek culture, but does that similarity really mark a semiotic *relationship?* Or is it simply a fortuitous coincidence into which Whitman and other Homeric scholars have read rather too much? If redundancy were lacking—if symmetrical or ring composition were discernible only in the Iliad (or certain parts of the Iliad) and in only a few Dipylon vases—we might well judge that the similarity between them is just coincidental rather than marking a semiotic relationship. But if we do find a high degree of redundancy we can be confident that we have indeed isolated a semiotic relationship of significance for the culture. In the present example this would involve detecting symmetrical composition in epics other than the Iliad, determining it to be a common structure of design in ceramics, and discovering further transformations of it in yet other segments of the culture. Whitman is able to demonstrate a good deal of redundancy in support of the hypothesis: he shows that not only the Iliad as a whole but also many of its component parts are organized according to ring composition, that the same structure is visible in the Odyssey (although less systematically than in the Iliad), and that for both the Iliad and Dipylon ware the symmetry is most strict at the edges of the composition (the borders of ceramic design, the beginning and ending books of the epic)—as might be expected with a framing device.[22]

Hypothesized semiotic relationships can also be tested by tracing through the cybernetic processes in which they participate. The investigator attempts to formulate the message communicated by the semiotic relationship, and then searches in the culture for other components which might also be seen as members of the set which communicates that message. Insofar as this investigation is a fruitful one, yielding insights and suggesting associations among cultural components that had not been previously perceived, confidence increases that a real semiotic relationship has been identified and its message correctly interpreted. But if the analysis leads to a dead end it is likely that what was hypothesized to be a semiotic relationship was only a fortuitous and nonsignificant association, or else that the interpretation of the message communicated by the relationship is faulty.

Native Awareness and the Reality of Cultural Principles

The fulcrum of the model presented here is the notion of cultural principles. These have a determining effect on reality as experienced in that cultural components are logical consequences of them. Conversely, the messages communicated by semiotic relationships among institutions are messages about those cultural principles. Hence it is important that we be clear about the nature of such principles. One thing can be stated unequivocally at the outset: cultural principles of the sort we are discussing are rarely verbally articulated by members of the society under study. Informants cannot provide the anthropologist with a neat list of the axioms upon which their culture is predicated. The anthropologist must infer them, and this is done by the same process that we have described for the manner in which the world affects people's minds. That is, the anthropologist observes or experiences patterns of institutionalized behavior and, from semiotic relationships among them, receives messages about the cultural principles underlying them. The main difference between this and the native's experience of living in and learning about his culture is that the investigator makes the entire process explicit.

The inability of members of society to articulate the principles raises a serious question about their reality. Instead of claiming, as we have been, that they really exist, one view is that they have no reality in the culture under study but are heuristic abstractions created by the investigator to assist in anthropological analysis.[23] If this were true, our model with its contention that cultural components are logical consequences of such abstracted principles would be highly vulnerable to the criticism that it reifies abstractions and then considers those abstractions to have a determining influence over the very things from which they were originally abstracted.[24]

Our position, however, is that the principles are far more than just the analyst's abstractions. They are objective characteristics of culture. One way to account for the fact that members of society cannot articulate them is to locate them in their unconscious minds. Gregory Bateson has explained this in terms of the economy of mental resources.[25] The conscious mind has a finite capacity: there is a limit to the number of things you can think about, appreciate, plan or decide in any given span of time. Habits contribute immensely to the economy of mind in that they enable us to do certain things "automatically," allowing attention to be focused on other matters. For instance, you can think about what you will eat for breakfast or what you will say in a lecture while you are tying your shoe, because that operation has become so habitual that it no longer requires your attention to accomplish it. That task, as Bateson would say, has been "sunk" in your unconscious mind or "primary process." A child of four, on the other hand, has not yet accomplished this sinking and must devote the full resources of conscious mind to getting the shoe tied properly.

Only those procedures which are invariably the same can be sunk in primary process. You can think about other things while you tie your shoe but not while you select which of several pairs of shoes to wear. The latter task has variable outcomes, and so the flexibility of consciousness is required to deal with it. Hence the mind approaches maximum economy and efficiency when those things which are unchanging and deemed to be permanently true are sunk in primary process (and so drop out of awareness), thus freeing consciousness to focus its attention on the contingent and variable elements of experience. People are not aware of their most basic cultural principles because, as the firm foundations upon which their behavior is predicated, they are sunk in primary process.[26] "The premises may, economically, be sunk," Bateson wrote,[27] "but particular conclusions must be conscious."

This is a useful way to conceive of the nature of cultural principles as long as we keep in mind a pair of provisos. For one, it must not be taken as an implication of the terminology Bateson uses that all things which are "sunk" in primary process were originally on the surface, available to consciousness. Sometimes, indeed, they have been. Our example of learning to tie one's shoe is a case in point: initially a child laboriously learns and repeats rules about loops or "bunny ears," but as the skill is mastered the rules are "sunk" and the act alone remains on the surface. (Of course, in this particular case the rules are not sunk so deeply as to be irretrievable if, for example, one wishes to teach the skill to someone else.) But a great deal of culture is acquired with the rules never having been explicit. The rules governing gestures, facial expressions, body positioning in social interaction, and language are clear examples. To say that these rules are sunk in primary process does not entail that during the learning process they were conscious.

The second proviso is that we must resist the common assumption that the inhabitants of mind (conscious or unconscious) are first and foremost propositions. It is very easy to fall in with this assumption. Bateson speaks of premises which may be sunk and conclusions which remain conscious; we have repeatedly used terms like principles and rules, and all of these are conventionally stated in the form of propositions. But a statement or description of something is not that thing; as Korzybski was careful to point out, the map is not the territory.[28] The unarticulated cultural principles which are sunk in native primary process are not a bunch of shadowy propositions that never quite get said. They belong more to the realm of action than to the realm of speech. Wittgenstein, who characterized cultural principles as rules which are simply accepted without grounds, wrote: "As if giving grounds did not come to an end sometime. But the end is not an ungrounded presupposition: it is an ungrounded way of acting."[29]

In their own right, cultural principles provide the ground for conventional behavior. The principles which appear in proposition form in our analyses are statements of those principles. While not identical with them, to the extent that they are accurate descriptions or maps, our analytic principles are vital tools for understanding the structure and working of human cultures.

Notes

1. Wilhelm Dilthey, *Pattern and Meaning in History* (New York: Harper and Row, 1962), p. 120.
2. Mary Douglas, *Purity and Danger* (London: Routledge and Kegan Paul, 1966), pp. 66-72.
3. Attributions of meaning to the physical environment may be found in all human societies; Australian aborigines are especially famous for it.
4. Here we are very close to Geertz's claim that cultural systems are models of and models for reality. "Culture patterns," he wrote, "have an intrinsic double aspect: they give meaning, i.e., objective conceptual form, to social psychological reality, both by shaping themselves to it and by shaping it to themselves." (Clifford Geertz, *The Interpretation of Cultures* [New York: Basic Books, 1973], p. 92.) Our stress has been on the latter part of this formulation, not so much because we think it is more important as because it has been less generally recognized. It has been recognized quite clearly, however, in the phenomenological approach to sociology inspired by Alfred Schutz. (Alfred Schutz and Thomas Luckman, *The Structure of the Life-World* [London: Heinemann, 1974], pp. 5-6, 243-50.) For a lucid, full-scale treatment see Henry L. Berger and Thomas Luckman, *The Social Construction of Reality* (Garden City, N.Y.: Doubleday, 1966).
5. The designation of independent and dependent variables in consequential relationships is not immutable. It is entirely possible, in a chain of relations, that a variable that is dependent with reference to one variable is independent with reference to another (as the furnace burner in a house heating system is dependent with respect to the thermostat and independent with respect to the amount of heat in the house). In cybernetic systems, with feedback, it is even possible that a dependent variable may affect its independent variable and thus, at a later time, be independent with reference to it (the burner affects the amount of heat in the house, which in turn affects the thermostat). In our terminology, however, all such relationships are termed consequential if, for any pair of relata at any point in the system, one can be termed the independent variable and the other the dependent variable.
6. See William Dray, *Laws and Explanation in History* (London: Oxford University Press, 1957); Dray, *Philosophical Analysis and History* (New York: Harper and Row, 1966), and Carl G. Hempel, "Explanation in Science and in History" in Dray, *Philosophical Analysis,* for a debate on the nature of the relationship. An excellent extended treatment of this and allied issues may be found in Rex Martin, *Historical Explanation: Re-Enactment and Practical Inference* (Ithaca, N.Y.: Cornell University Press, 1977).

7. Some philosophers restrict logical relationships to links between propositions. As this example makes clear, our use of the concept is broader: propositions may be logically related to actions.

8. David Hume, *Enquiries Concerning Human Understanding and Concerning the Principles of Morals* (Oxford: Clarendon, 1975), p. 24.

9. See Ferdinand de Saussure, *Course in General Linguistics* (New York: McGraw-Hill, 1966), pp. 122-27; Oswald Ducrot and Tzvetan Todorov, *Dictionnaire Encyclopédique des Sciences du Langage* (Paris: Seuil, 1972), pp. 140-46; Roland Barthes, *Elements of Semiology* (New York: Hill and Wang, 1968), pp. 58-59; Roman Jakobson, "On Aphasia," in *Fundamentals of Language* by Roman Jakobson and Morris Halle (The Hague: Mouton, 1956).

10. Claude Lévi-Strauss, *La Voie des Masques* (Genève: Skira, 1975), and *La Pensée Sauvage* (Paris: Plon, 1962), pp. 163-69.

11. Barthes, unstinting in his use of jargon, put it this way: "Any metaphoric series is a syntagmatized paradigm, and any metonymy a syntagm which is frozen and absorbed in a system; in metaphor, selection becomes contiguity, and in metonymy, contiguity becomes a field to select from." (Barthes, *Elements of Semiology*, p. 83.)

12. Marie Jeanne Adams, "Structural Aspects of a Village Art," *American Anthropologist*, LXXV (1973), pp. 266-71.

13. As Weaver put it, "in this new theory the word information relates not so much to what you *do* say, as to what you *could* say." (Warren Weaver, "The Mathematics of Communication," *Scientific American*, CLXXXI (1949), p. 12; Weaver's italics.)

14. A. A. Milne, *The World of Pooh* (New York: E. P. Dutton, 1957), pp. 48-49. The misspellings here are examples of what is called "noise" in information theory: signals in the message which the sender did not intend to transmit.

15. Of course, this is not a static model. Behavior changes over time, leading to changes in the components which ultimately affect changes in the messages about cultural principles, and so on through the cycle again.

16. J. M. Bochenski, *The Methods of Contemporary Thought* (Dordrecht, Holland: D. Reidel, 1965), pp. 92, 99-100.

17. Mary Hesse, *Models and Analogies in Science* (Notre Dame, Indiana: University of Notre Dame Press, 1966), and Rom Harré, *The Principles of Scientific Thinking* (Chicago: University of Chicago Press, 1970).

18. Cedric H. Whitman, *Homer and the Heroic Tradition* (Cambridge, Mass.: Harvard University Press, 1958), pp. 89-99, 252-84.

19. Whitman, pp. 92, 94.

20. Whitman, p. 77.

21. Clifford Geertz, "Art as a Cultural System," *MLN*, XCI (1976), p. 1499.

22. Whitman, pp. 98, 258-59, 265, 287-91.

23. See Jacques Maquet, "Some Epistemological Remarks on the Cultural Philosophies and their Comparison," in *Cross-Cultural Understanding: Epistemology in Anthropology*, F. S. C. Northrop and Helen H. Livingston, eds. (New York: Harper and Row, 1964), p. 17. A similar but more subtle view advanced by Peter Caws maintains that while such principles (or "structure") may objectively belong to a social or cultural system, in some cases it is the anthropologist's analysis which confers the structure upon the system (Peter Caws, "Operational, Representational, and Explanatory Models," *American Anthropologist*, LXXVI [1974], pp. 1-10). For the debate sparked by this proposition, see F. Allan Hanson, "Models and Social Reality: An Alternative to Caws," *American Anthropologist*, LXXVIII (1976), 232-34; Peter Caws, "The Ontology of Social Structure: A Reply to Hanson," *American Anthropologist*, LXXVIII (1976), pp. 325-27; Caws, "More on the Ontology of Social Structure: A Reply to Rossi," *American Anthropologist*, LXXIX (1977), p. 916; Ino Rossi, "On the Notion of Social Structure: A Mental or Objective Reality?" *American Anthropologist*, LXXIX (1977), pp. 914-16; and Richard Paul Chaney, "Structures, Realities, and Blind Spots," *American Anthropologist*, LXXX (1978), pp. 589-96.

24. David Bidney, "On the Concept of Culture and Some Cultural Fallacies," *American Anthropologist*, XLVI (1944), pp. 41-43.

25. Gregory Bateson, *Steps to an Ecology of Mind* (New York: Ballantine Books, 1972), pp. 141-42.

26. This is not to claim that principles never change; obviously they do. But they are more resistant to change than consciously held ideas and explicitly planned behavior.

27. Bateson, p. 142.

28. Alfred Korzybski, *Science and Sanity* (Lakeville, Conn.: International Non-Aristotelian Library Publishing Co., 4th ed., 1958), pp. 58, 498, 750-51.

29. Ludwig Wittgenstein, *On Certainty,* G. E. M. Anscombe and G. H. von Wright, eds. (New York: Harper and Row, 1972), section 110. The relation between principles advanced in analysis and the cultural and mental phenomena they denote has been discussed more fully in: F. Allan Hanson and Rex Martin, "The Problem of Other Cultures," *Philosophy of the Social Sciences,* III (1973), pp. 191-208; F. Allan Hanson, *Meaning in Culture* (London: Routledge and Kegan Paul, 1975), chapter 3; and Martin, *Historical Explanation,* pp. 203-11.

Contributors

G. DOUGLAS ATKINS. Professor and Coordinator of Graduate Studies in English at the University of Kansas. A specialist in Restoration and eighteenth-century British literature, he has published widely on Dryden, Pope, and other figures and is the author of *The Faith of John Dryden*. Recipient of an ACLS grant and of Woodrow Wilson, Danforth, Clark Library, and School of Criticism and Theory fellowships, he has also recently published "Dehellenizing Literary Criticism" in *College English* and "J. Hillis Miller, Deconstruction, and the Recovery of Transcendence" in *Notre Dame English Journal*.

JONATHAN CULLER. Educated at Harvard and St. John's College, Oxford. Before coming to Cornell in 1977 as Professor of English and Comparative Literature, he was Fellow of Selwyn College, Cambridge, and Fellow and University Lecturer in French at Brasenose College, Oxford. He is the author of *Flaubert: The Uses of Uncertainty*, 1974; *Structuralist Poetics: Structuralism, Linguistics, and the Study of Literature*, 1975; *Saussure*, 1976; *The Pursuit of Signs: Semiotics, Literature, Deconstruction*, 1981; *On Deconstruction: Literary Theory in the 1970's*, 1981; and *Roland Barthes*, 1981.

RICHARD T. DE GEORGE. University Distinguished Professor and Co-Director of the Center for Humanistic Studies at the University of Kansas. A former holder of Fulbright, ACLS/SSRC, Rockefeller and NEH fellowships, he is the author or editor of thirteen books including (with F. M. De George) *The Structuralists from Marx to Lévi-Strauss*.

F. ALLAN AND LOUISE HANSON. Have done anthropological field research in Tahiti and Rapa islands (French Polynesia) and New Zealand. She received a Master's Degree from the University of Pittsburgh, has been Reference Librarian and Assistant Director of Libraries at Baker University, and has published a bibliography on the American author James Norman Hall. He is Professor of Anthropology at the University of Kansas where he specializes in the Pacific and theoretical anthropology. He holds degrees from Princeton University and the University of Chicago. Among his publications are *Rapan Lifeways: Society and History on a Polynesian Island* and *Meaning in Culture*. They are currently preparing a book on the semiotics of New Zealand Maori culture during the period of early European contact.

RUDOLF JANDER. Professor of Entomology at the University of Kansas. He received his Ph.D. from the University of Munich, did postdoctoral research at the Max-Planck-Institute for Behavioral Physiology and at Yale University, and has taught at the University of Freiburg and at the University of Frankfurt. His research on the dance language of the honey bee was published jointly with K. von Frisch.

JAMES P. MESA. Received his degrees in philosophy from Saint Louis University. His primary interests are in the areas of ethics and moral education; his doctoral dissertation was a study of the relationship between moral indoctrination and the virtue of prudence. He is currently Visiting Associate Professor of Philosophy at Seattle University.

LOUIS OLDANI. A member of the Society of Jesus and Associate Professor of English at Rockhurst College. He received the Ph.D. from the University of Pennsylvania and has been awarded grants from the Lilly Foundation and from the National Endowment for the Humanities. His articles on 20th-century American writers have appeared in the *Library Chronicle*, the *Dreiser Newsletter*, and *Research Studies*. He is editor of a three-volume series on Jesuit drama.

W. KEITH PERCIVAL. Professor of Linguistics at the University of Kansas. He studied at Uppsala and Yale and worked with the M.I.T. Mechanical Translation Group prior to teaching at Brandeis and then at the University of Wisconsin-Milwaukee. He is presently engaged on a documentary history of linguistics from Antiquity to the twentieth century.

LEON SATTERFIELD. Teaches in the English Department at Nebraska Wesleyan in Lincoln. In addition to the Andrew Mellon fellowship he received to participate in the 1979 Semiotics Seminar at the University of Kansas, he had an NEH Summer Seminar fellowship at the University of Pittsburgh in 1977. He has read papers at four professional meetings, most recently at the 1980 convention of the Semiotic Society of America.

THOMAS A. SEBEOK. Distinguished Professor of Linguistics, Professor of Anthropology, and Chairman of the Graduate Program in Semiotic Studies and of the Research Center for Language and Semiotic Studies at Indiana University. He has received Guggenheim and Fulbright Fellowships and was a Fellow at the Center for Advanced Study in the Behavioral Sciences. He is the author or editor of a great many works, including

Approaches to Semiotics; Sight, Sound and Sense; A Profusion of Signs; Contributions to the Doctrine of Signs; The Sign and Its Masters; and (with Jean Umiker-Sebeok) *Speaking of Apes.*

JOHN K. SHERIFF. Received his M.A. from the University of Illinois in 1967 and his Ph.D. from the University of Oklahoma in 1972. He began teaching English at Bethel College, N. Newton, Kansas, in 1967 where he is currently Chairman of the English department.

ARTHUR SKIDMORE. Associate Professor of Philosophy at the University of Kansas. While he was a graduate student at the University of Texas at Austin, his interest in Peirce was sparked by Charles Hartshorne's seminar. His unpublished Ph.D. dissertation is entitled "Studies in Peirce's Theories of Logic." An article of his, "Peirce and Triads," appeared in the *Transactions of the Charles S. Peirce Society* (Winter, 1971). His main teaching interests are in logic, philosophy of science, and philosophy of art.

ANDREW TADIE. Associate Professor of English at Seattle University, obtained a Ph.D. in 1972. He has been awarded a post-doctoral fellowship and several research grants. His research has dealt mainly with the areas of rhetoric and seventeenth century English drama and philosophy. He has published papers on early English travel literature, English Deism, and on William Davenant's *The Siege of Rhodes,* England's first opera.

TZVETAN TODOROV. Born in 1939 in Sofia (Bulgaria), works at the Centre National de la Recherche Scientifique in Paris. He has written numerous books on literary theory, of which *The Fantastic, Poetics of Prose,* and (with O. Ducrot) *Encyclopedic Dictionary of the Sciences of Language* have already been translated in English, while his *Theories of the Symbol, Symbolism and Interpretation* and *Introduction to Poetics* are forthcoming. He is currently working on a book on the Conquest of America.

UNIVERSITY OF KANSAS PUBLICATIONS, HUMANISTIC STUDIES

Edward L. Ruhe, *Editor*

The Humanistic Studies may be purchased from the Library Sales Office, University of Kansas Libraries, Lawrence, Kansas 66045. The series is also available to learned societies, colleges and universities, and other institutions in exchange for similar publications. All communications regarding exchange should be addressed to the Exchange Librarian.